THOMAS MANN AND ITALY

ILSEDORE B. JONAS

THOMAS MANN AND ITALY

translated into English

by

Betty Crouse

THE UNIVERSITY OF ALABAMA PRESS
University, Alabama

To the Memory of Lavinia Mazzucchetti

Translated into English from a revised version of *Thomas Mann und Italien,*
Copyright © 1969 by Carl Winter Universitätsverlag,
Heidelberg

Library of Congress Cataloging in Publication Data

Jonas, Ilsedore B
   Thomas Mann and Italy.

   Bibliography: p.
   Includes index.
   1. Mann, Thomas, 1875-1955--Knowledge--Italy.
2. Mann, Thomas, 1875-1955--Appreciation--Italy.
3. Mann, Thomas, 1875-1955--Influence. 4. Italian
literature--20th century--History and criticism.
I. Title.
PT2625.A44Z6613   833'.9'12   79-9779
ISBN 0-8173-8063-9

CONTENTS

PREFACE

The longing of the northerner for Italy springs from a desire for completion through the atmosphere of the south, which is contrasted to the north in many respects. It is a longing that drew Thomas Mann to Italy again and again, since he too, as he expressed it in his address to his brother ("Vom Beruf des deutschen Schriftstellers in unserer Zeit"), felt "the insufficiency in oneself, the need for completion and deliverance through the completely other, the south, the brightness, clarity and lightness, the gift of the beautiful."

This study undertakes to show whether and to what extent the land of Italy as well as Italian culture and people exercised an influence on Thomas Mann's literary creativity, and to investigate what kind of reception Thomas Mann and his work found among his Italian readers and critics, and whether and how much present-day Italian literature has been influenced by the German writer. Although Thomas Mann himself tended to minimize the extent of Italian influence on him and on his work, our detailed study reveals significant influences of the south on his literary creativity and, reciprocally, examines Italy's reception of Mann and his works, and the extent of his influence on Italian literature.

My special thanks go to the Director of the Thomas Mann Archive in Zürich, Dr. Hans Wysling, Professor at the University of Zürich, for his kind assistance in my endeavors. Until her death, Lavinia Mazzucchetti followed the realization of this work with warm interest and, in most generous fashion, placed her unpublished Thomas Mann letters and other manuscripts at my disposal. Dr. Marco Forti in Milan made possible my utilization of the rich contents of the archives of the publishing house of Arnoldo Mondadori. I owe special thanks to Professors Wilhelm Emrich, Erwin Koppen, and Horst Rüdiger for numerous valuable suggestions and constructive criticism. Not least, I am greatly indebted to three Italian Thomas Mann specialists, Sergio Checconi, Italo A. Chiusano, and Roberto Fertonani for their helpful advice. My sincere thanks go to the American Council of Learned Societies, the Philosophical Society of America, and the Maurice and Laura Falk Foundation for the awards of research grants in support of this work.

Pittsburgh, Pennsylvania   ILSEDORE B. JONAS

TRANSLATOR'S NOTE

Unless otherwise noted, matter quoted in *Thomas Mann und Italien* has been translated to English directly from the original language of the quotation, and does not derive from an existing published translation. This procedure applies both to passages in German (as from various novels by Thomas Mann) and to matter (such as letters) whose original language is Italian or French.

BETTY CROUSE

Thomas Mann and Italy

I
Mann's Encounters
with the Italian World

1. Mann's Sojourns in Italy (1895–1954)

In his twentieth year Thomas Mann visited Italy for the first time, from July until October 1895. On his journey he experienced Rome and, in particular, the environs of the Eternal City. His older brother Heinrich was already settled in Italy at the time, and from there he invited the four-year-younger Thomas to join him for a few months. "I went," he reported, "and we spent, as few Germans do, a long, scorching summer together in a little provincial town in the Sabine Hills—Palestrina, the birthplace of the great musician."[1]

In October the brothers returned to Munich, where Thomas wrote the novella *The Will to Happiness (Der Wille zum Glück)*. The south drew him again the following year, and in October 1896 he spent three weeks in Venice. From there he continued on to Ancona, Rome, and Naples, where he was probably already at work in November on the novella *Disillusionment (Enttäuschung)*. Although Thomas Mann complained in a letter to Korfiz Holm that the prices in Italy were far too high, he was delighted with the magnificent view of the bay and Vesuvius, which he enjoyed from his room at Via S. Lucia 28. Only then, on his second stay in Italy, did he really have the feeling of being in the south, since in Neapolitan life there resounds "a distinct note of the Orient."[2]

In December 1896, Thomas joined his brother Heinrich in Rome, where they both remained until the summer of 1897, "as lodgers of a good woman who, in the Via Torre Argentina, possessed a flat having stone floors and straw chairs."[3] The brothers lived in total seclusion and encouraged no communication with their fellow man. As Thomas reported many years later in *A Sketch of My Life (Lebensabriss)*, they passed their days alone in their rooms, were regular patrons of the little restaurant "Genzano," drank good Italian wine there, and in the evenings played dominoes together in a café. In those Roman days Thomas Mann lived in his own world, isolated from the colorful life of everyday Italy. The extensive reading he pursued in his room would become important in his development as a writer: indeed, in Italy he read not Italian authors but the great French and, above all, the Russian and Scandinavian writers of the nineteenth century. "The historical and aesthetic impressions which the city (Rome) has to offer I respectfully assimilated, but not precisely with the feeling that they had anything to do with me or had immediate benefit for me."[4]

Because of the extreme heat, the brothers left Rome in August (1897) and again went to Palestrina, that small, grey mountain town on the steeply rising south slope of Monte Ginestro, which belongs to the Praenestine mountain chain.[5] There Thomas Mann inwardly prepared himself for his first novel, whose action would take place in far-off Lübeck.[6]

In the small, modest hotel "Casa Bernardini" in Palestrina,[7] where the brothers rented rooms for a few months, Thomas Mann began his first great work, *Buddenbrooks*. Almost fifty years later, Heinrich reminisced: "In our large, cool room of stone, halfway up a street of steps, the novice, unacquainted with his own self, began a work; soon many would know it; decades later it belonged to all the world."[8]

While the Italian landscape with its intense colors and luminous sunsets became for Heinrich a deeply felt experience, Thomas remained little susceptible to these impressions. In thought he was bound to the North; the atmosphere of Palestrina—even the house in the street of steps leading from the piazza and the Cathedral up to the hill of the temple—finds no mention at all in Thomas Mann's first novel. While Heinrich made Palestrina the setting for his work *The Little Town (Die kleine Stadt)*, it was not until forty years later, when Thomas wrote *Doctor Faustus*, that reminiscences about the stay in Palestrina appeared in an important scene in the book.[9]

In May 1901 Thomas Mann again visited Italy, this time principally Florence, where he became friendly with two young English girls. Of the two sisters, holiday guests in the same pension, he found the elder to be congenial, while the younger, named Mary or Molly, enchanted him with her charm: "A tender liaison unfolded, which we discussed cementing through marriage."[10] Nevertheless, out of common sense they parted, and in the writer's work the only clearly recognizable consequence is the dedication of his novella *Gladius Dei* to his former love: "To M.S. in remembrance of our days in Florence."

A stay in Venice in June 1901 ended this Italian trip; yet on July 10, only a short time after his return to Munich, Thomas Mann again went to the south: together with his brother Heinrich he travelled to the South Tyrol, at that time Austrian and today Italian, where the two of them passed their holidays in Mitterbad, above Merano. Thomas Mann set out on another Italian trip that year on 5 November 1901; as so often in later years, he went to Riva on Lake Garda in order to undergo treatment at the Villa Cristoforo from the physician Dr. von Hartungen, with whom he was friends.

Apparently Thomas Mann remained away from Italy for some years before he travelled in May 1907 to the Lido at Venice, whose atmosphere now so captivated him that he even stayed away from the première of *Fiorenza* at the Schauspielhaus in Frankfurt, because "the sea held me fast."[11]

In the Spring of 1909, in the company of his brother Heinrich, he undertook another trip to Italy, this time to Livorno (Leghorn), and in May 1911 he travelled with his wife to the island of Brioni, off Istria, where the news of Gustav Mahler's death reached him. As Thomas Mann wrote, in an unpublished letter to Hans von Hülsen, "Brioni was nothing for a long stay,"[12] and so the couple decided to go on to Venice. During their stay on the Lido from 26 May to 2 June in the Hotel des Bains, the novella *Death in Venice (Der Tod in Venedig)* was conceived. "It was not the first time we passed, my wife and I, a part of May on the Lido. A succession of curious circumstances and impressions had to fuse with a secret watchfulness for new things in order that a productive idea might result, which had then found its materialization under the name of *Death in Venice*."[13]

From 19 June to 12 July 1913 Thomas Mann spent a holiday in Viareggio, and on his return to Munich he felt so greatly strengthened that, even though hesitant, he could begin the difficult work on *The Magic Mountain (Der Zauberberg)*. "A three-week stay by the southern sea has again done me great good. Nevertheless, I am neglecting my strange novel[14] still further and am first of all preparing a novella which looks to become a kind of humorous counterpart to *Death in Venice*."[15]

Owing to the years of war and inflation, Thomas Mann could not set foot in Italy during the following decade. Not until October 1923 did he again travel to the south, to the Tyrol, which in the meantime had become Italian. He spent a few weeks' holiday at the "Hotel Austria" in Bolzano, and as Fate would have it, Gerhart Hauptmann was likewise a guest there during that time. Up until then the two writers had known each other only casually, but as a result of their daily encounters a closer acquaintance began, which gradually led to a personal friendship and great mutual esteem.

In the following year, in October 1924, Thomas Mann and his wife spent several weeks in Sestri Levante. For the first ten days they were joined by their friend Ernst Bertram, who taught at the University of Cologne as professor of German literary history. On 27 October, Thomas Mann wrote to him from Sestri: "Two afternoons we had rain, one morning magnificent breakers, enjoyed being on the cliffs at Chani and on the beach. . . We positively will come again."[16]

At the invitation of the Stinnes Line, Thomas Mann participated in a Mediterranean cruise in March 1925 on the ship "General San Martin," which carried him from Venice to Turkey and Greece, via Egypt, and ended at the harbor of Naples. In his article "Unterwegs," written for the *Vossische Zeitung,* he gave a detailed account of his impressions and experiences and dwelt with particular affection on the description of his reunion with Venice. The atmosphere of his novella *Death in Venice,* which that city inspired, came alive again in this article.

> My God, with what emotion did I see the beloved city again, after having borne it in my heart for thirteen years long. The slow journey in the gondola from the railway station to the steamer, with strangers, through night and

wind, I shall always count among my most beloved, most fantastic remembrances of it [Venice]. I listened again to its stillness, the mysterious lapping of the water against its silent palaces, its deathly elegance enveloped me again. Church façades, square and steps, bridges and alleys with solitary pedestrians appeared unexpectedly and vanished. The gondoliers exchanged their calls. I was at home.[17]

Thomas Mann could not see enough of the fabulous splendor, the oriental-like silhouette of the city:

The steamer, which lay before the Piazzetta, did not sail until the next evening. In the morning I was in the city, on the Piazza, in San Marco, the alleyways. I stood on deck the entire afternoon and contemplated the beloved composition: the columns with the lion, the Saint, the Arabic-bewitched Gothic of the Palace, the splendid protruding flank of the fairy-tale temple; I was certain no sight of the coming journey would be able to surpass, in my soul, this picture; I departed with genuine sorrow.[18]

Just two months later, in May 1925, Thomas Mann was once more in Italy, together with the classical philologist Ulrich von Wilamowitz-Moellendorff, in order to represent Germany at the "International Culture Week" in Florence, at which he delivered his lecture *Goethe und Tolstoi*. Joined onto this was an eight-day stay in his beloved Venice and the Lido. "We are back again . . . and congratulate ourselves warmly for it,"[19] he wrote on 17 May to his friend Ernst Bertram, who in his book on Nietzsche had devoted a special chapter to the city of Venice, mentioning, to Thomas Mann's delight, his novella *Death in Venice*.[20] Mindful of this fact, he wrote gratefully to his friend: "Is it not unseemly that we were never here together? We both find fault with this almost daily."[21]

Although the Manns had originally planned a holiday in Forte dei Marmi with the two youngest children for September 1925, they decided instead upon a visit to Casamicciola on Ischia. The colors there and the climate of the Mediterranean island seemed to the writer decidedly African, as he wrote to Bertram:

This south, which is now really almost completely "Africa" in its blueness, whiteness, harshness, dusty pungency of smells. We live high up, below is a little beach at which we bathe. . . Day after day clearness and heat. The grapes and figs are delicious. But there are *pulci* and so it plays havoc with sleeping in a way completely unfamiliar to me.[22]

A year later, from 31 August to 13 September 1926, Thomas Mann with his wife and the two youngest children spent the holiday intended for 1925 at Forte dei Marmi, the "Torre di Venere" of his first political novella *Mario and the Magician* [*Mario und der Zauberer*]. Exhausted and nervous, the writer would gladly have rested at home if the Italian atmosphere and above all the renewed encounter with the Italian people had not drawn him strongly: "I would prefer, really, to stay here," he wrote, "but also look forward again to the sea and to the sight of southern people."[23] The stay in Forte dei Marmi passed far less dramatically than portrayed in the novella appearing four years later,[24] but evidently Thomas Mann was not happy in Italy that time. To be sure, in a letter to Bertram he attributed his dissatisfaction more to external circumstances—"the children were bliss-ful, but not I, since the heat was frightful and I had to write"[25]—but it probably is not wrong to assume that it was far more the political climate of the Fascist state, which even a German tourist like Thomas Mann, who read no Italian newspapers, could hardly shut out. He felt disagreeably affected by the many symptoms of an aggressive, arrogant nationalism and the activity of Fascist agitators, and so it is significant that he then for some time avoided a trip to Italy; indeed, he even apologized to Enzo Ferrieri and Milanese friends of the journal and literary circle *Convegno* for his staying away, with the explanation that the Italian atmosphere had induced him to postpone a projected meeting until later.[26] On his second trip to Egypt, for which he set out from Genoa with his wife in mid-February 1930, he touched Italian soil only very briefly.

Four years were now to pass before the writer, who in the meantime was living in exile in Zürich, again came to Italy. Not as a tourist, but as a participant in the "International Art Congress," he was in Venice in July 1934. Once more the beauty and the singularity of this city fascinated him, and he hoped for an early return:

> The profit was the reunion with the city and its beach island, always deeply loved for profound and complex reasons, where a certain story, now already twenty years old, took place. For half of this time I had not been there again, but this chance visit has broken the ice, and I hope next Spring, if we live and the situation in Europe permits, to spend a few weeks there without fruitless babble on such topics as "L'Art et l'état" or "L'art et la réalité."[27]

For Thomas Mann, similarly as for Platen and Nietzsche, Venice again and again possessed the ambiguous, magical atmosphere of the fantastic which events of the time were incapable of touching. As Platen sought Venice in the land of dreams, so Thomas Mann felt an inner bond to this city as to no other in Italy. In a letter to his children Erika and Klaus, staying in Venice in May 1932, he expressed himself clearly about his relationship to this city:

> . . . since the place is so significant to me and I am glad to know you are there and in spirit am leading with you that life, occurring nowhere else, between the warm sea in the morning and the "ambiguous" city in the afternoon. Ambiguous is really the most moderate epithet that one can give to it . . . but in all its layers of meaning it suits it [the city] quite splendidly, and among all the absurdity and corruption which has taken possession of it, and which also irritates you, this musical magic of ambiguity nevertheless remains alive or at least has hours wherein it triumphs. You state: In the middle of the last

century it would have been beautiful. But Platen even then said: "Venice lies only in the land of dreams." Nonetheless, he loved it immeasurably, as it was in those days, just as Byron, as later Nietzsche, as still later and very insignificantly your Herrpapale. There is an unequalled hovering relationship-melancholia, which for certain souls links itself with the name Venice, full of home-like familiarity—a familiarity which today is spiritually also fairly corrupt and dulled, that I confess (Godfather Bertram has not gotten beyond that); but still my heart would beat violently if I were there once more. . .[28]

In the first nine years after emigrating from Switzerland to the United States, Thomas Mann had no opportunity to visit Italy; yet on his first trip to Europe after the war's end, the author accepted an invitation from his Italian publisher, Arnoldo Mondadori. On 30 July 1947 he and his wife left Zürich to stay four days in Meina on the Lago Maggiore, where a house was at their disposal in the park of the Villa Mondadori. This leisure time in the lively Italian family circle of the Mondadoris was interrupted only for one afternoon through interviews with Italian and German journalists. How well Thomas Mann felt, in spite of "African" heat, among the friendly family of his publisher Mondadori is clearly apparent from pictures by the photographer Federico Patellani.[29]

At the end of June 1952 Thomas Mann returned to Europe to settle definitely in the vicinity of Zürich. In September of that year he once more visited Venice, where at the UNESCO Congress he delivered his speech *Der Künstler und die Gesellschaft (The Artist and Society)*.

In April 1953 Thomas Mann saw Rome again for the first time in decades, in order officially to express his thanks to the "Accademia Nazionale dei Lincei" for the international Antonio Feltrinelli Prize bestowed upon him on 12 June 1952. Full of excitement, he set out on this trip which was to bring him back to the city to which so many old memories bound him: "It will be strange to see the city again where many, many years ago I lived with my brother and wrote on *Buddenbrooks*."[30]

Originally he had wanted to travel to Rome in September 1952, but owing to the overstrain of work the seventy-seven-year-old had to postpone the realization of this plan until the following Spring. The ten days spent in the Eternal City, from 20 to 30 April, were for Thomas Mann a deep spiritual experience. Countless memories awoke in him as, after more than half a century, he tried to rediscover the traces of his youthful years in Rome. But he no longer found the house at Via Torre Argentina 34, since previously (between 1923 and 1926) it had yielded to the temple excavations on the Largo Argentina, which revealed many treasures of antiquity.

The experience again of the superabundance of art treasures of all epochs, the living coexistence of various cultures in Rome, made a strong impression on Thomas Mann:

These squares, churches, fountains, obelisks, arrays of columns, this mesh-
ing and coexistence of the centuries, of antiquity and early and high Christian,
this profusion of art creations of sensuous and mystical piety and
originality,—as in a dream, a dream of grandeur, I absorbed everything, and
like a very intense, soul-piercing dream, it influences and lives on in me.[31]

The long tradition of spiritual and artistic creation of the West, which
becomes manifest in Rome, should fill every European with pride in his
intellectual heritage. In a letter to his publisher and friend, Gottfried
Bermann-Fischer, Thomas Mann expressed these thoughts clearly:

I was stirred by the perspective of millennia which opens up there, and
strengthened through it in my European self-confidence. Ah, in the consciousness of its ancient dignity and historical probity the Continent should
find itself and carry its head higher, instead of fading away in servility before
money and foolish power.[32]

Thomas Mann was so enthusiastically welcomed in Rome by publishers,
authors, and the public that he was nearly overcome and, in comparison
with the charming Romans, fancied himself clumsy and stiff.

Those were rapturously rich days, crowded with impressions, on which I
reflect with emotion and from which, in spite of all my fatigue, which indeed
often disagreeably appeared, I have carried away a deep spiritual edification.
I cannot be thankful enough for the almost stormy reception full of honor and
congeniality which was allotted to me. . . . Only too conscious am I of my
social inadequacy, which, thanks to utter stupefaction owing to the mag-
nitude of the impressions which assailed my susceptibility in the mighty city,
has oddly enough been allowed to disclose itself.[33]

Even before setting out on the journey to Rome it was Thomas Mann's
greatest wish to be granted a private audience with the Pope. Thanks to the
intervention of members of the Academy, he was successful in being
received by Pope Pius XII; and the conversation with the head of Catholic
Christendom became a profound experience for the writer:

It was, after slowly progressing through the antechambers, a private conversation of a short quarter hour and yet for me a remarkable and moving
moment in life, to stand before the white figure which represents so much. He
was extremely cordial. . .[34]

The topic of conversation was the "Unity of the religious world, how the
homines religiosi are after all fundamentally of one mind and in the long run
the denomination is not of such great importance."[35]

The figure of the Pope was for Thomas Mann, however, still much more
than only that of a highly cultured conversational partner: it was the symbol
of a long spiritual tradition of Western history, before which the north
German Protestant, without compromising anything, might also kneel:

"The unbeliever and heir of Protestant culture, without the slightest spiritual inhibition, bent his knee before Pius XII and kissed the ring of the Fisherman, since it was no man nor politician before whom I knelt, but a white idol, which, surrounded by the most formal spiritual and courtly ceremonial, meekly and a little sadly represented two thousand years of Western history."[36]

From Rome, Thomas Mann undertook a trip to the mountains, in order to see Palestrina again after so many eventful years.

Almost a year later, in February 1954, Thomas Mann visited Italy for the last time. The almost eighty-year-old writer had doubts indeed concerning the distant journey: "In a few days we are supposed to travel to Sicily—why and for what purpose I do not quite understand. In Morocco there is snow, and in Taormina it will also be bitter cold, even if not as cold as here. . ."[37]

On the way south, the Manns stayed two days in Rome and on 6 February arrived in Taormina. On the homeward journey at the end of the month, Thomas Mann stopped again in Rome and then, accompanied by his wife and their youngest daughter Elisabeth Borgese, visited Florence and Milan.

A double visit to Rome, the reunion with the Bargello in Florence, a few pleasant days with Medi, and finally, together with her, an excellent performance of Verdi's *Otello* at the Scala in Milan have, however, compensated us so much in the end that we do not regret undertaking the trip.[38]

As is apparent from the above examples, Thomas Mann undertook numerous trips to Italy in the fifty-nine years between 1895 and 1954. Again and again it drew him south. Yet while Goethe beheld in the land of his longing a reflection of his long striving toward his own development, the land of lemon trees remained intellectually foreign to the "outsider" Mann for many years. Goethe could not rest in Italy until all forms of existence became a living concept for him. There he collected sensual impressions which no picture, no book, could convey; there he sought and found a new cognizance of nature and from the natural form arrived at the art form and from there to the zenith of an uninterrupted development. Quite different was the reaction of Thomas Mann, who in old age still maintained he did not consciously see the manifold aspects of Italy, or that he had not wished to see them. "Indeed I do not," he wrote in a letter to Karl Kerényi, "like the great Schiller, have to confess: 'Unfortunately neither Italy nor Rome in particular is any realm for me; the physical aspect of the situation would oppress me and the aesthetic advantages would give me no compensation, since interest and feeling for the fine arts is missing.' I have a devout passion for Rome, the beautiful treasures of the millennia which it contains, its majestic cultural vista, and . . . that it 'does not lack my proper respect' is also true. But a certain disquieting kinship with the poet is nevertheless present . . . Likewise for me the world of the eye is not really my world, and basically *I desire to see nothing*—as he.''[39]

But for all that, Thomas Mann did see and observe, even if at first as from the distance and without very deep personal involvement. During his early sojourns in the south, in the years 1895, and 1896 to 1898, contacts with the Roman world still remained on the surface, and he considered the Italian surroundings more or less as side-scenery. In fact, at that time he had consciously little concerned himself with Italian culture and Italian intellectual life. In Rome and also in Palestrina he believed himself as an artist to be wholly bound to the northern world. Yet the southern atmosphere, which surrounded him day in and day out, obtruded upon him more and more. And with advancing age the spirit of the Italian world also gained a constantly growing importance in Mann's development. Finally, in his later years, his love for Italy grew so strong that the experience of this land became a significant component in his artistic personality.

Thomas Mann's avowal that the world of the eye was not his world was also ultimately refuted by his own enthusiastic words with which he described his later journeys in the south. There can be no doubt that, very early, the writer insistently wanted *to see* and that he eagerly absorbed the impressions gained in Italy, pondered them over ''reflectively,'' and could never again free himself from them.

2. Mann's Relationships with Italians

In the preceding statements it was already mentioned how little Thomas Mann had become involved with the Italian people during his first sojourns in Rome and Palestrina in the last years of the previous century. In spite of his repeated flights to the warm south, the mentality of the modern Italians, as well as their contemporary intellectual and artistic creativity, did not consciously interest him in the beginning. The first traces of a recorded involvement are found in *Reflections of a Non-Political Man (Betrachtungen eines Unpolitischen)*, published towards the end of the year 1918, in which Thomas Mann pointedly disassociated himself from the political attitude of the *Zivilisationsliterat*. With loathing he saw this spirit personified in the figure of the Italian poet Gabriele d'Annunzio, ''the ambitious word-debauchée, whose talent 'rings all bells' and to whom Latinism and nationalism is a means of influence and filling with zeal as nothing else.''[40]

The extensive recognition found in Italy of d'Annunzio's works, written—according to Thomas Mann—only for effect, out of vanity and lack of a sense of responsibility, Mann believed could be explained by the naïve lack of discrimination of the Italians:

Was that perhaps only possible in a land which remained childlike, a land in
which all of the political-democratic criticism does not prevent it nevertheless
from lacking in criticism and scepticism in every greater way, a land, therefore, to which no criticism of reason or morality, but least of all a criticism of
the artistic gift, was known?[41]

With biting words Thomas Mann attacked the irresponsible adventurer,
who desired his ecstasy and his great hour, his "historical moment," his
marriage to the people, and nothing more,[42] which he [Mann] scorned so
much that he could hardly find words for his loathing. "But from where do I
take the word to designate a measure of lack of comprehension, astonishment, loathing, *scorn* such as I feel regarding the Latin poet-politician and
warmonger of the type of Gabriele d'Annunzio?"[43] Thomas Mann called
the Italian army "Gabriel's hosts,"[44] and he accused the Italian poet of
shameless war propaganda and considered him an accessory to Italy's
entry into the First World War.

In spite of his harsh rejection of this contemporary Italian poet, Thomas
Mann had a very positive attitude towards the older Italian literature,
which, to be sure, was familiar to him at that time only very slightly. In the
Munich periodical *Jugend,* in a special issue on Dante in 1921, he published
a short article about the poet of the *Divina Commedia,* whom he described
as the "prototype of prophetic poesy."[45] For him Dante is the representative of the humanistic era, which was both bourgeois and liberal at the same
time and which, in Thomas Mann's opinion, in d'Annunzio's day was
approaching the end. As Dante, with the help of the mystical guide Beatrice
and of the "Famoso saggio" Virgil, strove after ever higher spiritual
knowledge, so also should we of the present aspire to renewal and continual
growth: "But should freedom, should individuality, personality at any time
cease to be the utmost happiness of mortals, then it will nevertheless
always be the significant personality in whose breast the alterations and
transitions of the spirit of the age occur—not easily, not boldly, but full of
difficulty, amidst struggles of conscience and pious inhibitions, in a way as
uniquely more dignified as it is uniquely decisive. May Dante's figure be for
us a symbol of reverence and contempt: reverence before death and renewal, and contempt for villainous, mindless barbarism."[46]

Not until the summer of 1920 did Thomas Mann finally come into personal contact with contemporary Italian intellectuals and the Italian literary world. On 1 February 1920 in the Milanese periodical *Secolo,* under the
title "Il romanziere della rivoluzione tedesca e suo fratello," the Italian
Germanist Lavinia Mazzucchetti,[47] who at that time was active as a journalist, analyzed the political attitude of Thomas Mann as expressed in his
Reflections of a Non-Political Man. She had set his views in contrast to
those of his brother Heinrich, whereby she sided with the political attitude
of Heinrich and criticized the strongly conservative stance of Thomas.
How delighted and at the same time amused the latter nevertheless was

over this first echo from Italy is clear from his letter on 4 July 1920 to his friend Bertram: "The *Secolo* of Milan recently published an article about *Untertan* and the *Betrachtungen,* with the conclusion that in their strange way the *Betrachtungen* are actually more interesting. That is humorous."[48]

In an acknowledging letter of thanks to the author of that first important Italian critique, Thomas Mann expressed his satisfaction at being branded by Lavinia Mazzucchetti as a conservative and not as a reactionary. Encouraged by the warmth of his words, she decided upon a first visit to Poschinger Strasse in Munich, which was to be followed later by numerous further visits there and also to Mann during his exile in Zürich. It was the beginning of a lifelong friendship which became through the years ever closer and more affectionate, and included not only the writer himself but also his wife. The Italian Germanist became for him an important connecting link with the land south of the Alps, whose more recent intellectual achievements had hitherto been remote to him.

On the other hand, thanks to Mazzucchetti's efforts concerning the work of Thomas Mann, the attention of Italy was drawn to him. Thus in May 1923 he was invited by the editor of the journal *Esame,* who was planning the publication in Italian translation of a collection of Goethe's critical writings on art and literature, to compile a selected bibliography of such works of Goethe and to assist him in his undertaking by furnishing particulars about the most important studies on the topic of Goethe as critic.[49]

In the year 1936 there appeared in the *Neue Zürcher Zeitung* Thomas Mann's *Offener Brief* to its feuilleton editor, Eduard Korrodi, in which, for the first time in public, the writer broke his previously strictly maintained silence concerning the outrages of National Socialism, renounced Hitler Germany, and before the world made a public declaration of his own emigrant status. This important document of 3 February was translated by Lavinia Mazzucchetti into Italian and circulated unpublished within the circles of the political opposition. In an unpublished letter, the translator not long afterwards wrote to the German author:

> I have allowed the article from the *NZZ* to make the rounds thoroughly and many were pleased, and I even had to quickly translate your words in order to convey them to some friends who admire you but are not versed in German. It is a great comfort to know that you are there at all, not only as an artist but also as a human being, and it is part of the many good things of these years that one retains some humanly reliable points of reference in the giddy collapse, and also that one need never have doubts about you. So! thank you! And even if we do not witness it so soon: your words live and endure and benefit the true Germanism. Almost with astonishment at my emotion and trembling upon reading your letter, I have discovered how much I am still attached to the real Germany through twenty years of cultural association . . . , although so often I thoughtlessly confuse it with the false one and revile it. And many are as I, and you have helped us all at the right moment. Grazie.[50]

Thomas Mann's sharp reply to the Dean of the University of Bonn, by whose letter the title of *Dr. honoris causa* had been taken away from him, likewise met with strong reverberations among Italian intellectual circles. Thus, for example, Toscanini[51] was deeply moved by Thomas Mann's firm attitude and wrote by return mail to the go-between, Lavinia Mazzucchetti:

> My dear and good friend. You are a treasure. I thank you infinitely for having sent me the translation of Thomas Mann's reply to the 'sehr geehrter Herr Dekan etc. etc. of Bonn . . .' Magnificent—moving—profound and humane. Thanks again for your noble toil on my behalf.[52]

A photocopy of this letter from Toscanini was delivered personally by Stefan Zweig into the hands of Thomas Mann. The echo from Italy, together with the "crescendo" from Toscanini's pen, proved to Thomas Mann the correctness of his behavior:

> Dear Friend: Accept the most sincere endorsement for my part that you are a tesoro [treasure]! Toscanini's crescendo gave me great pleasure, and I cannot thank you enough that you took the trouble of making a translation especially for the Maestro. Perhaps further use of one kind or another may yet be found for it privately.[53]

Through his decision to emigrate to the United States, Thomas Mann, for the first time, was forced to live and function outside the German-speaking countries. His hospitable home at Princeton soon became a center and rallying-point for Europeans who, like him, had to leave their homeland for political reasons. It is not surprising that he then also became associated with a circle of Italian intellectuals likewise living in exile. With one of them, the Sicilian writer, critic, and literary historian Giuseppe Antonio Borgese,[54] who had relinquished his Chair in the University of Milan and in 1931 emigrated to the United States in protest against the Fascist regime, he was linked not only by similar political views and philosophical concepts: through marriage in the fall of 1939 to Mann's youngest daughter, Elisabeth, Borgese also became Thomas Mann's son-in-law. Along with all the respect that the father-in-law felt towards the man seven years his junior, one nevertheless is conscious of a slight disapproval of his daughter's decision when he wrote to his brother Heinrich:

> Yes, we too have had a wedding. Medi has married her anti-Fascist professor, who with his 57 years would no longer have thought to win so much youth. But the child wished it and has had her way in it. He is a gifted, kind, and very well-preserved man, it must be admitted, and the most bitter hater of his Duce, whom, out of pure nationalism, he considers to be the worst of all.[55]

Thomas Mann was nevertheless deeply impressed by Borgese's views on the history and essence of the Fascist dictatorship, for indeed it had long been his own desire to call attention to the dangers of this movement which was so closely related to National Socialism. He never grew weary of expressing again and again his doubts and his grave concern: "It is the monstrous sin of the world that through weakness, apathy, and even a certain sympathy, it has allowed Fascism and National Socialism to grow. Now it lies in a battle of life and death with them, and the destruction of the enemy is the only means of making an end to his crime."[56]

At the time of his marriage, Borgese was professor of Italian literature at the University of Chicago, where he also taught political science. Time and again Thomas Mann and his wife were drawn to Chicago to visit their daughter, and on such occasions the two writers read from their latest works, as Mann once described in a letter to Erich von Kahler: "The Anti-Papist read forcefully from his Mexican opera libretto . . ."[57] When his granddaughter Angelica Borgese was born in November 1940, Thomas Mann jokingly called her "this little German-Italian counter-Axis."[58]

Collaboration between the two anti-Fascists grew even closer: in November 1941 both took part in a symposium at the University of Chicago, and at the beginning of February 1942, together with Albert Einstein, Bruno Frank, Count Carlo Sforza, Arturo Toscanini, and Bruno Walter, they sent a telegram to President Roosevelt with the entreaty to mitigate the status of "enemy alien" for declared opponents of National Socialism and Fascism.

Thomas Mann had already been in contact for some time with Count Carlo Sforza, one of the leaders of the democratic opposition in Italy. At the peak of a brilliant career in civil service and diplomacy—after one year as Italian Foreign Secretary he had, until 1922, represented his country as Ambassador in Paris—Count Sforza had resigned from his post shortly after Mussolini's accession and in 1926 emigrated to Belgium, from where he went to England and finally in 1940 to the United States. In 1941 in Montreal his work *Les Italiens tels qu'ils sont* was published, which he sent on to the revered Thomas Mann with the handwritten dedication: "A Thomas Mann—gran nome tedesco che non fa disperare dell'avenire—cordialmente Sforza."[59]

Thomas Mann thanked him with an enthusiastic letter in French, in which he declared:

> My dear Count, it is with extreme pleasure that I have read your book about Italy and the Italians. I thank you sincerely for having sent it to me and with such a flattering dedication as well. It would not be possible to treat with more wit, understanding, elegance, and authority a subject about which the world can never be enlightened enough—and about which it is so curious.[60]

Sforza advocated the view that Fascism was basically alien and unnatural to the Italian mentality and that the long history and tradition of the Italians would help them to create a new and better future for themselves. Thomas Mann applied these theories to his own fatherland, from which he was now estranged, and thus came to the conclusion that the conditions and prerequisites in Germany were, however, quite different from the Italian:

> You are fortunate! You are able to state that, for your country, Fascism is something alien and against nature. It would be difficult to prove that National Socialism plays the same rôle in Germany. . . . Your conviction that 'the long historical development of the Italians will enable them to be prepared for the greater plan which the future will create for all the peoples of Europe' is much better founded than similar hopes which our country and our people could inspire in us. And yet one is perhaps permitted to believe that the Germany of Dürer, of Bach, of Kant, and of Goethe, the Germany which has created 'Iphigenie,' 'Fidelio,' and the 'Ninth Symphony', has a breath of history which will go further than that of Nazism and racism. Finally one could even say that the German people, essentially non-political as they are, in a certain measure are predestined for the unified and depoliticized world which must be formed after the abolition of national autonomies and that, in such a situation, they would have the opportunity to display their best qualities.[61]

Over the years, Thomas Mann appears to have become somewhat skeptical regarding the clever elegance of the Count. According to his judgment—expressed in a letter to Agnes E. Meyer—he is only "an elegant, amusing, but, I believe, somewhat shallow man."[62]

Still another great Italian became closer to Thomas Mann during these years, Gaetano Salvemini, born in southern Italy in 1873, who after Mussolini's seizure of power emigrated to France in 1925, later to England, and in 1933 to the United States to teach as Professor of Italian history at Harvard University. He had already made a name for himself in Europe as the author of several significant works on Italian history and politics, as well as on prominent statesmen such as Mazzini, Francesco Crispi, and others, and his reputation had spread far beyond the borders of his own country. His greatest concern was to point out the dangers of Fascism: in 1928 after six years of Mussolini's dictatorship Salvemini's *The Fascist Dictatorship in Italy* appeared in London; and in 1935 in New York, his *Italy in the Throes of Fascism*. Salvemini, in addition to William Benton, Hermann Broch, Robert M. Hutchins, and Lewis Mumford, together with Thomas Mann and G. A. Borgese, was responsible for the drafting of the belligerent appeal *The City of Man*. Here these leading scholars and writers put forth their full energies for an unconditional defense of democratic values and goals, which were threatened by National Socialism just as much as by Fascism. On 28 January 1941 Thomas Mann sent this work to Eleanor Roosevelt with the following words:

> My dear Mrs. Roosevelt,
>   I am sending you a copy of *The City of Man*, a little book which a group of us prepared in all sincerity and humility as an attempt to outline the future world democracy and as a contribution to the solution of the fundamental problems facing all nations today. If the book appeals to you and you think it would interest the President, perhaps you will show it to him . . .[63]

In October 1943 Thomas Mann was welcomed to his lecture at Harvard University by Gaetano Salvemini, "whom I was pleased to see again, and who introduced me to the audience in the most winning way."[64]

Thomas Mann was also well acquainted with another leading anti-Fascist, the Italian author and lawyer Max Ascoli, who emigrated to the United States in 1931. Mutual respect, indeed esteem, united the two men, and moreover the active financial support of the Italian was of great help to Klaus Mann as founder and editor of the journal *Decision*. Thomas Mann wrote encouragingly to his eldest son: ". . .and if Ascoli then contributes an additional 5000 dollars, our child of sorrow might indeed be kept alive again for a while."[65]

Long before his emigration to America, Thomas Mann was linked in friendship with the great scholar and critic Benedetto Croce.[66] In 1932 the latter dedicated his *Storia d'Europa nel secolo decimonono* to Thomas Mann with the printed words "Thomas Mann" and a quotation from Dante's *Divina Commedia,* Inferno XXIII. In the second edition of Croce's book, published in 1950 in Stuttgart, these verses are rendered in German:

> Soeben traf dein Denken mit dem meinen
> In gleichem Schwunge sich, in gleichem Anblick,
> Dass ich aus beiden *einen* Ratschluss formte.[67]

> Just now thy thoughts came in among my own
> With similar attitude and similar face,
> So that of both one counsel sole I made.*

Thomas Mann was deeply moved by this recognition on the part of the respected Italian, to whom he felt quite inferior in the field of criticism. Fifteen years later he wrote to Hermann Hesse about his essay on Platen, "which, impressive for me, received Croce's applause. After all, he is a scholarly critic, which I by no means am. I like merely to offer private homages and thereby to tell tales a little out of school."[68]

In preparing for his essay "Germany and the Germans" *(Deutschland und die Deutschen)*, planned for the end of 1944 but only completed in Spring 1945, Thomas Mann thoroughly occupied himself with Croce's above-named work during November 1944: "Among all sorts of reading on German history, the Reformation and the Thirty Years' War, also from Croce's *Geschichte Europas,* I began on notes and preliminary remarks on this theme, without the proper will and resolve, by the way, to go on with it."[69]

Mann and Croce very often coincided in their views and convictions, a fact which Croce had also felt especially strongly and therefore expressed so impressively by using the Dante quotation in his dedication.

---

*Englished by Henry Wadsworth Longfellow (*The Divine Comedy of Dante Alighieri.* New York: The Nottingham Society, n.d.)

The interests and endeavors of both men ran parallel even in their youth: both made their more immediate home surroundings the object of their early studies. While Croce occupied himself with the political and cultural development of the old Kingdom of Naples, Mann became engrossed in the history of his own family and his Lübeck-Baltic Sea homeland. The essence of art and its place in the complex of human existence was the concern of Croce as well as of Mann, who again and again took up the problem of the relation of the artist to society. For Thomas Mann the artist was no longer—as in the romantic period or, in more recent times, in the circle of Stefan George followers—a superman, a prophet, a demigod, but a human being who because of his state as a poet loses contact with society yet who suffers under this isolation and yearns to return among the ranks of his fellow creatures. In Croce's aesthetics the artist even becomes characterized as the average man, whose gift accidentally points in the direction of the poetic. But this talent does not thereby entitle him to a special position in society; rather, he shares the same rights and above all the obligations of his fellow men. In Thomas Mann the parallels to this view are found in emphasis on self-conquest arising from the sense of responsibility and duty, as, for example, is clearly seen in the novel *The Magic Mountain*. In his *Storia d'Europa,* Croce designates the political backwardness of Germany as the reason for the destructive influence of German Romanticism with its mystical glorification of the German past. A self-isolation from the development of the rest of European literature, he believed, must be the consequence of this attitude. Thomas Mann was also convinced of this association and endeavored quite early to free German literature from its state of isolation and let it find contact with European literary creativity once more.

Mann's essay *Deutschland und die Deutschen* (1945) as well as Croce's book *Il dissidio spirituale della Germania con l'Europa* attempted to analyze the German problem and find a solution for it. Both writers were convinced that in the German soul good and evil lie close together and that the good may sometimes bring about evil. Independently of one another, both men saw proof of this theory in the figure of Martin Luther and his Reformation.

Coming to conclusions similar to Croce's, Thomas Mann set forth in his essay *Die drei Gewaltigen* (1949) that in Luther's soul and thereby also in the German soul the good and the evil are plainly intimately fused and that the good can frequently change into the evil. In Luther's separation of inner freedom from political freedom—in his strong nationalism, antisemitism, and anti-European thinking—Mann saw the germ of later developments in Germany.

The Italian scholar Benedetto Croce and the German writer Thomas Mann both denied the artist the right to withdraw into the ivory tower and to live a life of art for art's sake. Rather, they believed, the artist ought to yield to "the demands of the day" and strive for a synthesis of the ideal and reality. Therefore, Croce as well as Mann passed through a similar development from pure aestheticism to a consciousness of political responsibility.[70]

In 1942 the music lover Thomas Mann immersed himself with great zeal in the letters of Giuseppe Verdi, published by Franz Werfel and Paul Stefan; Mann admired Verdi's political instinct and farsightedness, for indeed after the French defeat in 1871 Verdi had already prophesied a great warlike confrontation in Europe. Mann was also deeply impressed by the noble sentiment of Verdi, who genuinely mourned the death of his rival Richard Wagner and ungrudgingly bestowed praise on him and his work, even though Wagner had shown him nothing but disdain.

While Thomas Mann was working on his great novel *Doctor Faustus,* Dante's *Divina Commedia* was included in his most serious reading. It is therefore not surprising that three stanzas from the second Canto of the "Inferno" were placed in the front as a motto for the book, which was completed after three years and eight months of strenuous and concentrated work, stanzas which in the translation by Thomas Mann's close friend, the Munich Romanist Karl Vossler, read:

> Zur Neige ging der Tag, die Dämmerung
> nahm allen Lebewesen auf der Erden
> ihr Müh und Arbeit ab, und ich allein
> begann mich einzusetzen in das Ringen
> mit meinem weiten Weg und schweren Herzen.
> Und nacherzählen will ich's ohne Fehl.
> Ihr Musen, hohe Geisteskräfte, helft mir,
> und du, die was ich schaute, hast verzeichnet,
> Erinnerung, jetzt zeige deinen Adel![71]

> Day was departing, and the embrowned air
> Released the animals that are on earth
> From their fatigues; and I the only one
> Made myself ready to sustain the war,
> Both of the way and likewise of the woe,
> Which memory shall retrace, that erreth not.
> O Muses, O high genius, now assist me!
> O memory, that didst write down what I saw,
> Here thy nobility shall be manifest!*

During his stay in Rome in 1953, Thomas Mann became acquainted with the Italian translator of *Tonio Kröger,* Emilio Castellani, a member of the management of the Italian radio. At that time the Italian was planning a film which was to be based on an early short story of Thomas Mann dating from 1904, *Ein Glück.* This project was, however, never carried out.

---

*Englished by Longfellow, *op. cit.*

Mann always possessed an active interest and deep sympathy for the difficulties with which the translators of his works had to struggle. Likewise with regard to his Italian linguistic interpreters, such as Ervino Pocar, he was always willingly prepared to explain obscurities with great patience, while on the other hand he gratefully looked into inconsistencies they discovered and into their suggestions for changes. It filled him with particular satisfaction to find that the Italian translator of the tetralogy *Joseph and his Brothers (Joseph und seine Brüder)*, Gustavo Sacerdote, was a specialist in Biblical history and was therefore able to examine the original German text extremely critically.

With the increasing circulation of Thomas Mann's books in Italy, public interest in the personality of the writer became ever greater. Lavinia Mazzucchetti, his oldest Italian friend and translator of his works, and the most active intermediary between the German writer and Italy, was the recipient of numerous letters from enthusiastic readers, who in Thomas Mann's writing rediscovered their own selves or admired his composition and style so much that they considered him to be one of the greatest writers of all time. Thus, for example, a Milanese printer, Daniele Manini, who described himself as "a simple worker," wrote of the profound impression that Thomas Mann's *Magic Mountain,* above all, had made on him.

> As far as it lies within my power (materially and in intellectual preparation), I am following with an interest truly new for me, the work of that man whom I consider (and may God correct me if I am wrong) the most highly gifted and complete artist of our time, Thomas Mann. I already made his acquaintance a long time ago in the course of my reading, and it was with *The Magic Mountain,* a novel which in my opinion exhibits stylistic perfection and exceptional narration. Later my knowledge grew richer, and the man who had appeared to me as one of the authors most difficult to understand (the conversations in the above-mentioned novel between Herr Settembrini and Naphta and Hans Castorp, and the ending, so distressing and unexpected, and all that atmosphere of sickness, of decadence and of ambiguity of the book) in brief, in the works which I read following that, Thomas Mann revealed himself to me as ever more fascinating and comprehensible.[72]

During his first trip to Europe after the war, in the summer of 1947, Thomas Mann finally made the personal acquaintance of his Italian publisher, Alberto Mondadori,[73] who came specially to Zürich to invite, in the name of his father, Arnoldo Mondadori, the writer and his wife to the Lago Maggiore, an invitation which both accepted with pleasure. Between Thomas Mann and the two Mondadoris there were numerous points of contact, and the friendship sealed in the publisher's villa in Meina, and nourished by a spate of letters exchanging thoughts, continued until Thomas Mann's death.

Mann's interest in the works of contemporary Italian writers and artists grew as his contacts continued to increase with artists of the south. This reached the point where he wanted to recommend to his American publisher, Alfred A. Knopf, that an Italian novel be published, Riccardo Bacchelli's *Il mulino del Po,* about which he had read a complimentary critique in a Swiss newspaper,[74] if Lavinia Mazzucchetti could give him a favorable judgment not only of the author but also of the work in question.[75]

The appearance of Thomas Mann's novel *Doktor Faustus* brought with it a controversy bordering on the painful with the German-American composer Arnold Schönberg concerning the parentage of the twelve-tone system, into which an Italian also intervened expressing his opinion, the conductor and composer Luigi Dallapiccola.[76] Since the latter was an admirer of Schönberg as well as Thomas Mann, he consequently presented the appropriate personality for the rôle of mediator between the two artists. It is no doubt owing to the mediating intervention of Dallapiccola and other mutual friends that a reconciliation between Thomas Mann and Schönberg, at least outwardly, gradually came to pass.

In the commentary to his Goethe songs, Dallapiccola referred to Thomas Mann's Joseph tetralogy, since the figure of Suleika treated there had suggested his "Canti" to him. For Thomas Mann's 80th birthday the Italian composer sent him the partitura of one of the *Canti della liberazione* with the handwritten dedication: "A Thomas Mann, per il 6 giugno 1955." The writer thanked him by sending the new edition of the Joseph novel, in which he wrote the following dedication: "Maestro Luigi Dallapiccola— Profondément reconnaissant pour son magnifique cadeau que je serai toujours heureux et fier de posséder. Kilchberg, 23 guigno 1955. Allerherzlichsten Dank! Thomas Mann."[77]

In 1950 Thomas Mann kept up an exchange of correspondence—brief, but highly interesting for both parties—with the prominent Italian philosopher Enzo Paci, who in July of the same year founded the Milanese journal for philosophy and culture, *aut aut.* In one of the letters Paci gave an account of his once fellow student, Gian Antonio Manzi, who was preparing a dissertation on Thomas Mann, but whose endeavors came to a sudden close through his tragic suicide in May 1935. Thomas Mann was deeply moved by this letter:

> I have underlined many passages in your letter, especially where you speak about the young friend who gave you Dürer's "Melancholia" and who took his own life. I share your grief for him. It is not yet two years since I lost my eldest son Klaus, a very gifted writer, who voluntarily gave himself to death. He could not live in a world such as that of which you speak in your letter saying some very true things.[78]

During his stay in Rome in 1953 Thomas Mann became acquainted with the archaeologist Ranuccio Bianchi Bandinelli,[79] who journeyed to Rome from Florence, where he represented his profession as a professor at the

University, in order to show Thomas Mann and his wife the special beauties and sights of the city. He guided Thomas Mann, who was particularly interested in the oldest vestiges of Western culture, through ancient Rome and in doing so felt like a copy of Eckermann.[80]

While in Rome, Thomas Mann also made the acquaintance of Giulio Einaudi, the founder and president of the important publishing house, who in previous years had published various works by Mann. A short time after the meeting, Einaudi sent the writer a lengthy report of his publishing activity, which was at the same time a critical and analytical essay on the modern, politically involved Italian literature. Einaudi publications of works by writers of the resistance against Fascism (such as Pavese, Gramsci, Pintor, and Ginzburg) accompanied the communication, for which Thomas Mann promptly and sincerely thanked Einaudi:

> On a trip to England and Germany I received your letter, which furnished me with such impressive and splendid insights into the formation of your publishing house, its moral driving forces, the spirit of its co-workers. I thank you just as cordially for this truly interesting information as for the rich gift of books which I found here. In view of my shamefully limited practice in reading Italian it will no doubt require some time until I have really made this spiritual endowment my own. But I look forward to the hours that will be devoted to its conquest and thereby to a most necessary expansion of my knowledge of the young literary Italy.[81]

Mann saw in the fate of the anti-Fascist writers of Italy a strong parallel to his own life, which owing to the First World War had been guided into other paths, to new perceptions and convictions.

> How greatly your description of the fates of all these martyrs to their own convictions moved me! It is pure reverence which I offer to their fighting and dying. The quotation from Pintor's letter to his brother seems strangely familiar to me: "Without the war I would have remained an intellectual bound up in prevailing literary problems, etc." For me, the one so much older, the First World War already played the rôle which fell to the Second for these young people. The crisis of my life found its expression in *Reflections of a Non-Political Man;* and thereafter I have not ceased to confront the apolitical cultural concept of my compatriots, the Germans, with the totality of the human, of humanitarianism, which of necessity includes the political.[82]

The inclination of many Italian intellectuals towards Communism, though, astonished Thomas Mann, who saw in politicalization of art and science a great peril to the free spirit. Is it not, he asked himself, the sign of a certain naïveté, when such a self-willed, mystically inclined artist as Cesare Pavese assumes that under a Communistic régime his freedom of creativity and thought could be preserved uncurtailed?

> It is indeed another matter with respect to the totalitarian politics which Communism embraces and enforces. Who would not have his doubts about

the cultural and pedagogical competency of a Communistic bureaucracy? About the fruitfulness of the official control of art and science by the Party state? These doubts have always kept me at a distance from the Communistic ideological world, and it does not take offense at me, apparently, because I refuse on the other hand to take part in the stupid Communist hunt à l'américaine. But I ask myself, how, for example, Pavese, with his interest in "the most delicate and most intricate topics of contemporary philosophy" and his inclination towards mythos, has imagined his personal existence in a Communist-disciplined Italy, in the straitjacket of Communist dogma. Has he believed that such sublime trivialities, including his weakness for my Joseph stories, would be *allowed* him under Communist rule? That would have been naïve.[83]

At about the time when Thomas Mann entered into closer relations with the publisher Giulio Einaudi, correspondence began with the critic Emilio Cecchi, with the Germanist of the University of Trieste, Guido Devescovi, as well as with other Italians, but it would be too much to examine them all here in detail. The indefatigable writer, who served his work to the last year of his life—indeed, was frankly possessed to bring it to a good conclusion—took the time, in spite of many-sided demands, not only to cultivate the old friendship with Lavinia Mazzucchetti but also to establish new bonds of friendship with a circle of Italian intellectuals, since precisely in Italy he found a sympathetic atmosphere of intellectual freedom and individuality which he sorely missed in the America of the McCarthy period and also in postwar Germany.

For Thomas Mann's eightieth birthday *Il Ponte* issued a special edition in honor of the German writer, who, following a prematurely concluded holiday on the Dutch coast, read it in the Zürcher Kantonsspital with pleasure and gratitude. On 10 August 1955, hence two days before his death, he wrote to Lavinia Mazzucchetti:

My present wretchedness was necessary to enable me to get down to a closer examination of the issue of *Ponte* which brought your fine birthday essay, and I am keenly aware of how much thanks I still owe you for this warm-hearted demonstration with regard to my personal being and our long-standing friendly exchange. Alas, this expression of thanks is not a letter which would be worthy of the praise that you bestow upon my written greetings in the commemorative article."[84]

This letter, in which he thanked his Italian friend of many years and the coworkers of the journal *Il Ponte* for their warm words of praise and affection, and which represents the last written document from the writer's hand, appears beyond any doubt to prove the fact that particularly during his last years of life Thomas Mann was attached to Italy and the Italians with a very special heartfelt sympathy.

3. Summary

In examining the documented encounters of Thomas Mann with the Italian world one comes to the conclusion that for the German writer and his work the contacts with the land and character of the Latins were at first of apparently slight, but then of increasingly greater, significance. While the early sojourns in 1895 and 1896 to 1898, primarily in Rome and Palestrina, allowed the young writer to remain intellectually in his own homeland and to keep almost completely aloof from closer contact with Italian culture and Italian intellectual life, his interest in the southern world nevertheless steadily increased in the following period, even if at first only with reserve and respect. But how thoroughly he absorbed his Italian surroundings, perhaps unconsciously, is proven almost fifty years after his stay there by the exact description of Palestrina and its inhabitants in *Doctor Faustus*.

Again and again Thomas Mann travelled to the land beyond the Alps, where Venice with its Oriental fairytale atmosphere so enchanted him and held him fast that he was absent from the première of his only drama, *Fiorenza*. Holidays on the southern sea became a cherished habit for him, until the years of war and inflation put a temporary end to these trips. In the twenties, under the Fascist régime, Italy lost much of its charm for Thomas Mann, and the writer's visits there became ever more infrequent.

During the period of his American exile and of the Second World War, Thomas Mann had no opportunity to visit Italy, but on his first trip to Europe after the war's end, in the summer of 1947, he once more went to the south at the invitation of his Italian publisher. In 1954, a year before his death, Thomas Mann was for the last time a guest in Italy, which through appointing him as a member of the Accademia dei Lincei and bestowing upon him the coveted Feltrinelli Prize had demonstrated a respect and love as had hardly any other country.

To be sure, in the course of time his contact with Italian people and Italian intellectual life had developed relatively slowly. In the period following the First World War, Thomas Mann's judgment of d'Annunzio was harshly negative, yet he could not withhold his admiration for the great Italian poet of earlier times, Dante. The mentality of the Italian people per se, however, still interested the German writer very little up to the twenties, and it is no surprise that in his early works, increasingly set in the south, the Italians exercised only a secondary function.

Not until his friendship with Lavinia Mazzucchetti and contact with the Italian intellectual and scholarly world in the twenties did Thomas Mann attain a much more positive attitude toward the Italian people and its great thinkers, an attitude which admittedly was clouded to a certain extent by the negative impressions which Thomas Mann received on a trip in 1926 from the people incited by Fascism. In his Swiss and, later, American exiles, however, the writer met many Italians who shared his views and hopes, so that occasionally in the political area a collaboration with leading Italian emigrants resulted.

Thomas Mann's understanding of the character and individuality of his Italian contemporaries then became ever greater, and ever closer friendships bound him to them, whether with the scholar Benedetto Croce, the world-renowned cultural philosopher, or with the publisher Mondadori, or with the various Italian critics and scholars who in their own country concerned themselves with his works. The steadily increasing and deepening correspondence with his Italian friends and acquaintances, among whom, to be sure, no poets or writers were found, was evidence of the close bond which tied Thomas Mann to the south. His love for Italy, which grew ever stronger in the postwar years, reached its zenith indeed with Mann's visit to Rome in April 1953, which brought honors and receptions of every kind to the German writer and also, at his request, an audience with Pope Pius XII.

There can be no doubt that this reverence on the part of the Italian public as well as on the part of Italian literary criticism during his last years had contributed greatly to an increase in the writer's sympathy towards Italy. On the occasion of his eightieth birthday and especially after his death, the Italian press in all fields, among them the Roman weekly journals *Il Mondo* and *Il Contemporaneo,* as well as the monthly publication *Il Ponte,* in numerous articles and essays lauded the great art of the man who by many Italians was considered as *l'ultimo grande tedesco,* the last great German.

Thomas Mann's sojourns in Italy and his encounters with Italian culture and Italian people, as well as with Italian cities and countryside, have found a more prominent deposition in his work than is at first imagined from the accounts and avowals of Mann quoted above. In the second chapter it will be shown how Thomas Mann's attitude concerning the Italian milieu was at first very reserved. Soon, however, the beauty of the south, so differently constituted from that of his northern homeland, wrapped him in its spell. His initial apparent indifference gradually developed into a steadily growing interest, particularly in the old Italian art and culture. The glorious past of this country then increasingly became for Thomas Mann a bridge to the Italy of the present. The continuously closer contacts with Italian contemporaries and the admiration which flowed to meet him from the land south of the Alps enabled the German writer to overcome all of his initial skepticism and evoked in him a steadily deepening love for Italy and its people, which was more and more clearly reflected in his subsequent work.

II
Reflections of Italy in Mann's Work

1. The Early Novellas

The Will to Happiness (1896), Disillusionment (1896), The Dilettante (1897)

Already in three early stories by Thomas Mann the scene of the action was, to a not insignificant extent, shifted to Italy: in the tale *The Will to Happiness (Der Wille zum Glück)*, appearing in 1896 in three consecutive issues of *Simplicissimus;* in the novella *Disillusionment (Enttäuschung)*, written shortly thereafter; and in the novella *The Dilettante (Der Bajazzo)*, published in 1897 in the journal *Neue deutsche Rundschau*. In the year 1898 these three stories, together with some others, were issued by the S. Fischer publishing house under the title *Der kleine Herr Friedemann*.

The Will to Happiness was the first in a series of novellas about artists that anticipated certain motifs later to be consummately treated by the writer in *Tonio Kröger*. Paolo Hofmann (the conflict of his nature and his destiny is already hinted at through the half-German, half-Latin name) is a painter who suffers from an incurable disease and in his situation is unable to cope with life. Restlessly he roams throughout southern Europe and especially Italy, where he sees again the friend of his youth, the narrator of the story. He meets him by chance in a café in Rome and then spends a month with him in the Eternal City. Thomas Mann's own experiences and impressions of his stay in Rome in 1895 are reflected in the description of Rome, which concerning his artistic work must have deeply impressed him even on this first trip to Italy, although at that time he would not admit this fact to himself.[1] Without a doubt Mann rejected certain aspects of the south during that period. The oriental-like superabundance of colors and sounds seemed too overwhelming for him and we might well consider the following statement of the young Paolo Hofmann to be a conviction of the writer:

> During the whole next month I wandered through the city with him: Rome, this superabundantly rich museum of all art, this modern metropolis in the south, this city, which is full of noisy, brisk, passionate, clever life, and yet into which the warm wind carries across the sultry inertia of the Orient.[2]

This atmosphere of the south, defined by the "sultry inertia of the Orient," had, nevertheless, undoubtedly affected Mann much more strongly than he was aware during the formative period of his first works. In his novella *Death in Venice*, not created until sixteen years later, this sensuously hot sultriness and oriental-like, nearly decaying beauty of the south became an important element, which in the deepest sense was a contributing factor to the plot.[3]

It is not only the works of art which the narrator of the story *The Will to Happiness,* and thereby Thomas Mann himself, admires in Rome, but also the landscape in the environs of the Eternal City, where the traces of antiquity form an harmonious unity with the broad plains bounded by hills and mountains.

> We took advantage of the wonderful late summer morning for a walk along the Via Appia and now rested, after following the ancient road a long way out, on a little hill with cypresses standing about, from which one enjoys a delightful view of the sunny Campagna with the great aqueduct and of the Alban Hills, which a soft haze veils.[4]

Paolo Hofmann, whose appearance is the pure image of his black-haired South American mother, also inherited from her a longing for the south. Yet Italy cannot bring him the longed-for happiness and inner peace; he is too strongly bound to his north German homeland through inheritance from his German father. He returns to Germany when he learns that the father of the girl he loves gives his consent to their marriage. But neither in the north is Paolo capable of living; he dies the morning after his wedding night—until the end a lonely man who, because of his inner conflict symbolized by his sickness, could find a home neither in Italy nor in Germany.

Thomas Mann's three-week stay in Venice in October 1896 left behind distinct traces in the novella *Disillusionment (Enttäuschung).* Once more the hero is a man on intimate terms with death, whose life is so lacking in love and purpose that he finds himself in a state of total isolation. His lonely figure forms a striking contrast to the colorful and gay scene of the Piazza San Marco, whose beauty and harmony had deeply impressed Thomas Mann, but by which the hero of the novella is disillusioned, as with all the impressions of his life. "On the broad square only a few people were moving about here and there, but from the many-coloured marvellous building, whose sumptuous and fabulous contours and golden ornamentations were set off in enchanting luminosity against a delicate pale blue sky, the standards floated in the light sea breeze; directly in front of the main portal a flock of pigeons had gathered around a young girl who scattered grain, while still more and more swooped down from all sides . . . A sight of incomparable shining and festive beauty."[5]

From this description of the Piazza San Marco it is clear that, as early as his first encounter with Venice, Thomas Mann must have felt a special admiration and love for this city. His relationship to this creation, which even then seemed to him like a fairy tale, grew to be ever more intimate in the course of his life. Undoubtedly, however, his impressions were also subject to certain changes: while on his first visit Mann emphasized the "festive beauty" and the "enchanting luminosity" of the city, in later years it assumed other aspects for him, which will be closely examined in the discussion of the novella *Death in Venice.*

The novella *The Dilettante* also deals with a psychological presentation of a lonely social outsider, again, as in the novella *The Will to Happiness,* of an artist who entrusts to his diary the ebb of his life, which ends in a state of complete alienation and isolation. While in his youth his sensitive, artistically refined mother recognizes her son's talent in the field of art, his unimaginative, prosaic father sees in him nothing but a "Bajazzo," that is to say, corresponding to the Italian word "pagliaccio," a dummy, a buffoon, a wag or clown such as one finds among tightrope walkers and acrobats. Hence his father describes his drawings merely as "clownery" and "joking." Against his will the youth is forced into a commercial career, for which, however, the artistically gifted young man is totally unsuited.

After the death of his parents he wins his long-desired freedom to make his own decisions. In order to escape complete isolation and find himself, he decides to leave his north German homeland. He hopes the trip will have a therapeutic effect and, like Paolo Hofmann and the stranger in the novella *Disillusionment,* roams through the world in the search for happiness and self-fulfillment. He, too, is immediately drawn by Italy, which by its color and gaiety seems to promise the lonely one a contact with life. From Verona the dilettante travels to Rome, where in passing he is impressed by St. Peter's, to Naples, and finally even to Palermo in Sicily, with which Mann was not yet acquainted at the time of writing this novella. Yet the dilettante is as unsuccessful in forming a bond with the pulsating life around him as is Paolo Hofmann or the stranger, and after his return from abroad his love for a young girl must remain unfulfilled, since the alien can no longer make contact with his fellowmen. It is significant that in the crucial scene at the bazaar Thomas Mann presents the girl whom the dilettante loves as dressed in colorful Italian costume: "In a little stall garlanded with fir branches she was selling wine and lemonade and was dressed as an Italian girl: with the colorful skirt, the white, square headdress and the brief bodice of a girl from the Alban Hills, whose blouse sleeves left her slender arms exposed to the elbow. A little flushed, she leaned sideways against the counter, toyed with her gay fan, and chatted with a number of gentlemen."[6] The brightly colored costume makes the girl seem still more lively and consequently still more unattainable for the dilettante.

In the three earlier novellas of Thomas Mann—*The Will to Happiness, Disillusionment,* and *The Dilettante*—the motif "Italy" therefore has a strongly symbolical meaning: it represents the pulsating life for which the hero longs in his state of isolation caused by his artistic talent or sickness. In Paolo Hofmann and the dilettante the longing for the south is further strengthened through inheritance from a Latin or artistically gifted mother. Yet the respective heroes, who grew up in the sober atmosphere of north

Germany, can find no deliverance in Italy either, since the paternal inheritance is too strong, and the chasm which yawns before them is too great to permit them the feeling of being at home in Italy.

None of the three wanderers succeeds in establishing any contact with his Italian surroundings and thereby any rescue from loneliness. In the main characters of these three novellas, Thomas Mann's own attitude towards Italy in that period seems to be reflected: he, likewise, found no contact at that time with the colorful animation of Italian life so little corresponding to his north German temperament.

Tonio Kröger (1903)

Six years after the completion of *The Dilettante,* in his novella *Tonio Kröger,* Thomas Mann once again raised the problem of the "straying bourgeois," the artist who seems to find no place in human society. Like Paolo Hofmann, Tonio Kröger also came of the marriage of a sober, north German merchant and an artistically gifted, sensitive Latin mother, whom his father "had once fetched from the bottom of the map."[7] Again the conflict in the soul of the young man is expressed through name symbolism: the north German family name forms a sharp contrast to the resonant Italian given name, a contrast which symbolizes the inner conflict of the young man.

Although Tonio loves and respects his dark-haired, passionate mother, she still seems to him at times somewhat "loose" in her behavior and not respectable or serious enough for the Kröger family. Tonio feels as disturbing the inheritance from his mother, which sets him apart from his contemporaries, in the same way as his given name, to his grief, sets him apart from the circle of his schoolmates. Tonio admires his mediocre and "normal" companions and longs to be admitted into their circle as an equal, just as he longs for the love of the blonde Inge Holm. Thus, Tonio stands "between two worlds" and is "at home in neither."[8]

Through a stay in the south where "the blood of his mother"[9] draws him, Tonio hopes to find his true self and a release from his isolation. He, too, perceives, just like Paolo Hofmann and the heroes of the earliest novellas, the possibilities and allurements of a liberation from the confinement of his self, suffered in his homeland, but he is not successful in sharing deeply in the southern rhythm of life either. Just like the other heroes, he remains an outsider. In his isolation he becomes ever further entangled in erotic adventures, which leave him with a feeling of intense guilt.

A loathing and hatred for the senses seized him and a thirsting for purity and respectable peace, while still he breathed the air of art, the mild and sweet, scent-impregnated air of a perpetual Spring, in which the secret rapture of procreation germinates and brews and buds. So it simply resulted that he, unsteadily flung to and fro between crass extremes, between icy intellectuality and scorching sensuality, led, under pangs of conscience, an exhausting life, an uncommon, dissolute, and extraordinary life, which he, Tonio Kröger, basically detested.[10]

As with Paolo Hofmann, with Tonio also the inheritance from his north German father is stronger than from his hot-blooded Latin mother, a conflict which prompts both young men to go south. Tonio confesses to Lisaweta his disappointment over it and at the same time his recognition that he does not fit in the south:

> God, get away from me about Italy, Lisaweta! I don't care about Italy to the point of contempt! It's been a long time since I imagined I belonged there. Art, no? Velvety blue sky, ardent wine and sweet sensuality. . . . In short, I don't like it. I renounce it. The whole *bellezza* makes me nervous. I also can't stand all those terribly lively people down there with their black animal gaze. These Latin peoples have no conscience in their eyes.[11]

Once more Italy symbolizes colorful, pulsating life, but this time Thomas Mann gives it distinctly negative undertones: the south is superficial and without conscience and is the opposite of the honest, upright circumspection of the north. Tonio Kröger can only go north, to his homeland, in order to find himself. But in order to become a great artist, his painful sojourn in the south was of great importance, since there Tonio Kröger developed the selective, refined discretion and taste which his northern artistry had lacked.

2. *Gladius Dei* (1902)

As a kind of preliminary stage to his first and only drama, *Fiorenza,* Thomas Mann wrote the novella *Gladius Dei,* in which the action takes place, if not in Italy, at least in a southern atmosphere imitative of Italy. Munich, the scene of the plot, is provided with all the attributes of an Italian city, specifically a city which evokes strong reminders of the Italy of the Renaissance, both through its architecture as well as through the works of art displayed in the antique shops. "Scattered everywhere are the little shops selling sculpture, picture frames, and antiques, from whose windows the busts of the Florentine *Quattrocento* women, full of a noble piquancy, gaze at you. And the owner of the smallest and humblest of these shops speaks to you of Donatello and Mino da Fiesole, as if he had received the right of reproduction from them personally."[12]

The Munich of the turn of the century is depicted as a city in which the joyously sensual intensity of life, the deceptiveness of an art of beauty and of love of life stand as the hub, just as it has been told to us about the Florence of the fifteenth century, where the emphasis on the pagan and sensual in the fine arts went so far that the churches were occasionally adorned with pictures of the Madonna which obviously were portraits of widely known prostitutes.[13] Even the south German people, although they whistle the *Nothung* motif from Wagner's "Ring," so popular around 1900, and in the evenings go to the modern theater, remind one of Italians of a light-hearted epoch.[14]

A strong contrast to this colorful sensuous atmosphere is formed by the figure of the haggard, gloomy young man Hieronymus, whose name corresponds exactly to Girolamo, the given name of the historic Savonarola (since the Italian translation of Hieronymus is Girolamo) and whose features exhibit an unmistakable similarity to those of Savonarola. His dark brows, the large and hooked nose, the strong, thick lips, the hollow cheeks and the square projecting chin are the characteristics of Savonarola which stand out in the portraits which have come down to us. Even the cowl is not missing, which he has drawn over his head, just as Fra Bartolomeo has presented him in the portrait which is now found in the monastery of San Marco in Florence.

> He gazed with an expression of knowledge, limitation and suffering. Seen in profile, this face closely resembled an old portrait from the hand of a monk, preserved at Florence in a narrow and austere cloister cell, out of which once issued a terrible and shattering protest against life and her triumph.[15]

This "protest against life and her triumph" finds its expression in Thomas Mann's sketch *Gladius Dei* in the unsuccessful attempt of the young man to induce the owner of a large Munich art shop to remove the reproduction of an extremely worldly portrayal of the Madonna from the display window and to burn it. For the youth sees in this painting the expression of the depravity of his time, just as Savonarola as a preacher of repentance had attacked the vices of the Renaissance epoch. On the eve of such a penitential sermon in the year 1492 Savonarola had a vision:[16] he heard loud thunder and beheld a sword which hung menacingly over Rome. On a commemorative medal which Ambrogio della Robbia created for Savonarola is imprinted the Latin wording of the vision: "Gladius Dei super terram . . . Cito et velociter." It is to be assumed that during his early sojourns in Italy, Thomas Mann had examined this medal and that the Latin words had so strongly impressed him that he ended his sketch with them. Hieronymus experiences the same vision as Savonarola: "Against the yellowish bank of clouds which was drawn up over the Theatinerstrasse and within which it faintly thundered, he saw a broad fiery sword, which in the sulphurous light stretched itself over the joyous city."[17] In great ecstasy he murmurs the Latin words, more than ever convinced of his divine appointment to extirpate the vices and vanities of his time with all the means at his disposal.

In Thomas Mann's sketch *Gladius Dei* the theme of the contrast and tension between the asceticism of the north and the sensuality and lively bustle of the south is dealt with again. The rebellion of Hieronymus against the triumph of life is again a rejection of the seductive Italian intensity of life which repels the "lonely one." Hieronymus protests against the sweet sensuality of the south, which did not have the power to deliver Paolo Hofmann *(The Will to Happiness)*, and from which Tonio ultimately turned away in renunciation. The passion with which Hieronymus declares his rejection and his protest is, however, evidence that he nevertheless has become deeply affected by the seductive wiles of this southern world.

3. *Fiorenza* (1905)

In the drama *Fiorenza* the setting shifts from Munich completely to Italy, to Florence. The Hieronymus of the novella changes in the drama to the monk Girolamo Savonarola, and the point of time of the action is now transferred from the turn of the nineteenth to the twentieth century into the Italian Renaissance, the brilliant epoch of Lorenzo il Magnifico.

Thomas Mann began to write the drama, which at first was to have the title "König von Florenz" ("King of Florence"),[18] in the autumn of 1900. This originally planned title was supposed to imply that the strong moral values of the monk overcame the Florentine vanity and outward splendor, which for Thomas Mann were synonymous with the seductive, pulsating life of Italy, which had already signified a danger for Tonio Kröger and by means of which Gustav Aschenbach would later be destroyed. The symbolism of the title "König von Florenz" was explained by Thomas Mann himself in a letter to his brother Heinrich in the following manner: "The ambiguity of the title is indeed intended. Christ and Fra Girolamo are one: namely, the weakness become genius attains dominion over life."[19] Moreover, the writer emphasized that the climax of the drama must be "The cruciamento delle vanità,"[20] the crucifixion of the vanities.

In further letters to his brother Thomas Mann reported on his copious study of sources on the subject. Above all he was occupied with Jacob Burckhardt's *Kultur der Renaissance*[21] and Pasquale Villari's work, *Savonarola e i suoi tempi,*[22] which appeared in German translation for the first time in 1886. Also the biographies of artists by Giorgio Vasari, *Vite de' più eccelenti pittori, scultori ed architetti,*[23] which he presumably read in German, brought the time of the Italian Renaissance closer to him. The visit to a large Munich art exhibition of copies of Florentine Renaissance sculpture gave Thomas Mann many significant hints: ". . . for me extremely interesting," he stated in a letter to Heinrich, "because through the portrait busts one becomes acquainted in such a pleasant way with the type of people of those days."[24]

Yet Mann had the feeling that a stay in Florence, which at that time he did not yet know, was absolutely essential for him in order to be able to complete his drama. "How much there must be to learn in Florence! If I might only go there, so that my soul's dream could be realized. I would like to express so many things in the play, but I am not nearly conversant enough with the externals of the affair; the necessary material cannot be gathered from a few books."[25]

In May 1901 the hoped-for trip to Florence was realized, and Thomas Mann was able to occupy himself thoroughly on the spot with Florentine history of the fifteenth century and with old customs and practices of the city. He visited the Uffizi and the Bargello several times and studied Vasari's portraits of Lorenzo il Magnifico and Pico della Mirandola in detail. In Santa Maria Novella his attention was particularly held by the paintings of Domenico Ghirlandaio, and the possibility appears to exist that Ghirlandaio's portrayal of Lucrezia Tornabuoni in the fresco "Birth of the Virgin Mary" in Santa Maria Novella had suggested the figure of Fiore to the writer.[26]

The writing of the drama was laborious and was only completed in January 1905, just before Thomas Mann's marriage. Up to the end the writer had doubts that he might not be equal to the form of the drama, but on the other hand he was convinced that the "dialectical, contentious and contradictory, profoundly discursive character of the material"[27]* demanded the sequence of dialogues and scenes.

Just as the monk Hieronymus (in the novella *Gladius Dei*), so Savonarola, in the drama, condemns the sensuality and licentiousness of his fellowmen. For both, the splendor and the joy of living of their epochs, as well as the abundance of artistic production, are only a deceptive illusion, behind which in reality a moral degeneration is hidden. While Hieronymus curses the corrupt people of Munich, Savonarola condemns dissolute Florence, whose symbol is the beautiful Fiore whom he himself once loved and desired, but by whom he had been laconically rejected. Through Fiore, Savonarola had hoped to overcome his isolation and alienation, just as Tonio Kröger had longed for a release from his existence as an outsider when he went to Italy. Yet both men become disillusioned: beauty and joy of living, as they are embodied one time by Italy *(Tonio Kröger)*, and another time by Fiore *(Fiorenza)*, prove to be only an illusion, behind which unrestrained sensual pleasure and depravity are hidden. Just as Tonio Kröger is filled with "loathing and hatred," Savonarola likewise feels his desire to be a disgrace. Yet, for both, this experience signifies a maturation process: they, who were in danger of abandoning their true self because of their encounter with southern eroticism, have only now truly found it.

In this drama Thomas Mann wished to express his views on the problem of the relation between life and spirit and at the same time to create the new ideal of a hero. Two adversaries face one another in this work: Lorenzo as the representative of life and Savonarola as the fanatical agent of the spirit.

---

*Englished by Richard and Clara Winston in *Letters of Thomas Mann, 1889–1955* (New York: A. A. Knopf, 1971), p. 684.

On a higher plane, however, these two mortal enemies are brothers in spirit, and the tragedy of the drama results from this conflict. For likewise Lorenzo, who symbolizes life, at the bottom of his heart really longs for the spiritual. Just as Savonarola, he also is sickly and ugly, but through enormous will power he has gained a beauty of his own. In Savonarola a similar miracle has occurred, "the miracle of reborn innocence."[28] This miracle means that spirit can become action and therefore spirit and power do not need to be an antithesis. Both protagonists represent a new ideal of a hero with Thomas Mann, men who by virtue of their spiritual strength, their will, and their energy become heroes. To Piero's question, "Is then, the one who is strong, no hero?"[29] Fiore replies: "No. Rather he who is weak, but of such a glowing spirit that he nevertheless wins the wreath,—he is a hero."[30]

Fiorenza is not an historical drama in the true sense of the word. The setting, Renaissance Florence, the external description of the main characters largely correspond with historical fact, but the presentation of the problems, the treatment of the central idea, the relationship of art to life, spring from the mentality of a more recent age. Thomas Mann himself admitted: "The rest is Nietzsche. For those two Caesars and 'hostile brothers,' who contest one another's right to the erotic possession of the symbolic city, Lorenzo and the Prior,—they are only all too much the dithyrambic and the ascetic priest, as they both appeared in the book" (i.e., in Nietzsche's *Genealogie der Moral*): "They embody it to such a degree that all efforts were understandably disregarded to present something further, more specific, less theoretical—to relate their psychological type to more intimate and burning problems."[31]

Although in the drama the dying aesthete Lorenzo wins the victory with the words "it is death, which you proclaim as spirit, and the life of all life is art,"[32] Mann's preference still belongs to Savonarola, as he confessed many years later in his work *Reflections of a Non-Political Man:* ". . . thus my real interest, my private intellectual partiality and curiosity, however, concerned the representative of the literary spirit and his clever trick of skilfully making himself into a theoretical demagogue by means of 'reborn innocence.' "[33]

The drama, in which the unities of time and place are strictly observed, occurs on the day of Lorenzo dei Medici's death, hence, on 8 April 1492, in the Villa Medicea at Careggi near Florence. A number of historical and fictitious characters appear, but the two main figures are seen only in the third and last act. Nevertheless, from the beginning of the drama the figure of Savonarola in particular stands at the center and comes to life at first by means of indirect reflection through the artists and writers. Fiore tells of his unhappy youthful love for her, the merchant Niccolo Cambi speaks of Savonarola's attacks upon the Medici, and finally Lorenzo himself relates the historically true episode of the summons of Savonarola to Florence as

Prior, for which, however, the priest showed no gratitude to the Prince at all. Pico della Mirandola describes the success of the preacher, and Lorenzo's son Giovanni is deeply impressed by the prophecies of Savonarola. When finally towards the end of the last act the admired or hated—depending upon the attitude of the commentator—man appears, a certain anticlimax is involved, since Savonarola is small and weak, and his face with the thick lips and the hooked nose is ugly. And yet from then on his presence entirely dominates the scene. Just as in the description of Savonarola, Thomas Mann also kept to historical tradition in the portrayal of Lorenzo and his dying hours.

On the basis of a detailed study of sources and occupation with the history and art of the city of Florence, the writer undertook the description of the milieu and the portrayal of the characters. The atmosphere of the Italian Renaissance is reproduced in its sundry aspects: the group of serious scholars finds its representatives in Lorenzo's former teacher Marsilio Ficino and the highly gifted Pico della Mirandola, while Luigi Pulci and Angelo Poliziano represent the art of poetry. A certain contrast to these dignified figures is formed by the group of high-spirited artists, who embody the sensual side of the Italian Renaissance. Their lively conversations are full of temperament and humor, and particularly in this group Thomas Mann succeeded well in the presentation of certain characterizations, treated not without irony. Thus he has disputes arise several times among the artists, which, typical for Italians, are based on local patriotism, for example when Aldobrandino reproaches Grifone with: "You hate me, I know it, you are my mortal enemy, because you are from Pistoia, from subjugated Pistoia, but I am a Florentine and by birth your master."[34]

As in the novella *Gladius Dei* the artistic representation of the Madonna is discussed. Savonarola had publicly attacked the all-too-sensuous portrait by the painter Aldobrandino and so stirred up the people against it that the artist was assaulted. But he defends himself in the spirit of the Italian Renaissance: "I cannot paint the Madonna as a worn-out miserable woman, as this mouther of Paternosters demands; I need color, I need brilliance. And since the most holy Virgin does not do me the favor of sitting personally for her likeness, then I must be satisfied if a worldly maiden will humor me."[35]

Despite the striking presentation of the atmosphere of the Italian Renaissance at the court of Lorenzo the Magnificent, Thomas Mann vigorously denied having glorified the Renaissance. Hence in a letter to a Catholic newspaper he wrote explicitly: "It has been said that in 'Fiorenza' I am a glorifier of the Italian Renaissance. That is an error. In it I am from the first to the last word a critic of the Renaissance—though one of the sort who completely assimilates the relative manifestation, entirely understands it and knows how to speak in its language. But that in these dialogues, which speak the language of the Renaissance, the Renaissance is meant to be criticized and by no means glorified, indeed follows from the fact that not Lorenzo of the Medicis, but his adversary, the monk Girolamo Savonarola, is the real hero."[36]

As in the previous novella *Gladius Dei,* in this drama Mann was also primarily occupied with the shaping of the contrast between asceticism and sensuality. In his early novellas the writer had already concerned himself with this contrast and in doing so equated the motif of asceticism with the atmosphere of the north, that of sensuality with the lively and noisy south. In the drama *Fiorenza* and in the prior sketch *Gladius Dei,* however, the conflict between the two opposites is carried on exclusively in the southern atmosphere. While until now the representative of asceticism and of the outsider was a north German, this role has now fallen to an Italian monk; and it is understandable that Thomas Mann's sympathies lay with this man partially endowed with northern traits.

The figure of the life-loving Lorenzo and the glittering world of Renaissance artists and scholars surrounding him were moulded by Thomas Mann with care and love of detail. And yet it is not hidden from the reader that this truly southern atmosphere is once again for the writer an *ambiente* which still remains foreign to his innermost self. Savonarola dominates the drama, and even though he makes his appearance for the first time only in the sixth scene of the third (and last) act, he is still unquestionably the principal figure of the drama, beside whom all of the other characters pale. "Yes, although the 'frightful Christian,' as Lorenzo calls him, only enters the stage near the end of the play, he is nevertheless, from the first word on, present on the stage in spirit; I proceeded from him, his life occupied the greatest part of my preliminary studies, his character received my most intimate psychological interest, his fate was for me the really inspiring motif. When in relation to him Lorenzo de' Medici seems important, charming, even occasionally superior, that is nothing but the expression of the striving for poetical justice, a striving to which nothing in the world is more foreign than precisely the inclination."[37]

In this drama, as well as in the two novellas *Gladius Dei* and *Tonio Kröger,* Thomas Mann for the first time added to the motif of the south the aspects of temptation and danger. In these three works Italy more and more strongly becomes the "courtesan," whose dangerous charms the hero must resist if he is to succeed in finding his own self.

4. *Death in Venice* (1912)

Six years were to elapse before Thomas Mann again began to write a work for which he chose Italy as the setting, although he visited that country several times during those years.

In the novella *Death in Venice (Der Tod in Venedig)* Mann assigned to the city of lagoons—which (as was discussed in our first chapter) was very dear to his heart and which, on his visits, had again and again deeply impressed him anew—a rôle important, actually crucial, to the development of the action. In the drama *Fiorenza* of 1905, the Italian landscape is still of very minor importance: in the second act the writer leads us into the garden of the Villa Medici, where "the open Campagna with cypresses, stone-pines and olive trees"[38] extended into the distance. The Florence of the Renaissance is only a backdrop in front of which the problematics of the characters are brought into relief. In the novella *Death in Venice,* on the other hand, the city of Venice and the landscape surrounding it—that is, in this case, the sea—are of determining significance; indeed, actually a part of the action itself.

Romantic Venice, the Venice of Platen, Wagner, and Nietzsche, reflects an older cultural epoch and is yet at the same time a city of the modern. And Thomas Mann, the stylistic artist, succeeds, through the help of the description of the real world, in fashioning a rich symbolism.

Before Aschenbach, the hero of the novella, decides upon his trip to Italy, he has, in Munich, the vision of a wild, exotic landscape: "a tropical swampland under a thick, steamy sky, humid, rank and monstrous, a kind of primeval jungle wilderness of islands, morasses and slime-bearing channels."[39] He decides to prepare for the trip, for a puzzling yearning has seized him, a longing for such a landscape which will enable him, after all his self-imposed discipline and narrow existence, to let all restraint fall away and to find his true self.

For Aschenbach there is no doubt that the south will bring him the fulfillment of his wish for self-release. Just as the heroes of Thomas Mann's early novellas—Paolo Hofmann, the Dilettante and Tonio Kröger— Aschenbach also travels to Italy, since by means of its colorful, spirited animation he promises himself deliverance from his previous isolation and self-discipline. Thus he comes to Venice, and on seeing this city recollections come alive in him of the poet Platen, that "melancholy and enthusiastic" poet, "for whom once upon a time the domes and bell-towers of his dreams had risen from these waters."[40]

With every fibre Aschenbach drinks in the fabulous beauty of Venice as he glides slowly on the ship through the canal of San Marco, and he is delighted that by the open sea he reaches this city, whose character is so strongly defined by the water surrounding and penetrating it:

Then he saw it again, the most remarkable landing place, that dazzling composition of fantastic structures which the Republic set facing the awestruck gaze of approaching seafarers: the graceful magnificence of the palace and the Bridge of Sighs, the columns with lion and saint by the shore, the splendid projecting flank of the fairy-tale temple, the vista of archway and clock of the giants, and looking at it he reflected that arriving in Venice by

land at the railway station is the same as entering a palace through a back
door, and that in no other way except as he was now, except across the high
seas, should one arrive at the most improbable of cities.[41]

Yet the impression of beauty and incredibility becomes supplanted by a
feeling of dread as Gustav von Aschenbach enters the gondola which is to
bring him out to the Lido. Suddenly he becomes distinctly conscious of
how much in form and color it (the gondola) resembles a coffin: "Who
might not have to subdue a fleeting terror, a secret aversion and uneasiness,
when for the first time or after a long absence the moment came to step into
a Venetian gondola? That peculiar craft, handed down completely un-
changed from balladesque times and so singularly black, as otherwise only
coffins are among all things,—it calls to mind silent and criminal adventures
in the plashing night, still more it calls to mind death itself, the bier and
mournful funeral and last, silent voyage."[42]

The sweet, exotic fullness of life which seduces the visitor from the north
into erotic adventures now becomes intimately fused with the motif of
extreme danger, indeed, of inescapable destruction. But simultaneously, in
this work Italy, for the first time for Thomas Mann, also signifies the land of
antiquity. He described the figure of the boy Tadzio with all the attributes
of a noble Greek sculpture, of the kind he had studied closely in the
museums on his first visit to Italy. "The head of Eros, out of the yellowish
mellowness of Parian marble, with fine and serious brows, temples and ears
duskily and softly hidden by the springing ringlets of his hair."[43]

The danger to Aschenbach from the ominous atmosphere of the city,
hidden beneath the magnificence and "splendor," emerges in the ever
more strongly emphasized picture of decay and putrefaction: "A loathe-
some sultriness lay in the narrow streets; the air was so heavy that the
smells which issued from dwellings, shops, eating-houses, oil fumes,
clouds of perfume and many others lay in exhalations, without dissipat-
ing."[44] Aschenbach begins to feel unwell, until finally he knows that he
must leave. "The longer he walked, the more agonizingly he was seized by
the abominable state which the sea air combined with the sirocco can
produce, and which is at the same time stimulating and enervating."[45] He
has himself conveyed to San Marco by gondola. Yet on the trip the fascination of Venice, which has become ambiguous for him, wraps Aschenbach
in its spell: "through the gloomy labyrinth of the canals, beneath delicate
marble balconies, past grieving palace façades."[46]

Aschenbach recognizes the danger in which he finds himself and decides
to flee; but he already begins to regret this decision on the way to the
railway station. The air seems to him suddenly fresher and more whole-
some, and it becomes clear to him how much he is in the power of Venice,
with its atmosphere at bottom so alien to him. "The Piazzetta revealed
itself once more in princely grace and was left behind, the great row of

palaces came, and as the waterway turned the magnificently spanned marble arch of the Rialto appeared. The traveller gazed, and his heart was torn. The atmosphere of the city, this faintly rotten smell of sea and swamp, which he had been so pressed to flee,—he breathed it now in deep, sweetly painful draughts. Was it possible that he had not known, not reflected, how much he was attached to it all?''[47]

The emotional conflict developed in his soul into a kind of physical defeat before this city. Once before he had to leave it hastily because of a sudden illness. If he now again departed, then it meant a parting forever, since he would "of course henceforth have to regard it as a place impossible and forbidden to him, which he was not equal to and which it would be foolish to visit again.''[48]

A chance occurrence comes to his aid and within a short time Aschenbach finds himself on the way back to the Lido. Inwardly he feels a deep sense of happiness and satisfaction to be "turned around and driven back by Fate to see again in the same hour places from which in deepest sadness one has just taken leave forever.''[49]

The weather indeed changes and in a true feeling of happiness Aschenbach enjoys the nearness of Tadzio and at the same time the southern surroundings, which form such a strong contrast to the coldness and austerity of his northern homeland: "Then it seemed good to him, as if he were transported to Elysium, at the ends of the earth, where the most carefree life is allotted to man, where no snow is or winter, neither storm nor streaming rain, but always gentle cooling zephyrs Oceanus commands to spring up and the days slip away in blissful leisure, effortlessly free from strife and wholly dedicated to the sun and its festivals.''[50]

Aschenbach has inwardly changed: while previously after a short period of relaxation he had always soon longed again for work, hardship, discipline, and order, he now allows himself to become completely caught up in the magic of enjoyment and idleness, "dreaming away across the blue of the southern sea, or in the mild night as well, reclining upon the cushions of the gondola which carried him from the Piazza San Marco, where he tarries long, beneath the vast starry heavens homewards to the Lido.''[51]

Aschenbach lives as if in a state of intoxication: Tadzio and the luminous sea, antiquity and present merge into a oneness, into perfect harmony. "He stood at the edge of the sea, alone, apart from his family, quite close to Aschenbach,—erect, hands clasped at the nape of his neck, slowly rocking on the balls of his feet, and dreamed into the blue, while little waves, which ran up, bathed his toes.''[52]

A vision of antiquity now rises within him: "Out of the murmur of the sea and the radiance of the sun a charming picture wove itself for him. It was the ancient plane-tree not far from the walls of Athens—that hallowed shady spot filled with the fragrance of the chaste tree blossoms, and adorned with sacred images and devout offerings in honour of the nymphs and of Achelous."[53] More and more Aschenbach becomes caught in his unnatural, forbidden love. And again it is Venice, the beguiling city, which symbolizes the enormous danger in which he finds himself owing to his passion for a fourteen-year-old youth. One day during a visit to the Piazza he notices a peculiar odor, "a sweetish-medicinal smell, which calls to mind misery and wounds and questionable cleanliness."[54] Even on his Sunday visit to the divine service in San Marco the warning odor seems to be present: "Then he stood in the background, on the cracked mosaic floor, in the midst of kneeling, murmuring people crossing themselves, and the compact splendor of the oriental temple pressed voluptuously upon his senses. In front the heavily adorned priest turned, gesticulated and chanted, incense welled up, it clouded over the feeble little flames of the altar candles, and in with the heavy sweet sacrificial odor another seemed to mingle faintly: the smell of the diseased city."[55]

But Aschenbach has once and for all fallen under the spell of Tadzio and Venice, and as he follows the trail of his beloved on the way home to the Lido, he himself recognizes the situation quite clearly:

> This was Venice, the fawning and suspect beauty,—this city, half fairy tale, half strangers' snare, in whose putrid air art once luxuriantly proliferated and which gave the musicians tones which rock and amorously lull to sleep. To the adventurer it was as if his eyes drank in the same voluptuousness, as if his ear were wooed by such melodies; he remembered also that the city was sick and concealing it out of avarice, and he peered more licentiously after the gondola gliding in front."[56]

In addition to the visual—the seductive exoticness of the city—the acoustic now also entered the scene, the magic of Italian music. In the evening a band of street musicians appears in the hotel garden to entertain the guests with their partly yearning-melancholy, partly rousing melodies. Aschenbach is transported by this music, "his nerves eagerly absorbed the piercing sounds, the vulgar and languishing melodies, for passion paralyses the sense of discrimination, and in all seriousness has dealings with entice-ments which sobriety would take humorously or indignantly reject."[57]

Death, which for Gustav von Aschenbach is a deliverance—deliverance from himself—does not come to him in the city of Venice, but on the beach, in view of Tadzio and the broad sea which Aschenbach loves, since it is for him "the experience of eternity, of nothingness and of death, a metaphysical dream."[58] In Venice he finds the perfect harmony of city with sea, such as he has longed for. The novella ends with Aschenbach's death just at the moment "when Tadzio beckons to him to follow him into the eternal infinity of the sea."[59] This motif, dealt with again and again in literature, was once expressed by Thomas Mann in another place with the words: "For love of the sea, that is nothing else but love of death."[60]

The Venice which Thomas Mann described in this work is to the smallest detail modern Venice. But at the same time he gave the city a timeless, romantic, exotic character, so that it is not only the background for the tragic event, but also has a share in determining the plot and, so to speak, itself becomes a part of the action.

The sensuous, seductive beauty of Venice is reflected for Aschenbach in the perfection of the boy, and owing to the exotic and fascinating atmosphere of the city the writer is particularly open to the attraction of Tadzio and willingly allows himself to become bewitched by him. One may assume that without the mystical force of the city of lagoons the encounter with the boy would not have become such a devastating experience for Aschenbach. Although in the case of Thomas Mann no such distinct equation of the figure of Tadzio with the concept "Venice" takes place as with Gerhart Hauptmann, in whose glass-factory fairytale Pippa and Venice become fused into a oneness, still the fascination of the boy is increased because of Venice, and perhaps even dependent upon it.

While the outward features of Aschenbach resemble those of the composer Gustav Mahler, of whose death Thomas Mann was apprised during a stay on the island of Brioni in 1911, the true image, however, was the poet August Graf von Platen, the proclaimer of the ancient ideal of beauty and of the close relationship between beauty and death, as he portrayed it in his poem "Tristan":

"He whose eyes have looked at beauty
Is a prey of death already."[61]*

Just as in Platen's fate, for Aschenbach, also, beauty and approaching destruction are closely interwoven, and in his love and passion for Tadzio one is reminded of the concept of the arrow of death, which Platen expressed in the second verse of his poem:

"He whom the arrow of beauty has ever hit
For him the pain of love endures eternally."[62]**

Beauty conceals deadly danger: Michel Hellriegel's eyes grow blind,[63] after he has beheld beauty; and Aschenbach, through his passionate love for the boy, is "a prey of death already." The three concepts—Venice, beauty, and death—become a mystical unity, and Aschenbach must suffer death because he has sought to become at one with beauty.

In *Death in Venice* Thomas Mann again dealt with the theme of the longing of the northern individual for the south. Tonio Kröger, as also the heroes of other earlier novellas, had succumbed to the temptations of Italy for some time; but then he had come to his senses, and precisely on account of his erotic adventures in the south and their ultimate conquest, had matured into an artist.

---

*Englished by Ignace Feuerlicht, in *Thomas Mann* (New York: Twayne Publishers, Inc., 1968), p. 124.

**Englished by Betty Crouse.

Aschenbach, to the contrary, had already concluded his important literary works when he is swept by an irresistible longing for Italy. The north suddenly seems to him too sober, too disciplined, and therefore cold and sterile. Like Tonio Kröger's nature, that of Aschenbach also exhibits Latin characteristics through inheritance from his southern mother, and because of this mixture the man influenced by "darker, fiery impulse"[64] is predestined to become an artist. For a long time he has suppressed his mother's inheritance through self-control and severe discipline, and the motto "hold fast" had become his favorite maxim and his life's rule of conduct. Now suddenly his literary existence appears questionable to him; he who for some time had become a model and teacher to his public because of the self-discipline reflected in his works, suddenly feels doubts about his profession as a writer, which at bottom is built upon an unnatural and therefore false basis.

So Aschenbach goes to Italy, to Venice, there to discover his true self in order to free himself from all restraint and self-punishment. In the south he desires to do justice to the previously suppressed inheritance of his mother, and through surrender to sensual beauty overcome the numbing of his personality that was brought about by his unnatural asceticism. He finds the fulfillment of his longing in Venice, which offers this beauty in perfect form, for indeed here Italian and fable-like Oriental elements are blended into a oneness. Visual impressions combine with the acoustic of the "languishing" Italian music.

While in the early novella *Disillusionment* Thomas Mann had emphasized the marvellous lucidity of Venice, which offers a "sight of incomparable shining and festive beauty,"[65] the Venice of Aschenbach is at the same time sinister and full of danger for the visitor intoxicated by this deluding atmosphere. The city has a conflicting character, for behind a façade of the greatest beauty and magnificence are hidden disease, immorality, and crime. Like Hieronymus in the novella *Gladius Dei* and Savonarola in *Fiorenza,* Aschenbach is conscious of this other side of the southern atmosphere; but while both of the moralists fought the evils with word and deed, Aschenbach lets himself be deluded and overcome by them. He does not possess the moral strength of resistance which made it possible for Tonio Kröger to flee from the dangers of the south by returning to his northern homeland.

Aschenbach, on the other hand, is already in a state of psychical and physical weakness while still in Munich, so that the sight of the stranger at the cemetery puts him in a state of "roving unrest" and evokes in him a "youthful thirsty longing for foreign parts,"[66] to which he completely surrenders; indeed, which within his soul heightens to an unrestrained vision. Also in the two encounters during the journey, one on the ship with the perverse old man behaving like a youth, as well as the one with the sinister gondolier, Aschenbach is incapable of resisting. To be sure, he realizes the danger he is in, yet in his exhaustion and susceptibility he lacks the strength to resist the temptation of a total abandonment. In reality, a longing, still unbeknown to him, for chaos, immorality, and death has already won the upper hand in his soul. In this condition Aschenbach is entirely delivered over to the alluring and seductive charms of Venice; indeed, the deceptiveness of the city increases his suceptibility to the utmost. In such surroundings the figure of Tadzio, the youth closely resembling an ancient statue, has to become for Aschenbach a deeply stirring experience. All the previously suppressed emotions are unchained and must lead to the destruction of the hero, to his death in sight of the city of Venice, the beautiful boy, and the infinite sea.

5. *Song of the Little Child* (1919)

If one examines Thomas Mann's attitude in relation to Italy as a whole, one is struck by the special place which Venice occupies: the writer loved this city as only few others, and again and again he was irresistibly drawn back to it. It signified to him an harmonious blending of East and West, as well as especially a union of North and South. In this Italian seaport he saw much that reminded him of his own native city of Lübeck, giving him a feeling of being at home. In the idyll *Song of the Little Child (Gesang vom Kindchen)* appearing in 1919 Mann amplified these thoughts about the close similarity between Lübeck and Venice and explored it from various aspects.

This poetic work, for which Goethe's *Hermann und Dorothea* and perhaps also the idylls of Johann Heinrich Voss might have furnished impetus, describes in hexameters the baptism of his youngest daughter, Elisabeth. At the same time it provides a description of bourgeois family life, into which, however, exotic elements are intruded, so that the homeland of the child is twofold: North German as well as exotic southern.

> Understand, you were begotten in the East. In fairy tales
> Nordic seafarer's blood begot you, lusting for adventures,
> Twofold is your homeland, north German and exotic.[67]

In just the same way, for the writer himself the northern city on the Baltic Sea as well as the southern city of lagoons are conjointly his native city:

> Just as to my mind my native city is twofold: once the
> Baltic port, Gothic and grey, yet once again as a miracle of the East,
> Transported, the Gothic arches bewitched by the Moors,
>
> In the lagoon,—most familiar heritage of childhood and yet
> Exotic as a fable, an extravagant dream.[68]

In both cities the writer breathed in the smell of the sea, in both the merchants rule, and even the architecture of the two proud free cities resembles one another with their arcades and loggias.

Did he not find, scenting the homelike smell of water, the
   arcades of the Town Hall,
Just like where they held the Exchange, the important burghers
   of his Free City—
Find it once more at the Palace of the Dᵒges, with its stocky portico,
Above which the lighter one floats in graceful arcades?
No, let no one deny me the mysterious bond
Between the trading ports, the noble city republics,
Between my homeland and the fairy tale, the eastern dream![69]

Thomas Mann gives an account, completely in the style of this popular and good-natured idyll, of a further binding relationship between Lübeck and Venice, namely, the partiality for marzipan, the name of which he brings into association with St. Mark, the patron saint of Venice, and the composition of which from the principal ingredients of almonds and rosewater he attributes to Oriental origin:

Did not the boy at Christmastide nibble on the delicious fare,
Famed throughout the land, which the local confectioners
Fashioned into tart shapes, imprinting the paste with the
Picture of the towered town gate; yet it of course, the sticky manna,
Comes from the Orient, a harem sweetmeat made from almonds,
Rosewater and sugar, and, named from St. Mark,
Came by way of Venice into my homeland. Mazapan is its name. . .[70]

Thomas Mann had already expressed quite similar notions in 1916 in a letter to Paul Amann, wherein he emphasized the exotic elements of Venice and linked the relationship between his two "homelike" cities with the motif of marzipan. There, also, it states: "Venice is still the most eccentric and most exotic place I know—and yet I regard it as mysteriously homelike: it is a Lübeck rendered into the Oriental-fantastic. I maintain there are quite remarkable, insufficiently investigated relationships between the two cities. As an immediate example, marzipan,—which after all quite obviously means Marci panis, St. Mark's bread, and hence comes from Venice, furthermore naturally from the Orient, since it is indeed a typical harem sweetmeat: almonds and rosewater!"[71]

As in the novella *Death in Venice,* so in the poetic idyll *Song of the Little Child,* Venice for Thomas Mann is therefore not only the timeless, romantic city of lagoons as Platen and Richard Wagner experienced it, it is the city which represents a close relationship between North and South and in which Thomas Mann saw a southern counterpart to his northern home city of Lübeck. In his address on 5 June 1926 for the 700th anniversary of the Free and Hanseatic city of Lübeck, Thomas Mann expressed his views at some length on this double bond:

Venice and Lübeck: some of you will recall that I have written a novella,
Death in Venice, in which I show that I am somewhat at home in the

seductive, death-linked city *par excellence*—and I use the phrase "at home" in its full, proper sense: in the sense, namely, of another literary work, a poetic idyll, which half-jestingly suggests hexameter and which speaks of how my native city is twofold to me: once the Baltic port, Gothic and grey, yet once again as a miracle of the East, transported, the Gothic arches bewitched by the Moors, in the lagoon.[72]

His whole life long, Thomas Mann was fascinated by the contrast and the affinity between North and South, and again and again this tension appears in his works, not the least of which are the important novels *The Magic Mountain* and *Doctor Faustus*. Since without a doubt Thomas Mann himself had quite strongly felt the temptations of the south, the force of attraction which from earliest times Italy has exerted on northern man became of special significance for his literary work. He clearly expressed these thoughts in his letter of thanks to his friend Ernst Bertram for sending him his *Nornenbuch:*

> North against South is a fascinating subject; passion for it constitutes a goodly share of that which binds us, and I suppose I can say I do not take any notice of material not relating to it. It is this which makes the 'Nornenbuch' dear to me. And finally, among all the unreliability is reliance upon myself, as with you reliance is upon a certain verse." I myself am clay of the North, and the North will always secretly fetch me home: 'In sound, as a whisper.' It is exactly that, upon which I myself rely."[73]

Aschenbach was intoxicated by the sensual beauty of the south, he had to succumb to its temptations, because he had abandoned his ties with the north, with his father's inheritance, and found himself in a state of moral exhaustion. Thomas Mann, to the contrary—like Tonio Kröger—was able to resist the temptations, he was too closely bound to the north and possessed the self-discipline to hold fast to his homeland.

6. *The Magic Mountain* (1924)

In almost all the works discussed up to now, Thomas Mann indicated the longing of the northerner for the south. Depending upon the disposition of the hero, this longing springs from a varying but great conviction that the intensity of life, the vitality and the sensuous beauty of Italy are able to bring deliverance from a self-discipline which has increased in degree to unnaturalness and repression. In the early novellas this longing for self-deliverance is still unexpressed and can only be surmised by the reader. Nevertheless, Tonio Kröger and also Aschenbach feel the burden of their northern heritage very distinctly and consciously. But while for Tonio this inheritance comes to his rescue in the face of the temptations of the south, in Aschenbach it is not strong enough to save him from destruction in Italy. In the novella *Death in Venice,* the eroticism of the south becomes heightened in the mysterious and the sinister, by whose power the artist

Aschenbach is defeated. Here one could lay down the equation South = destruction and death, as Thomas Mann himself did, in that he had equated the sea, and therefore also the southern sea, with death.

In the novella *Gladius Dei* and in the drama *Fiorenza,* the writer had concerned himself with the dangerous currents which are hidden beneath the surface of the Italian atmosphere, currents which in *Gladius Dei* referred to the moral aspect but in *Fiorenza,* on the other hand, already were tending to change from the moral over to the political. This theme was again taken up by Thomas Mann nineteen years later in his novel *The Magic Mountain* and finally dealt with once again in 1929 in the novella *Mario and the Magician.* But while in the two earlier works and in *Mario and the Magician* the moral and political aspect of the south meets with a negative valuation, in his novel *The Magic Mountain* the writer bestowed distinctly positive features upon the Italian element, in that he made an Italian schooled in the ideas of the Renaissance and the Risorgimento the representative of Humanism and Enlightenment. There can indeed be no doubt that, for Thomas Mann himself, occupation with the figure of the open-minded, liberal Italian Lodovico Settembrini, who was influenced by Dante and Petrarch, was of great significance in the development of his own political attitude.

Although in *The Magic Mountain* the setting is never transferred to Italy and only a single character represents this land of the south, nevertheless this very Italian element plays an important, even decisive rôle in the novel.

It is therefore not to be wondered at that the intelligent, astute Italian exerts a great power of attraction on the young man of the north, Hans Castorp, right from the first meeting; indeed, that through this representative of the south a new world of ideas becomes opened up for the young man; and that through the Italian he receives knowledge that has the greatest influence on his maturation and remains of decisive importance for his entire life.

Settembrini

On the first day of his stay on the magic mountain Hans Castorp meets Herr Settembrini, who immediately makes an impression on the young German by his cultured and lively facial expression, his black eyes and his slightly mocking smile. As a typical representative of his land the Italian has a natural gift for spirited rhetoric, of which he himself is also aware at all times. It strikes Hans Castorp very quickly how well-turned Settembrini's speech is, which he describes as "plastic," a word that the somewhat vain Italian had suggested to him. Hans later expresses his opinion to his cousin Joachim: "I always have the impression that for him (Settembrini) the purpose is not entirely only for the sake of instruction, perhaps that is only of secondary importance, but especially for the sake of talking, how he makes the words spring and roll . . . so resilient, like rubber balls . . . and that it is not at all disagreeable to him, when one also especially notices it."[74] Settembrini's delight in the handsome expressive gesture corresponds to his fondness for well-chosen plastic speech.

Settembrini is a keen, lucid thinker, a rationalist, who systematically and occasionally skeptically dissects problems. Although a sharp critic of his surroundings, he is still fundamentally an optimist, who firmly believes in the progress of mankind: "criticism means the beginning of progress and enlightenment."[75]

The element of temptation and seduction, which Thomas Mann equated with the Italian atmosphere in his novella *Death in Venice,* is represented in *The Magic Mountain* by the people of eastern Europe, principally by the Russian Mme Chauchat and the Pole Naphta. And to the representative of Italy, strangely enough, falls the role of warning the young German of these dangers and, as far as his influence permits, of rescuing him from them.

In the character of Herr Settembrini, Mann has created an unusually vigorous and spirited figure. The writer himself often speaks through him, but often he is not taken entirely seriously by Mann or is subjected to severe criticism, and sometimes the reader does not know whether he should admire him in his highmindedness and his high humanitarian ideals, or whether he should laugh at his gossipy and idle outpourings. A few critics even conjecture that the worldwide popularity of *The Magic Mountain* is in large part attributable to the figure of Settembrini. In Hans M. Wolff's obviously too one-sided view "his character is spirited in the highest degree, indeed we may venture the assertion that the figure of Settembrini has contributed the most towards the great success of the novel, for in his unshakeable conviction, to be refuted neither through logical arguments nor through practical examples, that the spirit is an essential life-promoting force, he embodies an eternal hope, which even the most extreme skeptic is unable to shun completely."[76]

Lodovico Settembrini sees himself as a link in a chain of family members who champion the same ideals and—each in his own way—tried to realize them.[77] In typical Italian family tradition he feels closely bound to his forefathers, and time and again he speaks willingly and full of love about his father and grandfather, who, just as he himself, had had in mind as the highest concepts those of freedom and "universal brotherhood of the people in testimony of reason, science, and justice."[78] "These ideas, ideals, and aspirations of the will were family traditions in his house. For to these all three had dedicated their life and their spiritual energy, the grandfather, father, and grandson, each according to his fashion: the father no less than the grandfather Giuseppe, although unlike the latter, he was not a political agitator and freedom fighter, but a quiet and sensitive scholar, a humanist at his desk."[79]

The qualities of the historical Luigi Settembrini appear in Thomas Mann's fashioning to be distributed between two persons, namely, father and son. Whereas the ideals represented by Lodovico of tolerance, reason, and liberalism correspond to the political thinking of the Italian independence fighter, the latter's other characteristics, those of the humanistic scholar, quite clearly found their deposition in the figure of Lodovico's father, that literary historian and cultivated scholar, whose "tiny, warm little study" was so snugly warmed through, when outside "the cutting tramontana blew . . . The little room was crammed with books and manuscripts, among which were objects of great value, and amidst the treasures of the mind he stood in his dressing-gown of blue flannel at his narrow desk and dedicated himself to literature."[80] He was a Romanist, a "Latin stylist," an "uomo letterato after Boccaccio's heart."[81] His fame spread from Padua throughout all of Europe, so that scholars from afar sought him out in order to seek his counsel and to render him their veneration. But at the same time he was also a writer, "who in his leisure hours composed tales in the most elegant Tuscan prose,—a master of the idioma gentile."[82] Lodovico's father was no agitator, no freedom fighter, and yet in his quiet way he was a fighter, and indeed a fighter for the ideals of humanitarianism. From the words of the son echoes his great reverence for his father, for whom he even now, as a grown man, still has the same admiration as he did many years ago, when as a little boy he visited him in his study. Thus after his father's death as well he tries to create a similar familiar atmosphere in his own study. Daily he spends many hours at his dead father's work desk, and also "the wicker chairs, the table and even the carafe had been in his possession."[83] In this atmosphere full of memories of the beloved deceased, Lodovico is able to concentrate with all the fibres of his soul on his work, which he will call "Soziologie der Leiden" ("Sociology of Suffering"). Father Settembrini was the prototype of a scholarly humanist in the manner of Erasmus of Rotterdam, who in his subtle and astute way championed western intellectuality over against the backward ideas of scholasticism. When through the words of the son Thomas Mann describes him as a small, delicate figure and endows him with the attributes of a fine, long nose and thick, grey hair, then the reader is tempted to ask himself whether the well-known portrait of Erasmus from the hand of Holbein might not have served the writer as a model for fashioning this scholarly figure.

Lodovico also speaks of his grandfather Giuseppe with the same reverence, and in this figure as well reminiscences are found of the historical Luigi Settembrini, who must have lived at the same time. Just like the latter, Giuseppe became a great patriot, also a ringleader and conspirator, who "desired to know his native land united and free."[84] In contrast to his son he was a warlike man," patriot and political agitator, who put his entire life into the service of revolutionary slogans such as freedom, progress, and the promulgation of democratic ideas and who, not only in his homeland but in other countries also, had fought for the revolution."[85] Only with difficulty did he escape imprisonment by Prince Metternich, but had to go into exile. In Spain as well as in Greece he had stood by the patriots in the battle for their freedom, helping with word and deed. His German-born wife, whom he had married in Switzerland, followed him to the various countries and brought their son into the world in Greece, "probably on account of which he then also became such a great humanist and lover of classical antiquity."[86] Finally when, after a ten-year exile, the family was permitted to return to Italy, Giuseppe became a lawyer in Milan, where he appeared only "in black mourning clothes among his fellow-citizens," since "he was a mourner, he said, for Italy, his fatherland, which languished away in misery and servitude."[87] To the end of his life he was politically active and tried with all the means at his disposal "to summon the nation through the spoken and written word, in verse and prose, to freedom and to the establishment of the united republic, to draw up government-overthrowing programs with a passionate dictatorial ardor, and in a clear style to proclaim the union of the liberated people for the establishment of general happiness."[88]

The grandson looks up full of honest admiration to his grandfather, who as a carbonaro was permitted to help actively in the liberation of his fatherland and of mankind. He cannot imitate him, "but since he, the sick one, lacks the ability to fight, he hopes, in this respect following the example of his father, the quiet humanist, to improve mankind and make it happy by means of the spoken and written word."[89] He has joined the "International League for the Organization of Progress," which has members the world over, who from the Darwinian theory of evolution derive the philosophical concept "that the deepest natural calling of mankind is its self-perfection."[90] Also, out of genuine conviction Settembrini has become a Freemason, for he hopes that the League can bring about the brotherhood of mankind. He has the "Rivista della Massoneria Italiana" constantly at hand, and with pride he tells of illustrious names, "whose bearers had been Masons or were today, including Voltaire, Lafayette and Napoleon, Franklin and Washington, Mazzini and Garibaldi, among the living even the King of England and a great many men besides, in whose hands lay the affairs of the European states, members of governments and parliaments."[91]

Thus the sick Lodovico endeavored to carry on the tradition of the Settembrini family and to fight for freedom and humanitarianism; that is, not on the battlefield, but through his writings and no less through his long discussions with Hans Castorp and his cousin Joachim, since it is reserved for youth to shape the future according to its ideas. "Therefore let us bless the Fate which has driven you into this horrible region, but which at the same time gives me the opportunity to act upon your plastic youth with my not unpractised, not wholly feeble discourse and to make you aware of the responsibility which it, which your country bears in the face of civilization."[92]

In Settembrini's argumentative discussions with his adversary Naphta, the bellicose spirit of his grandfather Giuseppe occasionally comes to light. Then sharp words are exchanged, and the two philosophies of life dash roughly against one another. Settembrini does his utmost to protect the young people from the seditious, destructive ideas of Naphta: "My words will fit the facts precisely, if I state that your manner of intellectually disquieting youth, which is unsteady anyhow, of seducing it and morally debilitating it, is an infamy and cannot be given a severe enough tongue-lashing."[93] Thus he cries out in protest against the "indecency" of the topic dealt with by Naphta that glorifies the "German-romantic longing for death"[94] in political romanticism at the time of the German war of independence, which the Jesuit "is disposed to consider as the intellectual beginnings of a modern German nationalism."[95] Yet Naphta's pride has been assailed too severely, he believes he must do the only thing he can, and so he challenges Settembrini to a duel, to which the latter only reluctantly places himself at Naphta's disposal; for just as the historical Luigi Settembrini, Lodovico thinks too lawfully than to be able to assent to the duel as a form of judgment: "I regret the outcome of our outing, only every man must reckon with such incidents in life. In theory I disapprove of the duel, I think in a lawful way. In practice, however, it is another matter, and there are situations where—contradictions, which—in short, I am at this gentleman's disposal."[96]

Settembrini knows that because of his humanitarian ideals he will not kill his opponent; he shoots into the air. But Naphta commits suicide, by turning the pistol against himself. Settembrini is the first to reach him, and full of despair cries: "Unhappy man! For the love of God what are you doing!"[97] Naphta's death is a tragic outcome, and Settembrini is not permitted to enjoy to the full the victory over his adversary, as had been possible for his forefathers.

The figure of Lodovico Settembrini is Thomas Mann's own creation; yet certain strong parallels to the historical Luigi Settembrini can be established, as will be more precisely illustrated in the following investigation.

The historical Luigi Settembrini was born in Naples in 1813 and at an early age through his father, an enthusiastic patriot and freedom fighter, learned to love his fatherland and freedom above all else. After successful completion of his Ph.D. at the age of only twenty-two, the young Luigi taught classical languages and literature in Catanzaro. In spite of great popularity with his pupils, he was sometimes subjected to hostility in the circle of his colleagues. Criticism took him severely to task over his major work *Lezioni di letteratura italiana,* a polemic against the middle ages, the papacy, and the Jesuits. The book concludes with the hope that Italy may be able to find the way back to its former greatness through a renewed awareness of her ancient values and above all her art, which will bring freedom and peace to the Italian people:

Through their own fault and through destiny the Italians have lost liberty, independence, customs and all things most dear to man; and they retained only that which they could not lose, their nature, which is an harmony of concepts and a great appreciation for art. This harmony and this appreciation became a habit of the intellect, and applied to beliefs, to the sciences, to politics and to the various areas of life, it helped us become reborn. If we give up this habit, we will be lost for ever; if we preserve it, employing it in the things of life, we will acquire great importance among the nations. For a great many years we have worked with art, and we have succeeded in giving unity to our fatherland: we will continue to work with art to bring freedom and peace to the conscience of all Christians."[98]

Settembrini's style is distinguished by clarity and skill, his views about writers and written works are critical and well founded. In his opinion the character of Italian literature is defined by the attempt to overcome all the influences of a medieval mysticism in favor of a classical clarity and beauty, which can be attained only through close association with the ancient ideals. Settembrini is firmly convinced that the greatness of Italian literature lies in overcoming all prejudice and all superstition, and that the unique importance of its literary works rests upon the ideals of freedom and truth.[99]

Luigi Settembrini's greatest interest during his lifetime was politics. Already at an early age he founded a secret society, "Figliuoli della Giovine Italia." Because of his political activity he was in 1839 arrested for the first time and imprisoned for fifteen months. In 1847 he drew up a paper which became well known under the title *Protesta del popolo delle due Sicilie,* in which he turned full of hate against the Bourbon régime and caused a great sensation at that time both within Italy and abroad.[100] Shortly after the ensuing founding in 1848 of the "Grande Società dell'Unità italiana," Settembrini was denounced and again arrested. From prison he circulated his powerful *Difesa scritta da Luigi Settembrini per gli uomini di buon senso* and defended himself even at the police trial:

There are only two factions in the world: the honest men and the dishonest. I have always striven to belong to the honest, and I have never troubled about names, for I have seen many outrageous deeds committed by men called realists, liberals, absolutists, republicans or constitutionalists. I love freedom, which for me signifies the exercise of one's own rights without offending anyone, it signifies severe justice, signifies order, signifies respect and obedience to the laws and to authority. I love this freedom fervently, it is the freedom longed for by honest men: and if to love it is a crime, I plead guilty, and accept the punishment for it."[101]

The death sentence that had been pronounced upon Settembrini was changed to life imprisonment. Together with his friend Spaventa he was imprisoned until 1859 in Santo Stefano, the prison for murderers and criminals. During these long years he worked on the translation from the

Greek of the *Dialogues* of Lucian. In 1859 he finally obtained his ardently longed-for freedom again, received the Chair of classical literature in the University of Bologna, yet soon afterwards went to southern Italy. After the liberation of Naples by Garibaldi he succeeded to a chair in the university there and together with Francesco De Sanctis founded the "Associazione unitaria costitutionale," of which he became President. From that time on he led a quiet and happy life in the realization that the scholarly existence was suitable for him, to which he now devoted all of his energies. In 1876 he died, at the zenith of his academic career, in his birthplace, Naples. With a foreword by De Sanctis, his *Ricordanze* appeared posthumously, the avowal of a passionate love of Italy and the testament of a man aspiring to the highest moral ideals. "There one finds, mingled with many sketches, portraits and anecdotes, related with great mastery of art, the most sincere manifestation of a soul constantly and almost naturally pellucid and certain in its vision and in the realization of the good."[102]

As is clearly evident from the above statements, many parallels exist between the historical figure of Luigi Settembrini and the person of Lodovico Settembrini created by Thomas Mann in *The Magic Mountain*. Yet the question as to how much the writer was familiar with the historical model and created a memorial to him in the novel is still disputed, as is apparent from the following. Thomas Mann expressed his views on this subject several times, specifically in respect to inquiries from scholars who were occupied with this problem. Thus declared the writer in 1948 in a letter to Eberhard Barthold, who had sent him an unpublished study on the theme dealing with the names in Thomas Mann's works: "The name Settembrini is influenced by 'Venti Settembre,' a national revolutionary date."[103]

Two years later Thomas Mann stated his views on the same question in a letter to Harry W. Rudman, who had called Mann's attention to certain parallels in Italian history with the figure in the novel. Rudman describes the incident thus: "The Italian liberal politician and literary critic Luigi Settembrini (1813–77) [sic] was imprisoned by the notorious Ferdinand II of Naples in the period of reaction which followed the revolutionary setbacks of 1848, and narrowly escaped execution. Settembrini's case attracted wide attention and evoked the indignant support of Gladstone in his famous pamphlet, *Two Letters to the Earl of Aberdeen, on the State Prosecutions of the Neapolitan Government* (1851).

"Impressed by the parallel between the ideals of Luigi Settembrini and those of the Lodovico Settembrini in *The Magic Mountain,* I wrote to Thomas Mann to discover whether the historical Settembrini had suggested his use of the name." Mann gave Rudman permission to quote from Thomas Mann's letter of March 24, 1950:

> I am sorry to be unable to answer your question with any certainty. It is twenty-five years now since I completed *The Magic Mountain,* and I no

longer have a clear picture of the studies on which I had based the novel, and which covered many different fields. I remember vaguely that the name Settembrini had indeed its origin in a historical association, and that its choice was connected with the revolutionary date of the 'venti settembre.' However, it is entirely possible that a direct reference to Luigi Settembrini also played into it. At least my family asserts that I mentioned this historical figure at that time.[104]

Still a third communication concerns the subject of the historical model for the character of Lodovico Settembrini, an unpublished letter of the Italian scholar Cesare Cases to Heinz Saueressig, author of a study on the creation of *The Magic Mountain:*

> Now the recently deceased Lavinia Mazzucchetti once told me that after reading *The Magic Mountain,* Benedetto Croce requested her to inquire of Thomas Mann how this homonymy was assigned. At that time Thomas Mann had replied that the historical Settembrini had been completely unknown to him, that originally he had even wished to christen his character 'Ottobrini' (whereby it is possible that the recollection of the date 'venti settembre' mentioned in the letter to Rudman influenced the final choice of the name of the month). It would be interesting to ascertain when Thomas Mann made this oral remark. Lavinia Mazzucchetti is dead, and I can recall no place in her numerous publications on Thomas Mann where this story is related.[105]

From the passages quoted from the three letters, it emerges how vague and confused Thomas Mann's recollections were about the origin of the name and the model for the figure of the Italian in *The Magic Mountain,* and how much he contradicted himself in his comments on this topic.

A thorough study of the figure created by Thomas Mann for the novel, Lodovico Settembrini, and the historical personality Luigi Settembrini clearly reveals that the writer must have been acquainted with the historical figure and must have been thoroughly familiar with his character as well as his works. Without this source he could not have created the figure of his novel, since there are too many parallels and coincidences in both characters. To the historical Settembrini just as to the fictitious figure of Thomas Mann's novel belong the same eloquence mounting to rhetoric characteristic of a man who with every fibre of his heart believes in his ideals and defends them in the face of all adversaries, likewise the uprightness and consistency of his reasoning and his optimistic belief in the ultimate victory of the good and the noble. Luigi Settembrini was a convinced patriot who defended freedom and justice against all intolerance, and reason and enlightenment against lack of understanding and confusion. Thomas Mann bestowed very similar traits upon his Italian humanist, provided him with the same hopes and ideals, not without lightly caricaturing certain peculiarities such as eloquence and rhetorical fervor.

But it should not be denied that the name Settembrini also calls forth in the reader historical associations: 20 September 1870, when Italian troops marched in for the liberation of the city of Rome, consequently the "venti settembre" expressly mentioned by Thomas Mann in his letters to Barthold and Rudman. "An army corps, under General Raffaele Cadorna, marched, with many precautions of a political nature, upon Rome, after the negotiations initiated by the King with the Pope had failed. After a brief resistance the Italian artillery made a breach near Porta Pia. The Pope ordered the cessation of hostilities (20 September 1870)."[106]

In criticism of Thomas Mann the question has occasionally been raised why, in *The Magic Mountain,* Thomas Mann presented the agent of reason—that is, the "literati of civilization"—in the figure of an Italian instead of a Frenchman, and even Italian critics such as Cesare Cases have wrestled with this problem:

> To me (who contrary to you am—as you know—an obstinant and incurable ideologist, although with remorse), to me Settembrini is interesting really as an idea-bearing personage; that is, it interests me to see why, in order to incarnate the ideas of Settembrini, Mann specifically took an Italian (while logic would have demanded that he rather choose a Frenchman, a Frenchman being the typical 'Zivilisationsliterat' characterized in the *Reflections of a Non-Political Man* and at least partially rehabilitated in *The Magic Mountain*).[107]

An answer to the above-posed question, also treated by Cesare Cases, regarding the nationality of Settembrini as the representative of a specific intellectual attitude related to that of the *Zivilisationsliterat* is not easily given, but it still should be attempted. The presumption appears to be obvious that acquaintance with the work of the historical Luigi Settembrini inspired Mann with the person of the fictitious Lodovico Settembrini as the representative of an Italian humanism, embodying all those characteristic features which Mann once had in mind for the figure of the *Zivilisationsliterat*.

Therefore the assertion of Helmut Koopmann appears all the more misguided:

> Yet it is probably more likely that here in the case of Lodovico Settembrini it is a question of a copy of a Dostoevskian figure. In *The Brothers Karamazov* in a critical passage (1036) an account is given of a man in a rather worn suit: 'The checked trousers fit superbly, but on the other hand were too pale and somehow too tight! . . .' Other epithets also correspond strikingly with the description of Settembrini.[108]

Karl Kerényi is also convinced of the connection between the historical humanist Luigi Settembrini and the character in *The Magic Mountain,* yet as he confessed in a letter to Thomas Mann:

> How often while reading your novel was I obliged to find myself shockingly uneducated! Did I know perchance of the existence (outside of *The Magic*

Mountain) of a Neapolitan humanist Settembrini, until—much later—I discovered his writings at a second-hand bookseller's on the Campo di Fiori in Rome?[109]

In a letter of 30 January 1934 to Pierre-Paul Sagave, Thomas Mann himself gave his opinion on the question regarding possible models for Settembrini and his antagonist Naphta, whose discussions Sagave investigated in a sizeable study, as yet unpublished:

> "The figures of Settembrini and Naphta are as good as freely invented; human reality offered only superficial points of reference. I had really never heard of the communistic Jesuit, but that the combination is possible and plausible, seems to me to be proven by the intellectually very closed view of life of Naphta. The human characters of the two 'emissaries,' for which, as I said, faintly suggestive models had crossed my path, resulted from their dispositions, the cheerful-humane of the one, the ascetic-brutal of the other. Or, better said: they harmonized with these models and in the realm of imagination matched them. Because first and last it was for me after all a matter of presentation of people, and as far as Herr Settembrini in particular is concerned, he would assuredly not be himself without his convictions; but yet he himself is more important and more amusing than these."[110]

But while Thomas Mann continually more or less evaded a precise answer to the question about the source for his Settembrini, in his *The Magic Mountain* he makes a series of prominent historical figures from Italian intellectual and cultural history come alive in the conversations between Hans Castorp and Settembrini. These writers, thinkers, and statesmen of the Italian past have, according to Lodovico Settembrini's and undoubtedly Thomas Mann's own view, had a not insignificant influence through their works upon the intellectual development of the West. Historical personages such as Dante and Petrarch, Carducci, Leopardi, and Garibaldi are repeatedly mentioned and discussed by Settembrini, so that these historical representatives of the Italian heritage of thought are also of consequence in the education and development of Hans Castorp.

In the following sections these Italians and the interpretation of their thoughts and deeds by Thomas Mann's Settembrini, and consequently by the author himself, will be more closely investigated.

Carducci (1835–1907),
Mazzini (1805–1872), Garibaldi (1807–1882)

That figure of Italian intellectual life whom Thomas Mann's Lodovico Settembrini admires the most is a great poet and scholar of the nineteenth century, Giosuè Carducci. In addition to his scholarly works he published numerous translations and also poems, which in part expressed bitter attacks against the papacy and also against the Italian government. In his Hymn to Satan (of September 1863), however, he stirred his readers to the core, for this poem contains a vehement invective against the traditional Christian religion and a glorification of reason, life, and progress which are symbolized by the Satan concept. The poem ends with two rebellious stanzas:

Salute, o Satana	Hail, O Satan
O ribellione	O rebel
O forza vindice	O avenging force
De la ragione	Of reason
Sacri a te salgano	Consecrated to thee ascend
Gl'incensi e i voti!	Incense and prayers!
Hai vinto il Geova	Thou hast vanquished the Jehova
De i sacerdoti.[111]	Of the priests.

Settembrini frequently quotes this hymn, "a magnificent song"[112] he terms it, since it expressed his own ideals: rebellion against all oppression and glorification of freedom of thought and enjoyment of life in the sense of Prometheus, whom he designates as the first humanist, "and he is identical with that Satan to whom Carducci composed a hymn."[113] This devil has little in common with Mephisto: "He is precisely the idol of Settembrini's rational humanism and is on the best of terms with the spirit of work, progress and instructive criticism."[114] Lodovico Settembrini was himself a pupil of the great poet Carducci: "In Bologna I sat at his feet," he reports. "I may thank him for what culture and joyfulness I call my own."[115] But the greatest honor for Settembrini was when he was allowed to write an obituary on the venerated poet for the German newspapers. "I had the honor of telling your countrymen about the life of this great poet and freethinker, when it was concluded."[116]

Carducci was a harsh critic and foe of romanticism. He rejected its vagueness, since for him clarity and truth were of the greatest importance. He propagated intellectual and political independence as well as discipline in thought and in poetical feeling for language. In his letters Carducci set down his thoughts regarding a new conception of art and its realization:

> We must make art realistic: to represent that which is real in more natural terms, with truth. We must do away with the ideal, the metaphysical, in order to represent man, nature, reality, reason, freedom. The study of the ancients, who are realistic and free, Homer, Aeschylus, Dante, and of popular poetry, must be united with modern thought and art.[117]

Settembrini concurs with this anti-romantic attitude of Carducci with all his heart: "I affirm, I honor and love the body, as I affirm, honor and love form, beauty, freedom, gaiety and pleasure, as I represent the 'world', the interests of life, against sentimental withdrawal from life,—Classicism against Romanticism."[118] Full of admiration, he gives an account of Carducci's public comments against Manzoni, the principal representative of

Italian romanticism: "Ah, by heaven, the cousins should have heard the old enemy of the church jeer and storm in Bologna against the Christian sentimentality of the romanticists! Against Manzoni's sacred songs! Against the shadows-and-moonlight poetry of romanticism, which he compared to 'Luna, Heaven's pallid nun'. Per Baccho (sic), that had been a treat!"[119]

Carducci was not the only poet who for Lodovico Settembrini, and consequently also for Thomas Mann, understood how to transform the spirit of the Risorgimento into poetry. Giuseppe Garibaldi (1807–1882) and Giuseppe Mazzini (1805–1872) also glorified national pride and the struggle for freedom in a similar fashion. As early as 1827 Mazzini was a carbonaro, founded various secret societies, and had to spend a great part of his life in exile. Perhaps he was "the most passionately political of all the writers of the time, and the most profoundly poetic in spirit of all the many men who devoted themselves heart and soul to the cause of Italian liberation."[120] Garibaldi, the hero of the Risorgimento, could be considered as a great rhetorician in his proclamations, but basically he was primarily a man of action, who fought for his ideals with indescribable bravery and self-denial.

The glorification of the figure of Mazzini in *The Magic Mountain* demonstrates that Thomas Mann's attitude towards this statesman as well as the Italian Risorgimento in general had fundamentally changed since the time of the First World War when he fell into a violent political controversy with his brother Heinrich. Thomas was enraged at that time over the liberal attitude of Heinrich, whom with disgust he called a *Zivilisationsliterat*. At that time Thomas Mann found the same spirit embodied in Mazzini, whom he sharply attacked in his *Reflections of a Non-Political Man:* "When I wish to read something which makes my stomach turn, whereby everything within me is transformed into contradiction (and sometimes that can be useful), then I open the volume of Mazzini, which one day, quite without my merit or assistance, fell into my hands as if Heaven-sent, and to which I not only originally owe my morsel of insight into the essence of political virtue, but which also taught me whence the German *Zivilisationsliterat* really derives the style, gestures, breath control, and passion of his political manifestoes. Here I have the Latin freemason, democrat, *Revolutionsliterat* and Progressive rhetorician in the purest form and in his prime."[121]

During the writing of *The Magic Mountain* an inner transformation took place in Thomas Mann: the earlier ideals of a narrow-minded nationalist were gradually relinquished in favor of an enlightened, liberal outlook, to which the Italian Risorgimento with its three representatives, Carducci, Mazzini, and Garibaldi, formed an important bridge. In *The Magic Mountain* these three men are great examples for Settembrini, to whom emulation of their high goals and aspirations is a profound legacy, something of which he desires to impart to his young German friend.

Dante (1265–1321) and Petrarch (1304–1374)

The two great poets of the Trecento are likewise continually present in Settembrini's thoughts. Settembrini is particularly fond of inserting references to the *Divina Commedia,* be it that he designates Hans Castorp's beloved, Mme Chauchat, as "Beatrice," be it that he threatens with the horrors of Dante's Inferno. "Are you not afraid of the hurricane of the second circle of hell, which tosses and turns the sinners of the flesh, the wretched ones, who sacrificed reason to lust? Gran Dio, when I think how you will be driven fluttering here and there head over heels, then out of distress I could collapse as a dead body falls."[122] No wonder that Settembrini considers himself as "Virgil" in relation to Hans Castorp and is pleased with himself in this rôle: "Your Beatrice returns? Your guide through all nine circling spheres of Paradise? Then, I do hope that you will not entirely disdain the friendly guiding hand of your Virgil."[123] As Dante once revered Virgil and chose him to be his guide, so Settembrini also admires this ancient poet: "Ah, Virgil, Virgil! Gentlemen, he is unsurpassed. I believe in progress, certainly. But Virgil has epithets at his command as does no modern."[124] Among the interpreters of Dante, Settembrini above all admires his great teacher Carducci, who extolled Dante as the citizen of a great city and "who had stood up for revolutionizing and world-reforming activity, against asceticism and negation of the world."[125]

In Petrarch, on the other hand, Settembrini, as Mann, sees the representative of a new humanism.[126] Already in one of the first conversations Settembrini imparts, in the process, to his young friend Hans Castorp his motto "placet experiri," "the valid symbolic term for Hans Castorp's pleasure in experimenting ideologically,"[127] which becomes a significant leitmotiv in *The Magic Mountain.*

Brunetto Latini (1230–?1294)

As an early representative of humanistic thought, Settembrini also admires Brunetto Latini. "Whether, he asked, his audience had ever heard of Brunetto, Brunetto Latini, notary of Florence around 1250, who wrote a book about the virtues and the vices? It was this master who had first given the Florentines polish and taught them how to speak, as well as the art of guiding their republic according to the rules of politics."[128] In point of fact, Latini was an important political personality in his native city of Florence, he was entrusted with diplomatic missions and for a long time lived in France, where he wrote both of his great encyclopedic volumes, the *Tresor* (*Le Trésor*) and the *Tesoretto,* works which already in his lifetime were translated into several languages and imitated by writers in France and abroad. He was a true educator of his people, and one of his grateful pupils was Dante, who memorialized him in the *Divina Commedia.*

Settembrini, of course, seizes his explanations about Latini as an occasion to expound his own ideas, to some extent as if the early writer had already expressed them: "For the word is the glory of mankind, and only this makes life have dignity. Not only humanism,—humanity altogether, ancient human dignity, human regard and human self-respect are inseparably bound up with the word, with literature—and so also is politics bound up with it, or rather: it results from the alliance, the unity of humanity and literature, since the beautiful word begets the beautiful deed."[129]

Pietro Aretino (1492–1556)

On the day when Hans Castorp and his cousin first meet the fellow lodger of their friend Settembrini, Leo Naphta, Settembrini quotes a passage by the Renaissance writer Aretino. It seems as if Settembrini must overcome a certain reserve, and in order to conceal his embarrassment he gives the appearance of being in a gay mood and mentions that sixteenth-century author, who really has nothing at all in common with Settembrini's way of thinking, who to the contrary was a swindler and blackmailer who shrank from no expedient to obtain money.[130] It seems strange that Settembrini, usually so fastidious in using his quotations, makes himself the spokesman for Pietro Aretino, but the light mood of Spring has overpowered him: "Joyfulness, said he, 'holds brilliant court in the salon of his breast,' as Aretino had expressed himself, and it was to the honor of Spring, to a Spring to which he commended himself."[131]

Giacomo Leopardi (1798–1837)

As already mentioned, Settembrini is proud of his sonorous, melodious speech, and even when his listeners do not understand him he readily recites Leopardi, "while he let the beautiful syllables melt upon his tongue, moved his head to and fro and now and then closed his eyes . . . Obviously it was for him a matter of enjoying his memory and his pronunciation and to impress his audience."[132]

Settembrini feels profound compassion for the poet Leopardi, who was sorely tried by Fate, when he reflects about the latter's life full of sickness, privation, and disappointment. "An unhappy poet of my land, an humpbacked, ailing man with a soul once great, but through the misery of his body continually more humiliated and dragged down into the depths of irony, whose laments rend the heart."[133] The love of a woman was denied to Leopardi, "and it was probably this, particularly, which made him incapable of controlling the atrophy of his soul. The glitter of fame and virtue paled for him, nature to him seemed evil . . . and he despaired of science and progress! Here you have tragedy, Engineer!"[134]

Leopardi, who died in 1837 in his fortieth year, is truly one of the most tragic figures of Italian literature.[135] Already at nineteen he was neurotic, his body was deformed, and depressions set in, from which he was to find only occasional release. With Leopardi, Settembrini concludes in his discourses, so to speak, the series of the great representatives of Italian intellectual life, by means of which he also displays his (and Thomas Mann's) knowledge of Italy's intellectual heritage.

Summary

Although in *The Magic Mountain* Italy is by no means the actual setting, yet in the novel a representative of the Italian intellectual heritage plays a very important rôle: the figure of Lodovico Settembrini, the rationalist and enlightened humanist, who becomes the preceptor of "Life's problem child" from the north and his greatest mentor.

The character of Lodovico Settembrini is actually one of the most interesting and most absorbing in the author's entire output, which also extensively reflects an important development in his way of thinking. That is, Settembrini not only appears as a representative of the land south of the Alps: he is at the same time an image of the *Zivilisationsliterat* for whom Thomas Mann had shown such a deep and vehement antipathy during the controversy with his brother Heinrich at the time of the First World War.

The Magic Mountain begins with a similar kind of negative attitude toward Settembrini and the world of his ideals. Hans Castorp sees the Italian as a "barrel-organ man," a "windbag." But gradually Castorp changes his opinion, similarly as within Thomas Mann himself a growing understanding developed for the world of ideas of his brother Heinrich, the *Zivilisationsliterat* par excellence. To be sure, it was not yet possible for Thomas Mann fully to overcome his skepticism regarding all forms of a democratic régime, but nevertheless he placed the representative of these ideas in *The Magic Mountain* in a substantially more favorable light than the representative of totalitarianism, Leo Naphta. In his lecture *The Years of My Life (Meine Zeit)*, given in Chicago in 1950, Thomas Mann confessed:

> Although the novel facetiously dissociates itself from democratic rhetoric, the political *bel canto* of the disciple of Mazzini,—it nevertheless displays the concepts of terror and subjugation of man in a far more sinister light, and I will confess—after many misunderstandings it seems to me the right moment for it—that this aversion to totalitarian dogmatism, this terror of terror, has remained in me for twenty-five years and that I can never become its partisan."[136]

Just as the ideas of Settembrini gradually meet with an ever stronger echo in Hans Castorp, so also the influence of his Italian mentor becomes of more decisive importance in the maturation process of the young German. Analogous to this development, occupation with the political and ideological ideals of the Italian humanist was also for Thomas Mann himself a path to his own transformation from a narrow-minded nationalist to an open-minded democrat and a future anti-Fascist, as he appears before the reader in the novella *Mario and the Magician*.

7. *Mario and the Magician* (1930)

While in the years following the First World War a liberal political attitude was opening up within Thomas Mann, in his novella *Mario and the Magician*, as mentioned above, his anti-Fascist attitude became clearly evident. During the summer of 1926, at Forte dei Marmi, he came into personal contact with the spirit of Fascism, against which a few years later, in 1929 and 1930, he expressed his views in two important speeches. But the impressions gained in Forte dei Marmi find their written record in the novella *Mario and the Magician*, in which his great interest in Italy and his anxiety about the political developments in this country are expressed. How thoroughly he had occupied himself at that time with the characteristics of the Italian people is demonstrated by the fact that in this work Mann repeatedly makes use of the Italian language and that in addition his style and sometimes even the choice of German words take on a strong Italian coloring; for example, he translates Italian concepts literally into German and in this way creates completely new German words.

In August 1926 Thomas Mann and his wife and the two youngest children, Elisabeth and Michael, spent a holiday in Forte dei Marmi, which three years later was described in every detail in the novella. According to reports by Lavinia Mazzucchetti, Forte dei Marmi in the twenties was already a well-known bathing resort, but was primarily visited by Florentines and Milanese, who met foreign visitors, and even those coming from other parts of Italy, with a certain mistrust.[137] In addition, at that time an intensified nationalism was unquestionably noticeable in Italy, since as early as 1922 Mussolini had seized power and subjugated the country to his dictatorship.

During his work on the novel *The Magic Mountain* and in his occupation with the figure of Settembrini, the change from his earlier conservative-nationalistic standpoint had taken place within Thomas Mann. He was by this time convinced of finding unity of state and culture only in a republic, and from democracy expected "the idealistic, fundamental turning away from death towards life."[138] Thomas Mann therefore observed with great apprehension the "rise of that wave of revolutionary obscurantism in the intellectual and scientific spheres, to me a thoroughly sinister movement, which set nationality against humanity and treated the latter as something waning, being left behind,—in short, . . . the rise of Fascism."[139]

During his stay in Forte dei Marmi, then, Thomas Mann had the opportunity to observe a people living under Fascist dictatorship and to record the negative effects on the character of man.

In the course of the twenties the danger of the spread of the Fascist spirit became ever greater in Germany as well. In his address to Munich students on 16 May 1929 on *Freud's Position in the History of Modern Thought (Die Stellung Freuds in der modernen Geistesgeschichte)*, Thomas Mann took pains over a comparison of true romanticism and the pseudo-romanticism of Fascism in the hope of being able to protect German youth from the dangers of Rightist ideology. A few months later, in August 1929, during a holiday sojourn in Samland, he began work on a novella which at first he entitled "Tragisches Reiseerlebnis" ("A Tragic Travel Experience") and only later named *Mario and the Magician*.

Concerning the origin of this novella, Thomas Mann reported in his *A Sketch of My Life [Lebensabriss]*:

> But since I am completely unskilled in unoccupied 'relaxation' and experience detriment rather than benefit from it, I resolved to fill my mornings with the easy realization of an anecdote whose idea went back to an earlier holiday trip, a stay in Forte dei Marmi near Viareggio, and the impressions received there: with a task, therefore, which required no apparatus and which in the most comfortable sense of the word could be 'plucked from the air.'[140]

According to the writer's own declaration, the occurrence with and because of the magician actually took place exactly as he described it in his novella, apart from one important fact: the hypnotist named Gabrielli, whom Thomas Mann, during his stay in Forte dei Marmi in 1926, was himself able to marvel at because of his amazing feats, was not shot at the conclusion of his performance, since the real Mario did not take his "degradation" so much to heart that he would have grasped at so radical a means of revenge:

> The 'magician' was there and behaved exactly as I have described it. Only the lethal ending is invented: in reality, after the kiss Mario ran out in comical confusion and on the next day, when he again served us tea, he was most amused and full of unbiased appreciation for Cipolla's work. In life it certainly happened less passionately than later through me. Mario did not really love, and the pugnacious youth in the parterre was not his lucky rival.[141]

In this period it was a serious concern of Thomas Mann to warn against the methods of a force "by which today Munich and tomorrow Berlin could be made Italian,"[142] as he explained in a further important speech on 17 October 1930.[143] In it he referred to some central motifs of the novella, when in the characterization of the national socialist movement he emphasized fanaticism, which becomes an "epileptic ecstasy": "Is fanaticism, the arm-flinging recklessness, the dissolute renunciation of reason, human dignity, spiritual conduct, really at home in some innermost stratum of the German soul?"[144]

In the novella *Mario and the Magician* Thomas Mann consequently tried to master the political questions deeply affecting him within by dealing with them in a literary way in this "story playing strongly over into the political sphere, a story which is intrinsically occupied with the psychology of Fascism—and of "freedom," its lack of will, which places it at such a great disadvantage against the robust will of the adversary."[145]

In the first sentences of the novella, the uneasy atmosphere of Italy in the twenties is indicated: "Anger, irritation, high tension lay in the air from the beginning,"[146] and by associating the shock "with this dreadful Cipolla" the "horrible ending"[147] is already intimated.

The disquieting conditions in the fictitious bathing resort "Torre di Venere," which unquestionably are closely related to the political situation in Italy, become further unfolded before the reader or, respectively, the listener.[148] The German family, which is spending its holiday there, has to be satisfied with a less desirable table in the diningroom, since the festive veranda is reserved for influential Italians. But the decisive reason for moving into a pension is the fact that at the instigation of some members of the Italian aristocracy the hotel management insists, in an humiliating manner, upon the German guests removing to other quarters in an annex. Even in the children's domain the nationalistic-Fascistic atmosphere and hostility towards foreigners becomes noticeable: a squabble arises over the flags, into which the adults intervene, and "phrases about the greatness and dignity of Italy"[149] become audible, by which even the children become affected. The twelve-year-old boorish, at the same time malicious and cowardly lad Fuggiero embodies the prototype of the political agitator, who repeatedly causes disputes among the children and thereby also among the adults. The parents try to play down the importance of the situation by explaining that "these people . . . are just now passing through something, a condition, something like a disease, if you will, not very pleasant, but probably necessary."[150]

Still another occurrence, in itself insignificant—that namely in her innocence the little girl from the north ran naked across the beach for a few instants in order to rinse out her bathing suit—causes a clash with the chauvinistic Italians, and it becomes ever more forcibly clear to the German visitors "that it had to do with politics, the concept of the nation was involved."[151]

Cipolla, the hypnotist, is a product and at the same time the image of the Fascist evil spirit. His glib rhetoric, coupled with great power of suggestion, produces a withdrawal of will in his public, which is promptly prepared to surrender all resistance against the seducer. Through hypnosis Cipolla compels his audience into a self-alienation and a complete letting-go. Only a gentleman from Rome dares at first to offer resistance to the "magician," but then he nevertheless is obliged to submit to him, since he lacks a positively directed will of his own and his negative and non-directed unwillingness is not sufficient to break the power of the demagogue's hypnosis.

Cipolla does not shrink even from cruel, inhuman experiments: be it a breach of the conjugal partnership of the Angiolieris, be it the undamming of orgiastic instincts among a group of spectators, be it the illusionistic exchange of two people, in that he leads the likeable waiter Mario to believe that his beloved stands before him and, in his hypnosis, Mario kisses the impostor. Upon waking from the trance, however, Mario avenges his violated human dignity by killing Cipolla and therewith gives an end to the demagogue: "An end with horror, an extremely unfortunate end. And yet a liberating end—I could and can not help but feel it to be so."[152]

Thomas Mann endeavored for a long time to deny the political purpose of the novella *Mario and the Magician,* as is apparent from a letter of 1932: "As for 'Mario and the Magician', I do not like to have this tale considered a political satire. Therewith it is assigned to a province in which at most it is at home with only a small part of its being. I will not deny that little political highlights and allusions of a topical nature are put in, but the political is a broad concept, which without a sharp boundary crosses over into the problem and realm of the ethical, and irrespective of the artistic, I would nevertheless rather see the significance of the little story in the ethical than in the political."[153]

Thomas Mann harbored no malice at all towards Italy, but wanted to point out the dangers of the Fascist régime in order to protect the country against greater harm. In further letters he expressed himself regarding his attitude towards Italy and its people, to which he felt strongly bound, but in whose political conduct he was conscious of something sinister and dangerous.[154]

Despite his sharp rejection of Fascism, Thomas Mann strove for a mediating position as to the Italian people, which is also clear from his attitude towards Bruno Frank's much-heeded work *Politische Novelle.*[155]

While in his early works set in modern times Thomas Mann had either placed German people in an Italian environment or Italians in a region outside Italy, in the novella *Mario and the Magician* he showed, for the first time, modern Italian people in their own land. The writer himself, as commentator, and his family are only passive witnesses to the event, which in this form could take place only among Italians of a particular epoch—that of Fascism. Although the writer observes and shapes the outcome of the "tragic travel experience" from the standpoint of a foreigner, in this novella he has nevertheless penetrated particularly deeply into the Italian character, the temperament and the traits of the Italians. In no other of his works does the employment of the Italian language play such an important rôle as here. In *The Magic Mountain* Thomas Mann indeed lets Settembrini interject an Italian expression now and then, chiefly in moments when the Italian is so overcome by an incident or emotion that German is not adequate for him to express his thoughts in words, as, for example, at the death of Naphta, when full of horror he cries out: "Infelice! Che cosa fai per l'amor di Dio!"[156] ("Unhappy man! What are you doing, for God's sake!")

It is quite different, on the other hand, in the novella *Mario and the Magician*, where the Italian people are allowed to speak in their own language. When the mother of the disobedient boy Fuggiero calls to him "Fuggiero, rispondi almeno!,"[157] then with this despairing "answer me at least" she stands before the reader as one of the typical Italian mothers who spoil their children from infancy, as runs in the tradition of the land. That she pronounces the name Fuggiero "atrociously stressed", with "harsh open è"[158] and what is more forms the "sp" in German fashion like an "schp," marks the woman as uneducated. The howls of pain of the boy, "Ohi!" and "Oimé!,"[159] which he employs upon an occasion of no import, display his cowardice and self-pity.

Italian expressions and idioms become particularly frequent during the performance of the magician, who of course directs himself primarily to his countrymen in his excessively great fluency: be it with inciting shouts, as "paura, eh!"[160] (afraid, eh!), or commands, such as "balla!"[161] (dance!), "una ballatina"[162] (A little dance). Cipolla's aggressiveness in relation to his audience frequently emerges in his delight in ironical insinuations. Thus he designates the young lad (giovanotto) as "donnaiuolo"[163] (ladies' man) or "questo torregiano di Venere,"[164] which can mean both an inhabitant of Torre di Venere as well as lookout of Venus, and calls his tongue, on the other hand, "linguaccia,"[165] hence coated tongue. Cipolla himself masquerades as "Cavaliere,"[166] a member of the nobility, and calls himself "Forzatore, Illusionista, and Prestigiatore"[167] (manipulator, magician, conjurer). From these few examples it becomes clear how thoroughly Thomas Mann, whose special interest always concerned the subtleties of the German language, must have occupied himself with Italian colloquial speech and particularly with its idiomatic peculiarities.

When he has Cipolla call the "giovanotto," who under hypnosis had to show his tongue to the public, "questo linguista di bella speranze,"[168] then one is conscious of the writer's pleasure in the play upon words, since *lingua* means both tongue and language, and it remains undecided whether his tongue or his fluency shows great promise. The Italian spectators admire Cipolla's glibness and also that of the "giovanotto," about whom one of the onlookers says in wonder: "Ha sciolto lo scilinguagnolo,"[169] that is, "he has a loose tongue" or "he has loosened his tongue." The writer even has his two children demonstrate their knowledge of Italian, although only through certain phrases which they have picked up from the natives during their stay in Italy. "Mario, una cioccolata e biscotti!" (Mario, a chocolate and biscuits!) they call to their friend in the hall, who, smiling, answers with "Subito" (at once).[170]

Thomas Mann had now become so very familiar with the Italian milieu and its idiom that even his German occasionally takes on a Latin coloring. Now and then he inserts into the novella Italian turns of speech that have been translated into German, when, for example, he has the magician call out "sieh ein bisschen"[171] (look a little), or "sage ein bisschen"[172] (say a little), whereby the appended "ein bisschen" (a little) doubtless represents a translation of the Italian "un po'." Also when Thomas Mann uses the term "Capannen"[173] (Italian "capanne") as the designation for bathing huts, or speaks of "Pineta-Gärten"[174] (Pinienhain-Gärten—Pine-grove gardens), forms the adjective "stakkiert"[175] out of "staccato," and above all when he renders the Italian phrase for shell-fishes, "frutti di mare,"[176] as "Meeresobst"[177] ("fruit of the sea"), one encounters new German word forms based on the Italian; that is, Thomas Mann's own, extremely original linguistic creations.

Since his youth, when he first lived in Italy for a long time, Thomas Mann had observed land and people and described them in several of his works, although sometimes only as relatively unimportant background. But in the novella *Mario and the Magician* he captured the Italian atmosphere especially penetratingly and in detail. In the description of the Italian summer weather, experienced from the viewpoint of the northerner, the reader has the sense of almost physically feeling the African heat: "the reign of terror of the sun as soon as one withdrew from the edge of the indigo-blue coolness,"[178] which at the same time is "the sun of Homer,"[179] the intense, often glaring colors, the dazzling light. The onset of the sirocco with its stifling sultriness and the faint rain is just as impressionably described, and no less the simultaneous flaccidity and inertia of the sea: the atmosphere in which the agitating event of this holiday time takes place is unmistakably characterized as Italian.

Against this background move the southern people: shrill-voiced mothers worried about their children, peddlers who offer the bathing guests coral, beverages, and "cornetti al burro"[180] (butter crescents), the manageress of the Pension Eleonora, whose life reached its zenith in friendship with the great actress Eleonora Duse. How deeply Thomas Mann had become absorbed with the soul of the Italian people is clearly shown by some characteristic traits that he has sketched out in the novella; for example, the awe of Italians for mastery of speech and their endeavor to manipulate it as artistically and beautifully as possible: "Among southerners, speech is an ingredient of the joy of life, which meets with a far livelier social valuation than is known in the north."[181] Neither has Thomas Mann disregarded the emotion of the person speaking, which frequently results from this attitude.[182] The childlike naive delight of the Italians in harmless ambiguous jokes appears in the episode of the number experiments, when a good-humored spectator suggests "null null" (zero zero) "and therewith had the merry success of which the reference to natural functions can be assured among southerners."[183]

The special attention which Thomas Mann gave to proper names in his works is generally known. In his early novellas, such as *The Will to Happiness* and *Tonio Kröger* he had, through the combination of an Italian given name with a North German family name, symbolically expressed the duality of a character. In the novella *Mario and the Magician* he additionally occupied himself thoroughly with Italian place-names and apparently found so much pleasure thereby that he even devised new place-names in Italian. In vain will one search for the names Torre di Venere, Portoclemente, and Marina Petriera on the map, since Thomas Mann made them up himself or fashioned them in analogy with existing names. The appellation Torre di Venere (Tower of Venus) was surely influenced by existing names such as Portovenere and Torre di Greco (Tower of the Greek) and at the same time is slightly reminiscent of Thomas Mann's real holiday spot Forte dei Marmi (Marble Fortress), which is not far from Portovenere. The name Portoclemente (Port of Clement) resembles the actually existing Porto Clementino (Port of the small Clement), and likewise for Marina Petriera (rocky coast) there is a series of equivalent seaside resort names. The given name Mario is very popular in Italy and in the novella gives the magician the occasion to allude to its ancient origin and simultaneously to insert a reference to "the heroic traditions of the Fatherland,"[184] in order then to strengthen this observation with the Roman salute. The name "Cipolla" (onion) is perhaps supposed to be an insinuation of the unsavory and grotesque appearance of the magician. But possibly Thomas Mann was influenced in the choice of this name by Boccaccio's *Decamerone:* in its tenth novella of the sixth day, which Dioneo tells to his friends, an account is given of a Frate Cipolla who not only in stature but also in his characteristics has many similarities with the "magician" of Thomas Mann.

> This Frate Cipolla was of small build, red-haired and a cheerful face, and the best rogue in the world; and besides this, having no education, yet such an excellent and ready speaker was he, that whoever was not acquainted with him would have not only esteemed him a great rhetorician, but would have said him to be Tully himself or perhaps Quintillian: and to almost everyone in the vicinity he was intimate friend, friend, or good acquaintance.[185]

Exactly like Thomas Mann's character, Frate Cipolla distinguishes himself through eloquence and quickness of repartee,[186] but at the same time, in contrast to the "magician," is friendly and liked in his surroundings. Common to both is the talent for influencing their fellowmen, and indeed often through unethical means. Boccaccio's Frate comes to Certaldo, the birthplace of the Italian writer, and wishes to deceive his audience, in that he makes them believe that he possesses a feather of the Angel Gabriel. Two wags, however, have stolen the feather from him and put coal in his basket, which he, in his quick-wittedness, immediately passes off as that upon which Saint Lorenzo was burned. With the statement that God himself has exchanged the feather for the coal, he impresses the crowd and reaps more admiration and alms than ever before. This influencing of his listeners seems to be very similar to the hypnotic art of deception of the modern Cipolla. But there is no doubt that the character created by Thomas Mann is substantially more complicated and problematical, since it has the traits of a demagogue and represents a danger to the world around it. The "Frate" on the other hand is a harmless fraud, to whom the reader can give his sympathy. Boccaccio tells his story in order to amuse his readers; Thomas Mann, on the contrary, in order to warn us against the figure of the demoniacal seducer of the people.[187]

In the novella *Mario and the Magician* Thomas Mann demonstrated his deep penetration into the life and thought of the Italian people. In his forcible portrayal of the dubious and sometimes menacing conditions under the Fascist régime there emerges not a rejection of the Italian people but rather a concerned sympathy and a warning addressed to his nation regarding a similar form of government.

8. *Doctor Faustus* (1947)

For the human and artistic design of *Doctor Faustus*, the Italian element is in a certain respect of just as great importance as for *Tonio Kröger* and for Aschenbach in *Death in Venice*. The hero of the novel, the composer Adrian Leverkühn, spends some time in Italy, like Tonio Kröger and Aschenbach, who travel in the south in order to free themselves there from the constraint and limitation of the north.

Exactly like Aschenbach, Adrian is also dominated before his departure by an inner unrest and the "desire for distant air." Analogous to Aschenbach, whose mind is completely receptive to the appearance of the stranger at the cemetery, Adrian also waits anxiously for a sign which should indicate to him the right destination, an environment in which he can find himself. "I am seeking . . . earnestly asking all around and listening for direction to a place where, really buried from the world and undisturbed, I could hold a conversation with my life, my destiny."[188]

It is significant that the direction guides him to Italy. For here, in the mysterious and gloomy atmosphere of the old Italian palazzo, that "conversation"[189] can take place which is of decisive significance for the rest of Adrian's life, just as Aschenbach's meeting with Tadzio in the seductive surroundings of Venice determined his fate.

As early as 1901 Thomas Mann had conceived the plan for the treatment of the Faust theme, yet a hesitation he could not explain held him back at that time from beginning the realization of these thoughts. His feelings told him that something sinister, plainly dangerous was connected with this theme. Not until forty-two years later did he again turn to his long-cherished plan; and in his perusal of old notebooks while preparing for the work, he chanced upon his "three-line plan of Dr. Faust from 1901."[190] Shaken, the author read his old notes "and along with looking them up again, and finding them again, goes an emotion, to say the least: excitement, which makes very clear to me how the scanty and vague thematic kernel had from the beginning been surrounded by an aura of the touch of life, an atmosphere of biographical feeling that, considerably far in advance of my discernment, predestined the novella to become a novel."[191]

If most of the works of Thomas Mann permit suspicions of autobiographical features, then the "atmosphere of biographical feeling" mentioned by the writer appears especially strongly in the novel *Doctor Faustus*. In addition to many other recollections, Thomas Mann assimilates the impressions and experiences of his stay in Palestrina into his great work which basically, as with the novella *Death in Venice,* presents an extensive self-analysis of the writer.

In November 1944 Thomas Mann wrote the "transitional chapter XXIV, taking place in Palestrina, in fourteen days."[192] Forty-seven years had gone by since he and his brother Heinrich had stayed in this small Italian town, but his memories of this time are precise and clear down to the details. Likewise in the novel a companion accompanies the hero: the friend Rüdiger Schildknapp is Adrian Leverkühn's housemate in Palestrina and Rome, just as Heinrich Mann had shared all experiences in Italy with his younger brother Thomas.

At the beginning of the twenty-fourth chapter, comprising only thirteen pages in the complete (German) edition, Serenus Zeitblom gives an account of his visit with Adrian Leverkühn and his companion Rüdiger Schildknapp in the summer holidays of 1912 and states that this was already the second summer which the friends had spent in Palestrina: "They had passed the winter in Rome and in May, as the heat increased, again sought out the mountains and the same hospitable house where, during a stay of three months the previous year, they had learned to feel at home."[193]

This description reminds one very much of the early Italian sojourns of Thomas Mann described in our first chapter, since he and his brother Heinrich had also spent the winter (1896–97) in Rome and in the summer (1897) returned once more to Palestrina, where they had already lived from July to October 1895.

Exactly as once the two brothers Heinrich and Thomas, so also now in the novel Adrian and Rüdiger live "three floors up in the Via Torre Argentina,"[194] take their main meal "in a neighboring Trattoria" and spend their evenings "playing dominoes . . . in a quiet café corner."[195] If one compares the description of the daily Roman routine of the brothers, which Thomas Mann gives in his *A Sketch of My Life* (*Lebensabriss*) appearing in 1930, with the portrayal of the life which Adrian and Rüdiger lead in Rome, one concludes that the true events fully coincide with fiction. Also the reserve practiced by Adrian and his friend in relation to their fellowmen is a motif which plays an important rôle in Thomas Mann's own recollections of his early trips to Italy.

After their sojourn in Rome, Adrian and Rüdiger return to Palestrina and are again guests in the small, old hotel where they had already felt very happy on their first visit. In the novel the historical "Casa Bernardini" becomes "the Manardi house, the lodging of Adrian and Rüdiger."[196] The description of the severe and fortress-like building situated on the narrow street of stairs corresponds to the account which Heinrich Mann gives in his reminiscences about the joint stay with his brother.[197] Thomas, on the other hand, amplified the description of the milieu much further and had the chronicler Serenus Zeitblom tell about the little black pigs and the mules with their wide loads which populate the lane in front of the house. There is indeed no doubt that both of the brothers Mann were again and again impressed, and certainly also somewhat repelled, by this street scene during their stay in Palestrina. Likewise one may well assume that the description of the rooms occupied by Adrian Leverkühn and Rüdiger in the Manardi house fully corresponds to Thomas Mann's own recollections, as do the furnishings of the "two-windowed livingroom of hall-sized proportions,"[198] which Heinrich described as the "stone hall"[199] in his reminiscences.

The description of the people living in the house also appears on the whole to be strongly modelled upon Thomas Mann's recollections of the inhabitants of "Casa Bernardini," although in the novel the names were changed. Around 1896 the hotel was managed by the daughter of the owner, Signora Anna Pastina, née Bernardini, who was already widowed at that time. In the novel the "stately matron of the Roman type,"[200] Nella Manardi, corresponds to her. Serenus Zeitblom reports in the novel about a thirteen- to fourteen-year-old daughter of Signora Manardi, Amelia, a child of slightly unsound mind, to whose peculiar behavior at table the guests soon become accustomed. The brothers Mann actually became acquainted with a little Amelia in Casa Bernardini, the granddaughter of the landlady, Anna Bernardini. However, the girl—according to an account by Karl Kerényi, who followed Thomas Mann's tracks in Palestrina step by step—by no means exhibited signs of mental illness. Kerényi stated she looks today very similar to a stately matron of the Roman type and can still remember a little about the guests Enrico and Thomas.[201]

In the novel, besides Signora Manardi and her daughter Amelia, there appear the two brothers of the landlady, the lawyer Ercolano and the perhaps forty-year-old farmer Sor Alfonso, called Alfo, who in the evenings rides home from the fields on his donkey. Both brothers, opposed in many respects in their philosophies of life, are portrayed as spirited representatives of Italian provincial small town life. Whether Thomas Mann had prototypes in real life for these characters is not certain, since neither in his nor in Heinrich's reports of their stay in Palestrina is mention made of acquaintance with similar Italians.

In the description of the landscape around Palestrina one again finds many reminiscences of impressions experienced by the author himself. Serenus Zeitblom tells about walks which lead him and his wife, together with Adrian and Rüdiger Schildknapp, out of the town into a typical Italian landscape, "with its olive trees and garlands of grape vines, its grain-fields partitioned into small holdings enclosed by stone walls in which almost monumental entrance-gates opened."[202]

Zeitblom, the humanistically educated chronicler, calls special attention to the antique mood of the landscape, above which "the classic sky" arches cloudlessly.[203] Zeitblom describes the impressions of the evening return to Palestrina with a mixture of sentimentalism and pedantry: "We looked towards the sunset, as we returned to the little town, and I have never seen a similar splendor of the evening sky. A thickly laid, oil-like coating of gold, edged with crimson, floated on the western horizon,— absolutely phenomenal and so beautiful that the view could indeed fill the soul with a certain exuberance."[204] That Adrian and Rüdiger do not share his awe and emotion in the presence of the beauty of Nature, but burst out into ironical laughter, wounds Zeitblom most deeply.

A parallel to this account is found in Heinrich Mann's essay about his brother Thomas, in which he describes a very similar occurrence during their stay together in Palestrina: "We descended, after the heat of the summer day, from our Roman mountain village to the main road. Before us, around us, we had a sky of solid gold. I said: 'Byzantine pictures are gold-grounded. That is not a metaphor, as we can see, but an optical fact. Just add the slender head of the Virgin and her much-too-heavy crown which look down indifferently from their plastic zenith!' My brother disliked the aestheticism in my remark. 'That's its external aspect,' said he."[205]*

Although similar references to art history do not appear in the novel, the basic mood of the occurrence and the effect of the natural phenomenon of the Italian sunset are nevertheless very similar, whereby Serenus Zeitblom reflects the attitude of Heinrich Mann, and Adrian and Rüdiger, on the other hand, embody the ironic skepticism of Thomas Mann.

Zeitblom is distressingly affected by the reaction of the two friends to his devout rapture: "Still it was slightly disagreeable to me when Schildknapp, pointing towards the wondrous display, shouted his 'Inspect that!' and Adrian burst out into the grating laughter which Rüdiger's humor always drew from him. For it seemed to me that he took the opportunity to laugh equally at my and Helene's emotion and at the grandeur of the natural phenomenon itself."[206] The discomfort of this honest and God-fearing chronicler seems to allude to an event which had already taken place before Zeitblom's visit in Palestrina, but which is not reported until the following

---

*Englished in *The Stature of Thomas Mann,* ed. Charles Neider (New York: New Directions, 1947)

chapter of the novel: Adrian Leverkühn's conversation with the Devil.

Leverkühn's solitary reading of Kierkegaard's reflections on Mozart's "Don Juan" in the salon of the Manardi house prefaces the appearance of the Devil. On the horsehair sofa suddenly sits—diffusing cutting cold around itself—a figure "rather spindly of build . . . reddish hair going back from the temple; reddish eyelashes as well, fringing reddened eyes."[207] This description of the Devil is very strongly reminiscent of a figure in the novella *Death in Venice,* that of the gondolier who conveys Aschenbach to the Lido. "Although rather slight of build . . . he handled the oar . . . with great energy . . . Reddish brows knitted together, he gazed out beyond his passenger . . ."[208] The gondolier, who symbolizes Death just as does the stranger at the cemetery, introduced at the beginning of the novella, and bestowed with very similar physical attributes, appears to have been in Thomas Mann's mind in connection with his conception of the Devil in Palestrina, and the assumption is natural that the writer wished to personify the dark forces of Death and the Devil through Italians. In a thorough inspection of the respective passages it becomes clear, however, that neither in the gondolier nor in the Devil in Palestrina did Thomas Mann wish to depict an Italian. The author himself emphasized that the facial features and the blond, curling moustache of the gondolier made him appear "not at all of Italian stock,"[209] whereby he therefore questions his origin and leaves it completely open. In this sense, in Thomas Mann's novel *Doctor Faustus,* the Devil also quite plainly refuses to speak Italian with Leverkühn, who upon seeing him bursts out with a startled "Chi è costà," indeed, he even gives to understand that his preferred language is German: "Do speak German! Only fine Old German spoken out without any pretense or dissimulation. I understand it. It is quite truly my favorite language. Sometimes I understand only German altogether."[210]

In addition to Italian people and the Italian milieu, Italian music and Italian literature play a certain rôle in Thomas Mann's *Doctor Faustus.* Since the novel is concerned with the destiny of a composer, music—its history and development—must naturally occupy a relatively large place. Thomas Mann is very conscious of the importance of Italian musicians and composers. In Palestrina (1525?–1594) he sees a significant pioneer in the evolution from liturgical singing to independent instrumental music, while he stresses the importance of Monteverdi and Alessandro Scarlatti for the creation of Italian opera. Leverkühn's "Faustus Cantata" is very strongly influenced in its style by Monteverdi, "whose music—again not without good reason—favored the echo-effect, sometimes even to becoming a mannerism."[211] Just as Monteverdi, in his "Lamento," knew how to transform deepest lamentation into music, so Leverkühn, in his cantata of the lament of Faust, takes pains over a work of variations based on the last words of Faust: "For I die as a good and bad Christian." "The return to

Monteverdi and the style of his time is exactly that which I termed the 'reconstruction of expression'—of expression in its first and original manifestation, of expression as lament."[212] In the compositions of Carissimi, Thomas Mann sees the highest form of the oratorio, and in the works of Vivaldi and Tartini a refinement in the instrumental music of the Baroque. Except for the mention of Paganini's violin concerto, which exerts a certain influence on Adrian's own composition of a violin concerto, Thomas Mann did not concern himself with Italian music of more recent epochs; from the post-Baroque period on, his interest is limited to German music and its development.

In Adrian Leverkühn's creative work in general, and particularly in his early work, the musical arrangement of lyric poetry, especially from the German, the English, and above all the Latin cultural sphere, plays a part. "He experimented now almost exclusively with the composition of lieder, short and longer songs, even epic fragments, for which he gathered his material from a Mediterranean anthology which, in a fairly felicitous German translation, included Provençal and Catalonian lyric poetry of the twelfth and thirteenth centuries, Italian poetry, visionary heights of the 'Divina Commedia,' then Spanish and Portuguese works."[213] The chronicler, Zeitblom, is particularly deeply impressed by the songs whose texts originated in Dante's *Divina Commedia,* especially from the "Purgatorio" and the "Paradiso." While Zeitblom admires the sublimation of the text through the music, he is repelled by some of the Dante verses, for example, by those which tell of the damnation of good and pure people who in spite of their innocence are banished to Hell because they are not baptized and consequently—although through no fault of their own—cannot share in mercy: "I was enraged by this renunciation of the human in favor of an inaccessible absolute predestination, and however much on the whole I acknowledge Dante's poetical greatness, yet I always felt repelled by his inclination towards cruelty and scenes of martyrdom, and I recall that I reproached Adrian because he had decided on composing music for the scarcely bearable episode."[214]

A composition which completely captivates Zeitblom is the musical setting of an episode from Canto XXII of "Purgatorio," which tells of a man "who in the night bears a light upon his back which does not light his way but illuminates the path of those coming behind him."[215]

In the case of this figure it concerns the "pagan" Virgil, whom the Latin poet Statius thanks for having shown mankind the way to Christianity, although it was not yet in his power to be a Christian.

> And he to him: 'Thou first directedst me
> Towards Parnassus, in its grots to drink
> And first concerning God didst me enlighten.

Thou didst as he who walketh in the night,
Who bears his light behind, which helps him not,
But wary makes the persons after him.'[216]*

Zeitblom then continues with his account: "But I was made still happier
by the exceedingly successful shaping of the address, composed of only
nine lines, of the poet to his allegorical song, which speaks so darkly and
laboriously and in consequence of its hidden sense has no prospect of being
understood by the world. Thus may it, charges its creator, implore people
to at least perceive its beauty if not its depth. 'Then heed, at least, how
beautiful I am!' "[217]

On the basis of Zeitblom's presentation, the reader has the feeling that
the lines from the *Divina Commedia* directly precede the poet's address to
his song and consequently form a part of Dante's work itself. In Dante's
time it was still quite customary to conclude a Canzone with a verse of
dedication in order to send the poem out into the world with the good
wishes of the poet. In the case of the "tornata" described by Thomas
Mann, it concerns, however, a dedicatory verse of the first Canzone in
Dante's *Convivio,* which addresses itself to the intelligences and angels
through whom the third sphere of Heaven is moved.[218] The Canzone begins
with the words "Ye who understanding move the third heaven,"[219] and in
Vossler's translation the verse of dedication reads:

Mein Lied, ich glaube, dass es Wen'ge sind,
Die deinen Sinn genau verstehen werden,
So dunkel sprichst du und so mühevoll.
Wofern es etwa dir begegnen sollte,
Dass du vor solche Leute treten musst,
Die stumpf für deinen tiefen Sinn erscheinen,
So bitt ich dich, mein liebliches Geschöpf,
Beruhige dich, indem du ihnen sagst:
So achtet wenigstens, wie schön ich bin![220]

My song, I believe that few there are,
Who will understand thy meaning well,
So darkly speakest thou and so laboriously.
Wherefore should it perhaps befall thee,
That thou must appear before such people,
Who seem indifferent to thy deep sense,
Then I implore thee, my lovely creation,
Comfort thyself by saying to them:
Then heed, at least, how beautiful I am!**

— ———

* Englished by H. W. Longfellow, *The Divine Comedy,* 319
**Englished from Vossler's German by Betty Crouse

Time and again Zeitblom mentions the great influence of Dante on the work of Leverkühn, not in the least on his composition "Apocalipsis cum figuris," which represents "an homage to Dürer,"[221] but at the same time, in addition to Michelangelo's interpretation of the Last Judgment, includes the representations of the Hereafter from Dante's *Commedia*.

In the novel, which has for its theme the descent into Hell of Doctor Faustus, Dante's *Divina Commedia* with its impressively horrible and gruesome scenes in the Inferno must play an important part. Thomas Mann could have placed no more fitting motto at the head of his Luciferian novel than the lines from the second canto of "Inferno," which indicate the close relationship between the modern German writer and the Italian poet of the early fourteenth century.

In summary it can be said that, in Thomas Mann's great novel *Doctor Faustus*, the Italian elements play an important rôle. Into the description of Adrian Leverkühn's sojourn at Rome and Palestrina the writer assimilated a large number of his own recollections of his early Italian trips with his brother Heinrich. In addition to observations about Italian landscape and Italian people, Thomas Mann also concerned himself in the novel with Italian music and Italian literature, above all with Dante. One of the most important episodes of the novel, the appearance of the Devil and the long conversation between him and Leverkühn, takes place in Palestrina. To be sure, at first glance it seems strange that Thomas Mann shifted this event, so significant to the novel, to Italy, although in the case of the Devil with his archaic language it clearly concerns a figure out of Old German times. And yet this large, gloomy room in the Manardi house, in which suddenly the coldness emanating from the Devil spreads itself, seems to be the right stage for the weird event. That this severe and fortress-like dark building is predestined for unusual and supernatural things is already apparent from the peculiar behavior of the thirteen- or fourteen-year-old daughter of Signora Manardi who at table occasionally asks about ghosts. While this slightly mentally ill young girl moves the spoon back and forth before her eyes she repeatedly asks: "Spiriti, spiriti?" Thus the house and the family circle of the Manardis are connected with something mysterious and murky, which once again corresponds to Thomas Mann's conception of an Italy whose dangerous undercurrents he had depicted in the novellas *Tonio Kröger* and *Death in Venice,* as well as in his drama *Fiorenza* and no less also in *Mario and the Magician*.

In contrast to Tonio Kröger and Aschenbach, for Leverkühn the temptation of the south lies, however, not in the realm of the erotic nor even, as in the novella *Mario and the Magician,* in the sphere of the political, but completely in the province of the moral. To be sure, the Devil is not of Italian origin, yet his arts of persuasion and seduction seem heightened by the Italian surroundings; on the other hand, however, through his stay in the south Leverkühn—like Aschenbach—is so strongly divested of his

northern inhibitions and powers of resistance that in this Italian atmosphere he succumbs without any hesitation to temptation by the Devil and
sells his soul to him.

9. *The Tables of the Law* (1944) and *Die Erotik Michelangelos* (1950)

The epoch of the Italian Renaissance with its highly developed artistic
level had very early interested Thomas Mann and inspired his novella
Gladius Dei and his drama *Fiorenza*. In addition to the prominent religious
and political figures of that time such as Savonarola and Lorenzo dei
Medici, Thomas Mann also let poets like Poliziano and a great number of
painters and sculptors have their say in his work. Included among the
important Italians of the early and high Renaissance with whom Thomas
Mann concerned himself in his works before and after *Doctor Faustus* is
also the sculptor and painter Michelangelo Buonarroti (1475–1564). Mann's
interest in this artist and his work undoubtedly goes far back into the
writer's youth. To be sure, during his first sojourns at Rome in 1895 and
1896, the young author still gave preference to ancient art over that of the
Italian Renaissance, yet at that time Michelangelo's "Last Judgment"
made a deep impression on him, indeed, not least because the powerful
fresco in the Sistine Chapel in its gloomy basic mood of the damnation and
downfall of mankind to a certain extent corresponded with the spiritual
state of the young Thomas Mann: "The ancient sculpture in the Vatican
meant more to me than the painting of the Renaissance. The Last Judgment
moved me deeply as the apotheosis of my thoroughly pessimistic, moralis-
tic, and antihedonistic mood."[222]

Strangely enough, however, the figure of Michelangelo made its way into
Thomas Mann's works only relatively late. In the Renaissance drama
Fiorenza his name is not once mentioned, although by the year 1492, in
which the action takes place, the sculptor had been a special protegé of the
Medici in Rome for three years and in spite of his youth had already created
some important works of art for the city.[223]

In the strongly autobiographical novel *Doctor Faustus,* however,
Thomas Mann returned to the great work of art which in his youth had so
strongly impressed him. Upon listening to the choral work "Apocalipsis
cum figuris," composed by Adrian Leverkühn, Serenus Zeitblom is in-
stinctively reminded of the representation created by Michelangelo of the
Last Judgment.[224]

Only in 1943 did Thomas Mann fashion the hero of the tale *The Tables of
the Law (Das Gesetz)* after the model of the great Italian artist and Renaissance man, and seven years later the artist became the subject of a character study in the essay *Die Erotik Michelangelos.* According to Mann's own
statement, the figure of Moses in the tale *The Tables of the Law* is com-

pletely modelled upon the historical Michelangelo, not only in his outward appearance, but also in his character and in his passions, his colossal creative power and his gift of artistic genius in the highest sense. In Thomas Mann's portrayal, Moses is "of burning senses, therefore he longed for the spiritual, pure and holy, the invisible, for this seemed to him spiritual, holy and pure."[225] Like Michelangelo in his art, Moses risks everything in order to attain the pure and the holy, and no effort, including self-sacrifice, is too great for the realization of his dream.

It has been assumed by various critics that Thomas Mann modelled his figure of Moses after the powerful statue of Moses which Michelangelo created for the tomb of Julius II and which is now found in the church of San Pietro in Vincoli. Nevertheless, the author had another model, as he admitted in a letter to Anna Jacobson: "The characteristics of my Moses are *not* 'borrowed from Michelangelo's mighty monument,' but from Michelangelo *himself*."[226]

A few years later Thomas Mann dealt with this theme once again and in his "Story of a Novel" ("Roman eines Romans"), in the journal *The Genesis of Doctor Faustus (Die Entstehung des Doktor Faustus)*, declared: "Probably under the unconscious influence of Heine's portrait of Moses I gave my hero the features—not of Michelangelo's Moses, but of Michelangelo himself, in order to depict him as a painstaking artist toiling laboriously over obstinate human raw material, and under disheartening defeats."[227]

Not only in character does the Moses of Thomas Mann resemble Michelangelo, but also in his outward appearance. It is reported that in a fight a fellow pupil in the Medici garden struck him a blow with his fist which shattered Michelangelo's nose. Similarly, in the story *The Tables of the Law*, Thomas Mann describes a scuffle between Moses and an Egyptian overseer, who ultimately is killed by Moses. Prior to that, however, Moses wished to have a discussion with the Egyptian, who has cruelly beaten a man: "Turning pale and with blazing eyes he called the Egyptian to account, who in place of any answer struck him on the nose, so that for the rest of his life Moses had a nose with a broken bone, smashed flat."[228]

Since in the moulding of his Moses, Thomas Mann continually had in mind the image of Michelangelo as a forming and shaping sculptor, he time and again calls the reader's attention to the hands of the great preacher and educator of the people. His discourses are often accompanied by uncontrolled fistshaking and thereby appear more impressive and more impelling.[229] Moses tries to make from his people, whom he has led out of Egypt, a better, indeed a holy people, by giving his fellow citizens rules of conduct and laws for their cultivation. In this attempt to guide and to mould them he is like the sculptor, who through hard work chisels a sculpture from the stone. "By the sweat of his brow he labored thereon at Kadesh, his workshop, in that his wide-set eyes were everywhere,—he hacked, blasted, formed and smoothed the unwilling block with stubborn patience, with repeated forbearance and frequent forgiveness, with blazing anger and punishing relentlessness."[230]

In 1950 Thomas Mann was sent a book which deeply impressed him: a German-Italian edition of the poems of Michelangelo, translated by the art historian and author Hans Mühlestein. Stimulated by this book, Mann composed an essay on the great Renaissance artist, which first appeared in the same year in the Zürich art journal *Du* under the title *Die Erotik Michelangelos (The Eroticism of Michelangelo)*, and a short time afterwards was again issued as a separate publication under the title *Michelangelo in seinen Dichtungen (Michelangelo in His Poetry)*. In a letter to Agnes E. Meyer, Thomas Mann announced the little study as follows: "On the whole trip I have worked on nothing but an article on 'Michelangelos Erotik,' apropos of an Italian-German edition of his poems, whose agitation moved me deeply. How inseparable from one another greatness and suffering are proven to be! The little essay will appear, only in German, in a Zürich art journal."[231]

What probably particularly impressed Thomas Mann about the poet Michelangelo was his ability to pour forth his feelings of grief and misery in poems which, although written in strict sonnet form, overflow with suffering passion: "It is poetic wild growth—indeed, although the obligatory sonnet form is often adhered to, we are even more dealing with the eruption of the grief, the bitterness, the love and the misery of a great, colossal, suffering soul striving to reach God through the beautiful, than we are dealing with poetry."[232]

The confessions of the Italian artist, which are proof of his great vitality, are concerned with a variety of themes: some of his poems speak of his sorrow over the downfall of the Florentine Republic and his loathing of the Medici dictatorship; others deal with his art, but the majority are love poems, to which Thomas Mann's particular interest was directed. The basic mood of Michelangelo is "*Love,* one which does not wish to end, a life-long love of the image, living beauty, human attractiveness—a persistence of the power of love and susceptibility to its blissful torture, as one also finds it in some other strong natures, sensitive and in whom sensuality endures, in Goethe and Tolstoi."[233] In this yearning sensuality, which at the same time strives after the pure and spiritual, Thomas Mann saw the basis for Michelangelo's sadness of life.

Like Goethe, the great Italian fell under the power of love into advanced years. Thomas Mann saw yet another parallel to Goethe: while in Frau von Stein Goethe found a guide and inspiration to higher things, for Michelangelo the union of souls with Vittoria Colonna was of the greatest significance for him as a person and as an artist. "In her ethereal quality and as a 'developmental experience' she is very reminiscent of Goethe's relationship to Frau von Stein, as he says to her in a sonnet that he came into the world twice: once only as a model of himself, in inferior clay, but then through her, through rebirth in stone, as a completed work, and indeed through the disciplining and subduing work which her goodness had performed upon his originally turbulent nature, adding what he had lacked, filing away what had been rough and excessive in him.''[234] But while Goethe, at the time of his love for Frau von Stein, was still young and capable of development, Michelangelo was in his sixtieth year when he began to love Vittoria and compose poetry for her. Thomas Mann was nevertheless convinced that this woman was likewise able to give the restless artist his longed-for happiness, in that she inspired him to great and lofty things and opened up to him a new world, transcending the senses. ''Yet it is undoubted, and the most intimate poetic documents testify to it, that his love for the woman whom he chose as his 'fragile life's heart and soul'—that this chaste and high-minded, reciprocated devotion had given him the most glorious exaltation, the most solemn marriage of the senses with the spiritual and the eternal, a happiness which, as its high-mindedness absolutely demands, pulls not earthwards, but heavenwards.''[235]

After Vittoria's death Michelangelo turned again to new love-affairs: into an advanced age he was a victim of his passions. He had to live according to his talent and his character, and it was not given to him to be a philosopher and to live as such. With great emotion Thomas Mann reported on the last years, marked by sickness and poverty, when in his wretchedness Michelangelo could find consolation neither in art nor in love, which once had meant so much to him.

The seventy-six-year-old Thomas Mann paid homage in this essay to the genius of an Italian artist whom he had admired since his youth. With deep understanding for his sublime spirit he plumbed the depths of the greatness and human weaknesses of Michelangelo, who recognized ''that work vanquishes time and death.''[236] Thomas Mann confessed that he never would forget the verses of Michelangelo which say ''that late, after many quests and ordeals, one arrives at new, sublime things and that then our course soon is at an end.''

Ch'all'alte cose nuove
Tardi si viene e poco poi si dura—[237]

10. *The Holy Sinner* (1951)

Thomas Mann's novel *The Holy Sinner (Der Erwählte)* is considered as the antithesis to his *Doctor Faustus*. While on the basis of his pact with the Devil, Faust must be damned, Grigorss can be redeemed on the strength of his remorse and repentance. He is the one chosen and favored by God, and who, like Joseph, must pass through the various stages of rise, downfall, and renewed rise in order, at the end, to ascend the highest possible step.

In reading his sources for *Doctor Faustus*, Thomas Mann was drawn especially strongly by the legend of Pope Gregory, which he found in a German translation, executed by Grässe, of the *Gesta Romanorum*. As Thomas Mann reported in his *Bemerkungen zu dem Roman Der Erwählte (Remarks Concerning the Novel, The Holy Sinner)*, he decided to expand this medieval tale into a separate work later on. "Actually, it pleased me so well, and seemed to offer such great story possibilities to my inventive fancy that at the time I at once resolved to take it away one day from the hero of my novel and to make something out of it myself."[238]

As in *Doctor Faustus*, in *The Holy Sinner* also, the story is told through a chronicler, the Irish Benedictine monk Clemens, who in the Cloister of St. Gallen writes down the story of the "virtuous sinner." Although in *Doctor Faustus* the Palestrina of the turn of the century, hence of modern times, comes alive for the reader, Thomas Mann nevertheless has a medieval figure, that of the Devil, play the main rôle therein. In *The Holy Sinner* as well, the period of the Middle Ages is conjured up. In contrast to the sinister and gloomy side of the south in *Doctor Faustus*, Thomas Mann now presents—since *The Holy Sinner* ultimately concerns a Christian legend—a festive and colorfully gay Rome: "Peal of bells, torrent of bells supra urbem, over the entire city, in its air glutted with ringing! Bells, bells, they sway and swing, roll and rock, surging up on their wooden beam, in their belfries, hundred-voiced, in Babylonian confusion. . . . They ring from the heights and from the depths, from the seven arch-holy places of pilgrimage and all the churches of the seven parishes flanking the twice-curved Tiber."[239] Only in Rome, the Eternal City, the center of Christendom with its countless churches and basilicas, can the peal of bells sound so overwhelmingly festive. "It rings from the Aventine, from the holy places of the Palatine and from San Giovanni in Laterano, it rings over the grave of him who bears the keys, in the Vatican hill, from Santa Maria Maggiore,/* in Foro, in Domenica, in Cosmedin, and in Trastevere, from Aracoeli,/* San Paolo fuori le Mura, San Pietro in Vincoli, and from the basilica of Santa Croce in Gerusalemme."[240]

Towards the end of his tale the chronicler once more tells of "this peal of bells and torrent of bells,"[241] this time, however, with a slightly ironically tinged exuberance: "Three days and nights long the bells of Rome were not to be contained with one accord they rang from every point with the greatest might, and to have this colossal booming and tinkling in one's ears all the time was no little demand on the people, the spirit of story-telling is clear about that."[242]

As so often in the work of Thomas Mann, in this novel, also, a certain

Translator's Note: The names as listed in the text, here marked by my addition of/, are only the geographical part of the full name, i.e. "in Foro" refers to Santa Maria Antiqua, which is in the Forum; the others are "Santa Maria" in Domenica, "Santa Maria" in Cosmedin, etc.

anachronism is established, in that various ages become concentrated into one and several centuries become compressed into one. While in Grigorss' life as a knight and in the service of love Thomas Mann allows the atmosphere of the high Middle Ages to be revived, the Rome he describes is unquestionably that of the fifth and sixth centuries, hence, around the turning point into the early Middle Ages.

In the chapter "The Disclosure" Thomas Mann transfers the action of the novel from northern Europe to Italy and reports on the death of a Pope, not specified by name, and on the resulting splitting of the people into two factions, each of which chooses its own leader as successor and crowns him as the Holy Father. "Symmachus was ordained in the Lateran, Eulalius in St. Peter's, and thus they sat, the one in the Lateran Palace, the other in Emperor Hadrian's round mausoleum-fortress, sang Masses, drew up Bulls and Decrees and cursed one another, while in the streets the weapons clattered."[243]

This incident is Thomas Mann's own poetical invention, since historically nothing is known of a double Papacy of Symmachus and Eulalius. To be sure, these two names emerge in connection with two schisms in the fifth century, once in the combination Eulalius and Bonifatius and a little later in the struggle between Symmachus and Laurentius over the triple crown. Yet in both cases there is no historical proof of a successor by the name of Gregorius.

For the writing of this work Thomas Mann had searched into and made use of historical sources, but so strongly transformed them into the mythical that the connection between historical reality and poetical invention is only vague. One of Mann's sources for the description of conditions in Rome of the fifth and sixth centuries was the historical work of Ferdinand Gregorovius, *Geschichte der Stadt Rom im Mittelalter (History of the City of Rome in the Middle Ages)*, whose eight volumes were published between 1859 and 1872. Thomas Mann took names such as Probus, Liberius, Chrysogonus, and others from this work of Gregorovius. Likewise, some of the noteworthy events of the novel originate, as Hermann J. Weigand has conclusively proven,[244] from the same source. Thus, for example, Gregorovius gives an account about Bishop Liberius who, after he has experienced a vision, hastens to his friend, from whom, to his astonishment, he learns that the latter experienced the same manifestation at the same time. In Thomas Mann's work "a pious man of an old family,"[245] Sextus Anicius Probus, has a vision: the Lamb of God announces a new Pope to him, Gregorius by name, whom Probus must bring to Rome. After consultation with his wife Faltonia he hastens to his intimate friend, the prelate Liberius, to whom the Lamb had appeared with the same tidings.

In *The Holy Sinner,* Thomas Mann was able in a few sentences to sketch a vivid picture of Rome at the time of the early Middle Ages. In spite of the

Christianization of the Roman population, the picture of the city is still considerably defined by statues and images of the pagan gods. Thus one finds in the gardens of Probus "a marble bench with heads of Pan, thickly pressed in upon by laurel bushes, from which, beyond a statue, fallen from its pedestal, of Amor, charming in body, with arrow and bow and no head, one gazed upon a little open meadow standing in colorful weeds."[246] Yet the traces of ancient Rome are ordained to decay and destruction; just as the gardens are found in a neglected state, so the magnificent ancient buildings have become ruins, and of the splendid marble statues of the golden age of Rome only fragments are left. Before the reader rises a Rome "whose streets wound among enormous ruins of magnificent buildings of other times, now lying half in rubble, and where everywhere marble statues of emperors, gods, and great citizens lay about mutilated, and waited to be thrown into the lime-pit so that mortar might be burned out of them."[247] This destruction under the weight and burden of one's own greatness also becomes evident in the state of deterioration in which the immensely vast estate of Probus is found. It lies "in the fifth region, on the Via Lata" and comprises "three hundred sixty rooms and halls, a horse-racing track as well as marble baths."[248] Yet "the baths were no longer supplied with water, the hippodrome was also long out of use and most of the three hundred sixty rooms empty and in a neglected condition,—not because the owner had lacked the means and serving hands to keep it all in order, but because to his eyes decay, disorder, and the collapse of the very great under the weight of its own greatness appeared as befitting the times, necessary and God-ordained."[249]

Once again towards the end of the novel *The Holy Sinner,* strong reminiscences are found of the historical work of Gregorovius, in the description of Rome at the entry of the new Pope. The novel states: "Not through the Porta Nomentana, one reads, did he enter, but came along the wall and then across the Milvian Bridge, in order thus to reach the Church of the Apostle."[250] The parallel passage in Gregorovius reads: "He probably did not celebrate his entry through the Porta Nomentana (Nomentian Gate), but moving along the wall, probably crossed over the Milvian Bridge."[251] The astonishing thing, however, is that the quotation from Gregorovius' work in no way refers to Gregorius, but to the entry of Charles the Great into Rome. In this description, therefore, we are dealing with the Rome of ca. 800, that is, an epoch several centuries later.

That the scene of the Papal entry into Rome is a montage of various passages from Gregorovius' historical work has been authenticated by Hans Wysling through a thorough study of Thomas Mann's copy of *Geschichte der Stadt Rom im Mittelalter.* The most important passages in this connection, which without exception originate in the first volume of Gregorovius' work, have been listed by Wysling as follows:

— Coronation procession of Charles the Great in the year 800, (coming) from
  Nomentum (Greg. I, 556/558).
— Reception of Charles the Great in Rome on 2 April 774 (Greg. I, 448/489).
— Entry of Honorius in the year 403 (Greg. I, 67).
— Hymn of Prudentius: "Ye people, rejoice all together . . ." (Greg. I, 44).
— Route of the Papal procession according to the Instruction of Canonicus
  Benedict from the year 1143 (Greg. I, 1217–1219).[252]

Naturally, the description of Rome in *The Holy Sinner* has nothing to do
with the reality experienced by Thomas Mann. In contrast to the Italy
portrayed in *Doctor Faustus*, which, as we have seen, is very heavily based
on autobiographical events and impressions, the picture of Rome sketched
by Thomas Mann in the novel *The Holy Sinner* rests on extensive studies of
various sources which are of importance for understanding the book's
milieu.

The Italy described in this novel does not, in its basic mood, correspond
to the land of darkly mysterious temptation and seduction as confronts the
reader in the novellas *Death in Venice* or *Mario and the Magician,* as well
as in the novel *Doctor Faustus.* Instead, in *The Holy Sinner,* Italy embodies
the spirit of gayness and cheerful joy in life, which among other things is
symbolized by the noise, all-too loud for northern ears (in the excessive
ringing of bells). Thus, in this work of his old age, Thomas Mann returned to
a view of the south which shows strong reminiscences of his presentation of
the Italian atmosphere which enticed the heroes of the early novellas, and
especially also Tonio Kröger, into their Italian journeys.

11. Summary

As shown in detail in this chapter, the significance of Italy for the work of
Thomas Mann sustained a gradual development.

In the earliest novellas the land south of the Alps is primarily a stage upon
which move German people with their problems. To be sure, again and
again in these early works the beauty of Italian cities and art is described,
yet the individualities and characteristics of the Italian people and their
milieu are disregarded. The Italian atmosphere still symbolizes cheerful-
ness, harmony, and joy of life, in which, however, the respective heroes of
the novellas, coming from Germany, neither seek nor can find any participation and therefore suffer from a feeling of being thrust out. Paolo Hofmann and also the Dilettante remain isolated in this cheerful and gay
environment as well, owing to their northern temperament and their status
as outsiders, occasioned partly through sickness, partly through artistic
talent, just as Thomas Mann himself during his first sojourns in Italy did not
desire and was not able to establish any contact with southern life and
southern people.

In the novella *Tonio Kröger,* also, the gaiety and cheerful bustle of Italian

life is described, yet here the image of the land is intensified in the erotic and
sensual which at first ensnares and intoxicates the German artist. Tonio
Kröger, who feels a misfit in his German homeland and hopes to find in the
south the longed-for contact with his surroundings, succeeds, as the first of
these uprooted artists in Mann's early work, in dipping into Italian life and
partaking in the southern enjoyment of life. Yet through his father's heritage Tonio is too strongly rooted in the north German spirit to find a
permanent home in the south and not to feel finally a strong loathing for the
exuberant vivacity and colorful splendor of the south, which are basically
alien to him.

In the novella *Gladius Dei* and the drama *Fiorenza,* Thomas Mann's
interest is concentrated on Italian history. He became engrossed in the
study of Vasari, Villari, and Jacob Burckhardt and fused it with the impressions of his own various trips on which he had become familiar with the
Italian Renaissance. For that reason the figures of these works outwardly
resemble Italians of the fifteenth and sixteenth centuries and move in an
environment which corresponds to the Florentine atmosphere of that time,
yet with their views and problems seem very modern. Just as in the
preceding novellas, Thomas Mann also deals here with the contrast between self-discipline and renunciation on the one hand and enjoyment of
life and sensual pleasure on the other, yet in the drama the contest over
supremacy between these two courses is decided entirely by Italian characters and on Italian soil, in the Florence of the Medici. As already with *Tonio
Kröger,* in the novella *Gladius Dei* and in the drama *Fiorenza,* Thomas
Mann also has the representative of discipline and asceticism win the
spiritual victory. The seductive, glittering outward aspect of Italian life, be
it the modern or be it the historical of the Renaissance, is at heart regarded
skeptically by Thomas Mann, just as he himself at that time still was not
capable of establishing any deep contacts with the land south of the Alps or
its people.

The intense fascination which Venice exerted on Thomas Mann from his
first visit has been set down in the novella *Death in Venice:* he has his hero
Aschenbach travel there, who, like Tonio Kröger, feels a strong yearning
for the south owing to the heritage of his Latin mother. In the hope of
freeing himself from the excessive constraint of his self-discipline and of
finding his true self, as Thomas Mann's heroes attempt time and again, he
decides upon a stay in Venice. But in this novella Thomas Mann allots to
the Italian element the motif of the greatest danger and menace: the erotic
and at the same time seductive and dangerous qualities of Venice become
an important pivotal point in the action; indeed, the blending of beauty and
destruction in the city of lagoons, which Platen already recognized, symbolizes, as it were, the fate of Aschenbach.

In Thomas Mann's great novel *The Magic Mountain,* Lodovico Settembrini represents the Italian element, which exercises a strong influence on

Hans Castorp's maturation. There can be no doubt that, in the figure of Lodovico, Mann had in mind the historical personality of Luigi Settembrini, with whom the character in the book exhibits a large number of mutual characteristics: the love of freedom and of fatherland, clarity of thought and purity of aspirations, eloquence which occasionally rises to rhetoric, the optimistic basic attitude and the high sense of duty with respect to his fellowmen. That Thomas Mann must have been familiar with the historical Luigi Settembrini is also shown by the fact that in *The Magic Mountain* he assigns further qualities and preferences of this prominent man to another character in the novel, the father of Settembrini. Thus, Lodovico Settembrini reports on the literary interests of his father, an important Romanist and humanistic scholar, which coincide extensively with those of the historical Settembrini.

Unquestionably, while fashioning the character of Lodovico Settembrini, Thomas Mann had also thoroughly gone into the literature and history of nineteenth-century Italy and in particular that of the Risorgimento. For by means of Settembrini's conversations with Hans Castorp the author discusses the important representatives of this time—Carducci, Mazzini, and Garibaldi. In *The Magic Mountain* Thomas Mann also erected a monument to the great poets of the early period, such as Dante and Petrarch and the still earlier Brunetto Latini. Italian literature and politics and Italian intellectual life come alive in the figure of Lodovico Settembrini and through his mediation play an important rôle in the education and formation of the young German, Hans Castorp.

In the course of countless discussions Settembrini guides his protégé ever more intensively into the world of ideas of humanism and liberalism. He teaches him to love life and to resist the temptation of death, to recognize his obligation towards his fellowmen and not to stand aloof from the problems of the European continent.

This young north German, who in his instability was incapable of enduring life, develops, through the instructions and advice of his Italian mentor, into an open-minded individual, qualified for life, who has learned to better understand his surroundings and life as such and who can now fearlessly expose himself to temptations and dangers.

Similarly to the way in which Hans Castorp is introduced through an Italian to what is for him a whole new world of ideas and of politics, the German seaside guest in the novella *Mario and the Magician* is also allotted a deeper understanding of the philosophy of life and of politics on the basis of his experiences in the Italian environment. In this novella Thomas Mann described events which befell him and his family during their stay in the Italian bathing resort Forte dei Marmi in 1926 and which had made clear to him the dark, destructive forces of Fascism and their pernicious influence on the soul of the Italian people. Thus he also—like Hans Castorp in his association with Settembrini—gained an awareness of the true facts and a clarification of his own point of view through contact with the Italian spirit and schooling through it. On the basis of the instruction ensuing by means of the Italian element, Hans Castorp, as well as the German visitor in Torre di Venere, became conscious of their own obligation, and from the spirit of the "non-political man" there developed within them the sense of a political responsibility.

Here, for the first time in Thomas Mann's creative work, the action is carried exclusively by modern Italian people in their own contemporary milieu, although the events are described by a German commentator from the point of view of the writer himself. In this short work Thomas Mann penetrated particularly deeply into the spirit of Italian life, for which the frequent insertions of Italian phrases into the German text bear eloquent witness. The writer has such a strong feeling here for the Italian language that even his German occasionally takes on a Latin hue. This appears above all in Cipolla's speech, but also in the loan-word translations (into German) created by Thomas Mann, based on typical Italian objects or concepts such as frutti di mare, capanne, and others.

As in the story *Mario and the Magician,* in the novel *Doctor Faustus* as well, Mann's own experiences were used as the basis for the description of the Italian milieu and of the Italian people. Although his sojourn in Palestrina already lay forty-seven years in the past, Thomas Mann depicted the small mountain town and its people very similarly to the descriptions which we find in his and his brother Heinrich's letters. The two brothers correspond to Adrian Leverkühn and his friend Rüdiger Schildknapp of the novel, who live in the same little hotel in Palestrina as did once Thomas and Heinrich. And the stay of the two friends in Rome, described in the novel, likewise clearly alludes to personal experiences and recollections of the writer Thomas Mann.

In *Doctor Faustus* Italian music, above all compositions by Monteverdi and Palestrina, and Italian literature come into play as important factors of development for the hero. The musical settings of Dante's lyric poetry and some parts of the *Divina Commedia* are deemed worthy of detail by Thomas Mann, whereby indeed a misunderstanding—which was alluded to—occurred on the part of the author.

In the essay *The Eroticism of Michelangelo (Die Erotik Michelangelos),* Thomas Mann thoroughly occupied himself with the lyrical poetic work of the great Renaissance artist, to whom he had already erected a monument seven years earlier in the story *The Tables of the Law.* The German writer could not help but compare the tirelessly creative Italian artist, who at an advanced age fell under the power of love, with Goethe, particularly since he saw a parallel between both men in their love and veneration for a mature woman: Vittoria Colonna and Frau von Stein had become a "developmental experience" for their respective great admirers.

Thomas Mann's novel *The Holy Sinner* once again brings the beauty and splendor of Rome before the eyes of the reader—this time, to be sure, the Rome of the historic early Middle Ages. Many traces of ancient statues and magnificent buildings are still in evidence, yet they are ordained to destruction and are close to ruin. This is not the Rome personally experienced by Thomas Mann, but the "Eternal City" as Ferdinand Gregorovius had described it in his great historical work *Geschichte der Stadt Rom im Mittelalter*.

In the writings of Thomas Mann from the earliest beginnings to the works of his old age, Mann's knowledge of Italy and Italians is reflected in two basic ways, with ever new variations: on one hand, the writer bases his descriptions on knowledge acquired through study of source material; on the other hand, his personal experience in Italy inspires his accounts of the land and the people south of the Alps.

As Thomas Mann confessed in a letter to Ernst Bertram, the relationship and tension between north and south meant a great deal to him; indeed, it plainly exercised such a strong power of attraction on him that he could write: "North against south is a fascinating subject . . . and I can certainly say I do not pay heed to any material which is not relative to it."[253]

III
Italy's Reception
of Mann's Works

1. Italy's Reception of Twentieth-Century German Literature

Italian interest in German literature of the twentieth century developed relatively slowly. Before the First World War it was German philosophy, history, and German music—especially the works of Nietzsche, Ranke, Treitschke, and Richard Wagner—that exercised a great influence on Italian culture of the time. In the endeavor to bring the German heritage of thought and particularly also the more modern German literature closer to Italians, the Florentine journal *La Voce* performed pioneer work in the years before the First World War. About this time some daily newspapers also began to publish instructive critical articles on Germany and literature north of the Alps, which were later collected in part and issued in book form. Thus in 1911 Giulio Caprin of Trieste published his book *La Germania letteraria d'oggi* and in 1912 the Sicilian Giuseppe A. Borgese published a collection of critiques under the title *La nuova Germania*.

After the First World War, at the beginning of the twenties, there appeared in Milan in the Treves Press (today the Garzanti Press), a journal, *I Libri del Giorno,* which concerned itself with the literature of Europe and reported in regular, detailed articles on new publications in individual countries. The revolutionary works of German expressionism, Rilke's *Sonette an Orpheus,* the works of Franz Kafka—until then completely unknown in Italy—and many other examples of contemporary German literature were here introduced to the Italian public for the first time.

The Milanese monthly journal *Il Convegno* also wished at that time to make the latest German literature known in Italy by letting the German writers themselves have their say in Italian translation, and dedicated special issues to various writers—Rilke, Thomas Mann, Kafka, Carossa, and others. Closely connected with the journal *Il Convegno* was the literary club of the same name led by Enzo Ferrieri, which, through readings by authors and lectures, furthered the appreciation and diffusion of German literature in Italy.

Likewise the journal *La Ronda,* appearing from 1920 to 1923, tried, with the help of its collaborator Marcello Cora, to support German literature by publishing in Italian translation contributions of such authors as Emil

Ludwig and Thomas Mann, the latter with a fragment of his essay *Goethe and Tolstoi (Goethe und Tolstoi).*

A short time later the journal *Il Baretti,* published from 1924 until 1926 and edited by Piero Gobetti, brought out not only important studies about contemporary German literature, but also Italian translations of German lyric poetry.

In general, however, in the twenties in Italy, German literature was reputedly too concerned with social and psychological problems and therefore not readable. Since at that time in the south there was more interest in problems of form and style, the attention of the general public as well as of the influential literary journals turned more to the French. On the whole, however, readers remained provincially focussed and to some extent kept aloof from the influence of other countries. In spite of this, some progressively oriented publishing houses now gradually began to issue works of German writers such as Thomas Mann, Döblin, and Kafka in Italian translation. These renditions distinguished themselves in part through deep understanding for Mann's style and choice of words, especially those of Alberto Spaini, born in Trieste in 1892, who in addition to the moderns also translated the German classicists and romanticists into Italian.

A young scholar from Gorizia, Enrico Rocca, at this time successfully introduced Austrian literature and the newest German dramatic works into Italy. His critical articles, especially those from the journals *Pegaso* and *Scenario,* were later, after Rocca's suicide in 1945, collected by his friends and issued posthumously in 1950 in book form by Sansoni in Florence under the title *Storia della letteratura tedesca dal 1870 al 1923.*

Another pioneer for German literature after the First World War was Leonello Vincenti, born in 1891, who in the twenties taught by the side of Vossler as Professor of Romanistics in Munich and in 1932 was called to the University of Turin as Professor of German literature. His articles appeared chiefly in the journal *Il Baretti* and, assembled by him in the book *Teatro tedesco del Novecento,* were published in 1925.

In the course of these years, interest in current German literature continually increased in Italy, and in growing measure the publishers endeavored to broaden their program by taking up foreign works. The largest Italian publishing house, Arnoldo Mondadori, produced the "Medusa" series of novels, whose German components were supervised by the Germanist Lavinia Mazzucchetti. The first volume of this exceedingly successful series was Hans Fallada's best-seller novel *Little Man, What Now? (Kleiner Mann was nun?),* which at once achieved high sales figures. Publishing houses such as Modernissima, Frassinelli, Garzanti, and others also had a considerable share in the publication of German literature in Italy during this intellectually very active period prior to the Second World War.

The Fascist régime at first did not interfere in the undertakings of the individual publishers. Not until the advent of the Berlin-Rome Axis in the year 1938 was a control of intellectual life in Italy instituted, forcing many Germanists to transfer the concentration of their research from the modern to the older epochs of German literature.

Towards the end of the Second World War, interest in the literary products of the Nazi-oppressed writers of Germany broke through with new vigor. Primarily in Milan, some small, new publishing houses secretly began to print books placed on the Index by Fascism. Thus the press *Rosa e Ballo* brought out a series of modern dramas by Wedekind, Toller, Kaiser, and Brecht, which ultimately led to a rediscovery in Italy of German expressionism. At the same time, especially after the end of the war, a particularly strong interest emerged for the works of Thomas Mann, which for years had been repressed by the Fascist censorship and withheld from the Italian people. Mann's political writings and warning cries to Europe from the time of his exile now met with a strong echo in Italy, and his novels and novellas were taken up by the Italians with an entirely new understanding. How, in particular, this deep and far-reaching admiration for the German writer came about will be shown below.

2. Mann's Works in Italy to 1930

In the following chronological presentation of the reception of Thomas Mann's works in Italy, a restriction to remarks of the leading critics is necessary, since an extensive analysis of the entire Italian secondary literature on the subject of Thomas Mann would go beyond the scope of this work.

The Italian studies primarily yield interpretations of works and biographical investigations. It is only in isolated cases that a specific theme with regard to Mann's work is dealt with. The relationship of the writer to Italy and its recording in his writings appears to have interested the Italian critic much less than one would at first suppose. Only the novella *Mario and the Magician*, as will be amplified later in this chapter, brought about a reaction to his attitude regarding Italy. However, it is noteworthy that the "north-south" tension emphasized in this study and ever recurring in Thomas Mann's life and work continued to be completely disregarded by Italian critics.

The first significant critical comment in the Italian language on the work of the Lübeck author is Alberto Spaini's article "Thomas Mann," which appeared in Rome on the first of January 1915 in the *Nuova Antologia*. Here, for the first time, the attention of the Italian public was drawn to the German writer who in the years since the appearance of his novel *Buddenbrooks* had attained an undoubted fame north of the Alps. Five years later, in 1920, Lavinia Mazzucchetti published an article about the two brothers

Heinrich and Thomas in the Milanese journal *Secolo;* and in the same year, in his journal *La Critica,* Benedetto Croce brought out an assessment of Thomas Mann's book published in 1919, *Reflections of a Non-Political Man,* which he called a particularly well written and carefully thought-out work. Croce concurred with most of the thoughts expressed by Thomas Mann; indeed, he also had to support him in his rejection of d'Annunzio as a warmonger and in his criticism of the politically immature Italy which hails the demagogues: "For my part, I have read it underlining with continuous approbation."[1]

In spite of these early critics in Italy, the Italians still had to wait some time before a work of Mann's was made accessible to them in their own language. In the press of G. Morreale, two shorter books of Thomas Mann finally appeared, in 1926: *Tonio Kröger,* translated by Guido Isenburg, and a rendition executed by R. Pisaneschi and Alberto Spaini of the early novellas *A Weary Hour (Schwere Stunde), A Gleam (Ein Glück), The Infant Prodigy (Das Wunderkind), At the Prophet's (Beim Propheten), The Wardrobe (Der Kleiderschrank),* and *Tristan (Tristan).*

A year later, already in advance of the first publication in book form, the novella *Disorder and Early Sorrow (Unordnung und frühes Leid)* appeared in the Milanese journal *Il Convegno* (1927), which relatively early supported the work of the German writer. Mann had allowed his Italian friend Lavinia Mazzucchetti to translate this novella into her mother-tongue, and had also presented her with the Italian rights. For a long time it seemed as if no prominent Italian publisher would set about bringing a work of Thomas Mann onto the market. Finally, however, Lavinia Mazzucchetti succeeded in interesting a smaller Milanese publishing house, Sperling & Kupfer, in Thomas Mann. As a result, in 1929 the publisher inaugurated a new series, "Narratori Nordici" ("Northern Story-Tellers"), with the translation of the two novellas *Disorder and Early Sorrow (Unordnung und frühes Leid)* and *A Man and his Dog (Herr und Hund)* as Volume I. The bestowal of the Nobel Prize to Mann in the same year contributed to the special success of the book in Italy. Thomas Mann was very pleased with the style of the Italian translation, especially in comparison with the almost simultaneously appearing French version, which, as he believed, was in no way suitable to the light touch of the story. In a letter of 9 August 1927 he wrote to Lavinia Mazzucchetti:

> Today I received your friendly letter and the copy of 'Convegno' with *Disordine* and yet hardly have time to thank you from my heart. . . . Thus, this time the opportunity is denied me, above all of seeing you, and then, in particular, to extend my hand to you in thanks for your translation, a product of the greatest accuracy and of twofold linguistic mastery. A fact which I appreciate so much more now that the same story, about which I like the light touch, was completely distorted in France. How much trouble you must have taken over the little songs alone! Also Saverio and Anna Viola seem to me

particularly successful. I am happy that your talent has presented mine to
your compatriots under a much more favorable light than that in which the
French have seen it on this occasion.[2]

Spurred on by this high praise, Lavinia Mazzucchetti also translated
other shorter writings of Thomas Mann for *Il Convegno;* for example,
Rede über Lessing (Lessing), which had appeared in February 1929 in the
journal *Neue Schweizer Rundschau.*

According to Lavinia Mazzucchetti, there already existed in the twenties
an Italian translation of *Buddenbrooks,* although very deficient, which
apparently was not preserved; yet in his bibliography, *Das Werk Thomas
Manns,* Hans Bürgin fixed the first publication of the novel in the Italian
language at 1930.[3]

3. Mann's Works in Italy 1930–1945

With the bestowal of the Nobel Prize upon Thomas Mann in November
1929 the German author became overnight, as it were, an international
celebrity whose work now advanced to the center of interest in Italy also.
The Milanese press Fratelli Treves, in a translation by Emma Virgili and
Paolo Milano, brought out *La morte a Venezia (Death in Venice)* and *Le
confessioni di un cavaliere d'industria (Confessions of Felix Krull, Confidence Man)* together in one volume in 1930, and in the same year *La
montagna incantata (The Magic Mountain)* appeared in a translation by
Bice Giacchetti-Sorteni from the Modernissima press.

In Italy *The Magic Mountain* became a particularly great success, not
only in intellectual circles but also among the youth at all levels of society,
who were seeking an antipole to the value concepts ever more intrusively
propagated by Fascism. Thus the essayist and critic Emilio Castellani, born
in 1912, who later translated Thomas Mann and above all the complete
works of Bert Brecht, recalled the impressions which the reading of *The
Magic Mountain* made upon him and his generation:

> Few books, of that I am certain, have exerted a more profound effect upon my
> generation. It saved a good part of our youth from spiritual death, which
> Fascism with its systematic adulteration of worth and its aggressive anti-
> humanism brought about in others. Enthusiasm for the magnificent work did
> not confine itself to intellectual circles; it also stirred the progressive
> working-class youth and directly became the tacit password for the genera-
> tion which soon was to play the decisive rôle in one of the decisive periods of
> Italian history.[4]

Not only in the Italian book market did Thomas Mann's new popularity,
furthered by the Nobel Prize, make itself noticeable: newspapers and
journals brought out articles on the German writer, among others the
Nuova Antologia, Italia letteraria, and *La Stampa,* in which Italian Germanists such as Leonello Vincenti and Bonaventura Tecchi expressed their

views about Mann's work. The already mentioned journal *Il Convegno* even dedicated a special issue to the writer. In the year 1931 from the Turin press Fratelli Bocca, a book by the Germanist Italo Maione appeared on contemporary German literature, *Contemporanei di Germania,* whose five chapters are respectively dedicated to prominent modern German writers. In addition to Dehmel, Rilke, Hofmannsthal, and George, Thomas Mann and his work is thoroughly discussed and analyzed. In his investigation Maione comes to the conclusion that the German author loved life in its diversity and, not without a considerable trace of irony, presented it with an almost classic purity. According to Maione's opinion, Thomas Mann's works are largely based on elaboration of self-experienced impressions which, through his art of representation, he invested with general validity:

> His art is all autobiographical: those tales of artists—of families—are his portrait and that of his family. But with an attentive surveillance he knows how to make himself independent from his own life:—elaborating on impressions and recollections of his childhood or youth, he knows how to divest them of every trace of tender sentimentalism and to objectify them in the essential form of a plastic organism.[5]

In the year 1933 two different translations of Thomas Mann's novel *Royal Highness (Königliche Hoheit)* were issued at the same time by two Milanese publishing houses: *Altezza Reale* appeared through A. Barion in the translation by Lamberto Brusotti and through the Corbaccio press in that by J. Douglas-Scotti.

At about the same time the first relations were opened between Thomas Mann and the Milanese press Mondadori, which later was to become the overseer of most of his works and also of the complete Italian edition. The initiative came from Lavinia Mazzucchetti, through whose stimulus a conference took place among Thomas Mann, his German publisher Bermann-Fischer, and Luigi Rusca, at that time the director of the Mondadori press. For the series "Medusa: I grandi narratori d'ogni paese" (The Great Story-Tellers of all Countries), the German writer was readily prepared to place at the disposal of the press his novel *Joseph and his Brothers (Joseph und seine Brüder),* whose first volume, *Le storie di Giacobbe (The Tales of Jacob)* appeared in the same year, 1933, in the translation by Gustavo Sacerdote. The second volume, *Il giovane Giuseppe (Young Joseph)* followed two years later from the hand of the same translator. *The Tales of Jacob* were such a great success in Italy that in the same year, 1935, the second edition was already issued, and two years later, in 1937, the third. At the same time, Mondadori published the third novel of the tetralogy, *Giuseppe in Egitto (Joseph in Egypt)* in a two-volume edition.

The first monograph dedicated exclusively to the work of Thomas Mann, *L'opera di Thomas Mann (The Work of Thomas Mann),* was published in 1936 by the Germanist Ladislao Mittner, who in chronological order analyzed the most important of Mann's works, from the novella *Little Herr Friedemann (Der kleine Herr Friedemann)* to the novel *Young Joseph*, and then made a general evaluation of the works and of the artist. As already expressed by the title of this last section, "Sebastiano: L'arco e la lira" ("Sebastian: the bow and the lyre"), Mittner regarded these two attributes in their indissoluble union as the most profound symbol for the writer Thomas Mann. Coldness and passion are not excluded from his personality or his work, as Thomas Mann had already acknowledged in his essay *Bilse und ich*. Mittner saw a further important indication of the art of Thomas Mann in the clarity and elegance of presentation, which he attributed to French influence. The Italian critic referred to the particular subtleties of expression which are evidence of Thomas Mann's unremitting striving after the appropriate word. Mann's significance as a creator of language can be understood from this passionate love of words.

> His art, conscious and conscientious, is the work of a chiseller and therefore art, above all, of the word. He loves the word with a passionate and maniacal love: each phrase must have the right weight, the right bulk, the right vibration. He is the creator, yet also observer of the appropriate and irreplaceable word, which contains, a little like the *Leitmotiv*, the secret of a soul.[6]

Similarly to Maione, Mittner also emphasized in his study the importance of the autobiographical element in Thomas Mann's works. But he went still further when he stated that Thomas Mann desired to convince the reader that the stories containing certain autobiographical passages presented a true happening which possibly took place not in real life, but rather within the writer's soul. In Thomas Mann, life and art continually overlap, as likewise the names of his closest relatives frequently appear in his works. With the greatest self-discipline Thomas Mann constantly struggled over his art, in which he wished to find his self-confirmation: "The root of the humanity and hence also of the Mannian art lies in that unmistakable and vigorous sense of active self-discipline which transforms aestheticism into a moral value."[7]

In the period from 1937 to 1945 no work of Thomas Mann was officially published in Italy. The Berlin-Rome Axis with its cultural agreements resulted in a coordination of German book production with the Italian, and the authors "forbidden" in Germany were likewise not allowed in print in the Italy of Mussolini.

4. Mann's Works in Italy, 1945–1950

Towards the end of the Second World War the situation changed. In 1945 a completely new interest began to grow in the German literature, which had been suppressed during the time of the Axis, and above all in Thomas Mann's work; and the individual publishing houses were feverishly engaged in making previously suppressed books accessible to the impatiently waiting public as quickly as possible. On the day of Italy's liberation, an entirely new translation of Thomas Mann's *Tonio Kröger* was published in Turin, and shortly thereafter followed publications of the essays and warning cries to Europe from the time of Mann's exile. On the occasion of the writer's seventieth birthday there appeared in the series "Narratori Nordici" of the Sperling & Kupfer press a deluxe edition of the two novellas *Disorder and Early Sorrow* and *A Man and his Dog,* accompanied by a foreword by Lavinia Mazzucchetti:

> For us, his Italian friends, it is a cause for particular emotion and pride to be able to give him a sign of devoted homage at the beginning of our somewhat tormented dawning, and precisely on the day on which in vigorous and industrious strength he reaches his seventieth year. We do it by issuing again in worthy dress these characteristic little masterpieces already dear to our public, thus in the best manner, in unabridged form, resuming the old series of the 'Narratori nordici.'

> We know and remember how much Thomas Mann has always respected and followed the true Italy of the underground of the last decades, rejecting from the beginning every illusion or indulgence for Fascist Italy, and therefore we are convinced that for the great European the return to his most loyal Italian readers will be a pleasure.[8]

The daily newspapers and the radio also carried commentaries and tokens of esteem in honor of Thoman Mann's birthday, and never before in Italy was admiration for the German writer so great as in this postwar period. Thus in 1945 the Milanese press "Istituto editoriale italiano" published Thomas Mann's first novel *Buddenbrooks* in the excellent translation of Ervino Pocar, while the Turin publishing house "Libreria editrice eclettica" issued the tragic Italian holiday experience *Mario e l'incantatore (Mario and the Magician),* translated by Anna Bovero and illustrated by G. Badio.

Through Lavinia Mazzucchetti, Thomas Mann was kept informed of his successes in Italy as well as of the fact that the Mondadori press had designated this friend of many years as general editor of his works. In a letter of reply he expressed his great satisfaction over this piece of news:

> I want to inform you that your friendly message of 10 November, with the interesting enclosures, the open letter in Italian and the article about *Mario,* have arrived safely. All this interested me greatly, especially the news that you, now, are officially named guardian of my works. It will surely be a burden for you, but you bear it by full rights.[9]

In 1946 two shorter books by Thomas Mann were issued by Mondadori: *Tonio Kröger,* in the translation by Emilio Castellani as part of the "Le Pleiadi" collection, and, translated by Lavinia Mazzucchetti in the "I Quaderni della Medusa" series, *Saggi,* a group of essays, among which were the well-known pieces *Sufferings and Greatness of Richard Wagner*

(Leiden und Grösse Richard Wagners), August von Platen, and *Chamisso.*
At the same time, the Milanese press Bietti brought out the Italian translation, by G. M. Boccabianca, of the novella *Death in Venice.*

At the beginning of 1947 the Mondadori press sent the writer the just-
published volume *Moniti all'Europa* which, with an introduction by André
Gide, and in the translation by Cristina Baseggio, contained a collection of
political essays such as *Attention, Europe (Achtung, Europa)* and *Germany
and the Germans (Deutschland und die Deutschen).* Thomas Mann was
very impressed by this book, as is evident from his letter to Arnoldo
Mondadori written in Pacific Palisades on 21 March 1947: "Today I received both copies of *Moniti all'Europa,* a very handsome book, well
selected, and with which I am intensely pleased."[10]

A still more important concern to the writer, however, was his thanks for
the news, already reported to him by Lavinia Mazzucchetti, that the
Mondadori press intended to publish his complete works in a ten-volume
Italian edition:

> Besides thanking you I want to reply to your long report, which reached me a
> short time ago, with regard to the complete edition of my works, which would
> be supervised and attended to by our friend Lavinia Mazzucchetti. This is, for
> me, a particular joy and satisfaction, since I have complete faith not only in
> Lavinia's general literary capacities, but also in her special sympathy for my
> personal work and in her excellent attitude towards this work.[11]

This was to be the first time since the publication by the S. Fischer press
of the complete German edition of Thomas Mann's works that a similar
undertaking was attempted, and Thomas Mann was pleased and grateful
over this planned edition precisely in Italy, the land of which he had so
many beautiful memories and which played such an important rôle in his
work:

> I cannot close this letter without once more expressing my sincere satisfac-
> tion regarding your fine project of a ten-volume edition of my "opera omnia."
> Since the time when the Berlin publisher S. Fischer published an edition of my
> works, likewise in ten volumes, this has not been done in any other country,
> and that now this will take place precisely in Italy, a land to which since my
> youth I have felt so closely bound, where I have often lived in the status of
> grateful guest, and which also in my works is an element which recurs so
> frequently, represents, for me, a particular joy.[12]

On 5 October 1947 the Accademia dei Lincei in Rome named Thomas
Mann as foreign member of the "Classe di Scienze morali, storiche e
filosofiche."[13] The writer was happy over this high honor, as expressed in
his letter to the President, Guido Castelnuovo:

> Honorable President:
> It grieves me extremely to reply with such great delay to your letter of 7
> October. Addressed to Zürich, which I had already left, it traversed long
> routes and detours before reaching my house in California.

I know how venerable and glorious the Accademia dei Lincei is. I therefore am cognizant, with grateful pride, of what an honor is reflected on me by the nomination as a member.

Foreign member, as you write me; but only in so far as it is possible to be a foreigner to Italy. As much as I was permitted, I have always been a mediator and devout admirer of Italian thought and art; nor have these bonds weakened, on the contrary, they have become reinforced with the distance and the years. I enjoy immensely the new opportunity which is now offered to me of feeling as brother, and I would almost say, not as a guest, but as a blood relative of the eminent spirits who, remembered or present, inhabit the rooms in which I hope to greet you personally.[14]

In the course of the year 1947 three short works of Thomas Mann again appeared in Italian translations: *La legge (The Tables of the Law)*, translated by Mario Merlini, *Mario e il mago (Mario and the Magician)*, translated by Giorgio Zampa, and *La morte a Venezia (Death in Venice)* in the translation by Emma Virgili that had previously appeared in 1930.

During this period Lavinia Mazzucchetti was occupied with the translation of the novel *The Beloved Returns (Lotte in Weimar)*, and Thomas Mann was surprised at her rapid progress, as he wrote in a letter to the faithful Italian mediator: "I am amazed that with *Carlotta* you are on the point of lacking only one chapter. I suppose it is 'the seventh' and I almost believe that you will not find it so difficult as it seems."[15]

In the following year, 1948, *Carlotta a Weimar*, with illustrations by Luigi Grosso, was published by the Mondadori press. Thomas Mann was enthusiastic about the quality of the translation, but with regard to the illustrations had strong doubts, which he frankly expressed: "Now *Carlotta a Weimar* has arrived, and I am amazed over the exactness of the translation which, so far as I can see, has not lost a single nuance of the original . . . And the illustrations? What do you say to them? I would not like to say anything. I think no author has ever been satisfied with the way in which his books were illustrated. My perplexity, therefore, does not signify much. And yet, and yet. . ."[16]

Likewise in his letter to Arnoldo Mondadori, Thomas Mann confessed that the illustrations appeared to him a little strange, but then, in order to soften his judgment, added: "But I can be objective enough to recognize the talent which is expressed in the illustrations for *Carlotta a Weimar*, among which I especially like the last one, the scene in the carriage, where the imaginary or dreamlike element of that encounter is reproduced by the artist with great understanding."[17]

In the year 1949 Mondadori published the last volume of the Joseph tetralogy, *Giuseppe il nutritore (Joseph the Provider)*, in the translation by Gustavo Sacerdote, and in addition, as the eighth volume of the *opera omnia*, Ervino Pocar's excellent translation of *Doctor Faustus*, introduced by Lavinia Mazzucchetti. In January 1950 Thomas Mann thanked his friend for her Foreword:

> *Faustus* has arrived, with your intelligent and brilliant Foreword, which puts various statements in the shade and which will be of the greatest help in Italy to this my so strange book. It is a beautiful edition, in spite of the ridiculous jacket, from which I have immediately freed my copy. The binding is very dignified and the type large and pleasant. All have truly done what is possible to lighten for the reader his hard task.[18]

5. Mann and the Feltrinelli Prize

In Spring 1952 the Jury of the Accademia dei Lincei met in order to select a suitable candidate for the International Literature Prize which, donated by Antonio Feltrinelli, amounted to the sum of five million lire (approximately $8000). Two members of the Academy, the art historian Ranuccio Bianchi Bandinelli and the literary historian Luigi Russo, proposed Thomas Mann, whose candidature was unanimously accepted in the session of 7 June in Rome. The well-known literary historian Franceso Flora, Professor of Italian literature at the University of Bologna, commented upon Thomas Mann's development in a letter supporting and explaining the proposal:

> In the work of this great writer two periods may be discerned . . . The first, which runs from about 1901 to 1928 and had outstanding recognition, is followed by the second, which extends from that date until today and corresponds to a substantial evolution in Mann (and was in fact called by some a conversion), which from a romantic and perhaps decadent individualism, whose emblem was a proud and solitary Germany . . . passed into a European humanism, where it was not the task of his tragic and great fatherland to subjugate the world, but to become European.[19]

In the course of his account Flora analyzed in detail the maturation of Thomas Mann as a person and artist and, in addition, his evolution from the first period to the second, in which, thanks to his active humanism, he acquired an international reputation:

> A clear testimonial to this first period is in the *Considerazioni di un apolitico (Reflections of a Non-Political Man)*, which, appearing in 1918, were the interpretation of a great part of his work as a storyteller in the German ivory tower, and a program which, although already disturbed by some doubts, lasted for many years; and he himself was to write later that the fixing of this, his position, through a vigorous analysis was already a first stimulus to renew himself on the basis of the attained clarity. The terrible events which Europe and the world experienced when his fatherland made its 'pact with the Devil,' raging against allegedly inferior races in order to create the abstract supernation (comparable to the misconceived superman), helped Thomas Mann to understand social responsibility, which no conscientious writer can evade.

This social consciousness deepened the soul and the art of Mann and brought to full light the humanism which was still latent. Now he was able to confirm that everything separatistic, anti-Roman, anti-European—and that is, every-thing, for that part, which Mann had pronounced to be extremely German—disturbed and frightened him, even when it presents itself as the evangelical freedom of a Luther.[20]

After a detailed discussion of some of the more important works of Thomas Mann, Flora reached the conclusion that above all in his later works, such as the Joseph tetralogy and *Doctor Faustus,* the writer had elevated his Germanism to a universally valid humanism and consequently gave orien-tation and direction to all those spiritually creating individuals:

Also the later work of Thomas Mann, including *L'Eletto (The Holy* Sinner), although with its medieval and ancient Oedipan material, is illuminated by the experience during which he comprehended the truth of art as a spiritualiza-tion of substance and complete humanism. To this renewed writer, who invokes in the world a new hope in pages where his great art has become deepened through more human truth, is directed our grateful admiration of today and the expectation of tomorrow.[21]

At first Thomas Mann heard only through rumor about the honor which was to be bestowed upon him; hence, for example, through Lavinia Maz-zucchetti, to whom, in a letter, he expressed his great pleasure, at the same time he also asked her for good advice and information about the Academy:

I confess that I am extremely happy. With all respect to Stockholm, 'Roma eterna' and the Petrarchian coronation makes still more impression on me. Up to now I have had no direct notice. Perhaps I am supposed to learn about it only when the thing is made public, that is, in June. This would be a calamity, since I must arrange my trip accordingly and know about so many things in time, besides preparing for the speech expected of me (in which language? German? French? Italian?), etc. *Readiness is all!* Privately, then, I must collect information and also know something about the history of the Academy.[22]

On 7 June 1952 Thomas Mann received in California the telegram from the Accademia dei Lincei with the news of his unanimous election as recipient of the Feltrinelli Prize. Since it was impossible for him to be present at the awarding of the prize in Rome on 12 June, he sent a return telegram in English to the Academy in order to express his regret over his absence, and on the day of the conferment of the prize itself sent a second, in whose composition in Italian Professor Panunzio assisted him: "I am present with you in spirit, proud of the unusual honor which you have conferred upon me. I hope to be able to personally express my deep gratitude during my proposed sojourn in Rome next summer. With respects to the glorious Academy, my most esteemed greetings."[23]

How proud and happy Thomas Mann was over the honor that Italy

bestowed upon him is apparent from a letter to Agnes E. Meyer which he
wrote on 20 June:

> In the official document drawn up by Professor Francesco Flora (of Milan) it
> states that with the prize not only my "powerful" literary work was to be
> honored, but more especially "the rare example of an attained *living
> humanism,* which spiritually transcends the dissension of our time and ac-
> cordingly gives direction to all spiritually creating individuals." This reason
> appears truly moving seen against the background of the character and the
> activity of the Academy, which are determined by a philological and
> ancient-archaeological humanism.[24]

On 12 July 1952 Thomas Mann thanked the President of the Accademia
dei Lincei for sending an official letter which set forth the reasons for his
selection as the first holder of this highly esteemed literary prize:

> Honored Professor,
> Accept my thanks for your letter of 1 July, which arrived in Zürich on the 10th
> and reached me here yesterday. The enclosures also were of great value to
> me, and above all the reason for conferring the prize, which is particularly
> beautiful. Also the yearbook of the Accademia Nazionale dei Lincei inter-
> ested me very much.[25]

Not until Spring 1953 was it possible for Thomas Mann to undertake the
trip from Zürich to Rome in order to officially accept the Premio Feltrinelli
of the Accademia dei Lincei. The German author was so tumultuously
honored by press and public that the demands placed on him almost
exceeded the strength of the seventy-eight-year-old. Receptions and interviews followed one another, and Thomas Mann had the opportunity personally to meet prominent representatives of modern Italian literature,
such as Giuseppe Ungaretti, Alba de Cespedes, Carlo Levi, Alberto
Moravia, and others. He had much in common with Ignazio Silone, whom
he already knew from Zürich, where he had described him as a "pleasant,
sometimes very droll man."[26] The great success and smooth course of his
visit to Rome were primarily due to the efforts of his two publishers,
Einaudi and Mondadori. After his return to Switzerland, Thomas Mann
wrote the latter a heartfelt letter of thanks in which he especially stressed
the warm reception which was prepared for him in Rome:

> The reception on the part of the intellectual circle of Rome—so overwhelm-
> ingly cordial—had on me the effect of a beautiful dream and I could not but
> remember the time in which, very young, I passed through the streets of the
> city: no one knew anything about me then and no one paid any attention to
> me. Now I have experienced honor upon honor and the visit with Pius XII
> was for me, the unbeliever and the pupil of a Protestant culture, a profoundly
> unique and moving event.[27]

6. Mann's Works in Italy, 1951–1954

In the year 1952 two different editions of the novel *Buddenbrooks* appeared in Italy: in the A. Mondadori press the translation by Ervino Pocar and in the Einaudi press of Turin a translation by Anita Rho. In addition *L'eletto (The Holy Sinner)*, translated by Bruno Arzeni, and *Romanzo di un romanzo (The Story of a Novel: The Genesis of Doctor Faustus)*, translated by Ervino Pocar, were published by Mondadori. The last-named work, together with the Italian translations of the two essays *Lebensabriss (A Sketch of my Life)* and *Meine Zeit* (partially translated as *The Years of my Life*), formed one volume in the "Medusa" series. Thomas Mann's satisfaction over this volume above all, and over the translation by Pocar, was clearly expressed in a letter to Alberto Mondadori:

> Accept my thanks for your kind letter of 24 September. I add the expression of my pleasure for the edition of *Romanzo di un romanzo* in the 'Medusa' series, an edition which seems to me particularly successful. I understand that *Romanzo di un romanzo* could not represent a complete volume and I find the addition of the other two autobiographical pieces very clever.[28]

In the following year, 1953, Mondadori brought out two further volumes of the *opera omnia:* Volume 2, *Novelle e racconti (Novellas and Tales)* in the translation by Emilio Castellani and Mario Merlini, as well as *Nobiltà dello spirito (Nobility of the Spirit)* translated by Bruno Arzeni and Lavinia Mazzucchetti, as Volume 10, which Thomas Mann especially praised to his publisher: "The beautiful edition of the Essays [*Saggi*] has given me a real pleasure and I hope to be able to see before me the completed *opera omnia* in your magnificent language."[29] Still in that year the same press republished Emilio Castellani's translation of *Tonio Kröger* and *Tristan*. Finally, also in 1953, three additional Italian publishers issued works by Mann: Rizzoli, in Milan, published Bruno Maffi's translation of *Royal Highness (Sua altezza reale);* Einaudi issued Clara Bovero's translation of *A Man and his Dog and other Stories (Cane e padrone e altri racconti)*; and the Istituto Grafico Tiberino of Rome issued the essay *The Artist and Society (L'artista e la società)* in the translation by Vittorio Libera.

During his stay in Rome, Thomas Mann met the prominent critic and journalist Emilio Cecchi, contributor to the most important newspapers and journals in Italy, editor of the works of De Sanctis, as well as member of the Accademia d'Italia and the Accademia dei Lincei. At the request of the publisher of the great Milanese newspaper *Corriere della Sera* he invited Thomas Mann, in May 1953, to contribute regularly to this newspaper. In the same letter he sent Thomas Mann a series of articles which he had published in that newspaper about the German writer, and which evoked Mann's pleasure and gratitude: "It has given me much pleasure to read in

the 'Corriere della Sera' the complimentary article which you wrote about
our private meeting, and the one so intense and alive about *Doctor Faustus*.''[30] The meeting and conversations with Cecchi were still vividly in
Thomas Mann's memory, for the impressive personality of the Italian had
indeed affected him especially strongly:

> When I received your kind letter of 2 May I was just preparing to write to you:
> I felt the need to tell you how happy I was to have made your acquaintance,
> and to thank you for the conversations which we had together. Among all the
> hundreds of persons whom I met in Rome, without doubt you number among
> the two or three most distinguished and most important figures. I am also very
> grateful to you for the insights and stimulations which I have gained from your
> interesting writings.[31]

But regarding the possibility suggested by Cecchi of his collaboration
with the *Corriere*, and his willingness to furnish contributions to him
regularly, Thomas Mann was skeptical:

> And now permit me to tell you that I feel very honored by the proposal made
> to me by the *Corriere della Sera*. If I were able to work faster, and did not fear
> the deadlines, I would most gladly accept this offer, and be happy to become a
> regular contributor to a newspaper of such broad circulation, and which
> numbers you among its collaborators. But as things lie, and being almost
> always engaged in labors which absorb all my energies, and committed to
> small daily tasks, I would feel frightened and oppressed by the responsibility
> of furnishing a new article each month, without mentioning that my talent
> is—after all—essentially oriented to a certain kind of narrative, and that the
> art of essay remains—more or less—a marginal activity.[32]

Yet Thomas Mann did not wish this explanation to be understood as a
definite refusal:

> This naturally is not an absolute refusal to the invitation of the *Corriere*. In
> fact, I will be unable to refrain from interrupting my literary work again with
> an essay—reflections on the problems of art and of life. And on that occasion
> I will certainly remember the *Corriere della Sera* and will offer them my
> article. I will therefore be very grateful if you will inform Dr. Mario Missiroli
> in this sense.[33]

Actually, in the course of the following years Thomas Mann placed
various articles, which, to be sure, had already appeared elsewhere, at the
disposal of the *Corriere della Sera* for reprinting; hence, for example,
Frammenti su Zola (31.7.1953), *Bernard Shaw, amico dell'umanità*
(22.11.1953), *Cecov* (10.2.1955), and *Teatro e cinema* (5.5.1955).

Toward the end of the year 1953, the Turin publisher Giulio Einaudi
approached Thomas Mann with the request to write a foreword for the
planned book *Lettere di condannati a morte nella Resistenza europea*
(*Letters of those in the European Resistance condemned to death*). The

selection and arrangement of these letters lay in the hands of Piero Malvezzi and Giovanni Pirelli, who, through the testimony of their last letters
from prison, were anxious to show representatives of the various European
nationalities, in their contempt of death, their irrevocable conviction and
willingness to sacrifice themselves. Thomas Mann was so impressed by
this idea that he felt obliged to comply with Einaudi's request, although he
was swamped with work and his strength, as he himself was aware, had
greatly diminished. By March 1954 he sent the manuscript of his foreword
to Einaudi: "Here is the requested foreword which I hope corresponds in
some measure to your expectations. It is the expression, nonetheless, of
the emotion aroused in me by this collection of letters, which certainly will
make a strong impression."[34]

The deeply moving book, which in 1955 also appeared in Switzerland and
Germany in German translation *(Letzte Briefe zum Tode Verurteilter aus
dem europäischen Widerstand),* was presented in a solemn ceremony to
high representatives of the Italian government as well as to diplomats of
sixteen countries. Through a misunderstanding, however, Thomas Mann
neglected to comply with the request of the two editors for a dedication in
the two copies sent to him, which occasioned from him a letter of apology to
Piero Malvezzi:

> Through a misunderstanding, an inadvertence, the two volumes sent to me
> landed in a library containing duplicates and dedicatory copies, and thus I did
> not sign them. I am truly sorry, and I beg you a thousand pardons. You can
> well believe me that I would have unhesitatingly fulfilled the so simple and yet
> moving wish of the two persons who have so well deserved it because of this
> so touching publication. It is *you* one must thank, not me. If my words of
> introduction should contribute a little to open the way for the book into the
> heart of the readers, that would constitute, for me, a great satisfaction.[35]

At the end of 1953 in the journal *Il Mondo,* published by Mondadori,
Lavinia Mazzucchetti's translation of Mann's novella *The Black Swan (Die
Betrogene)* appeared under the title *L'Inganno,* over which the writer
expressed enormous satifaction: "The translation gives me the impression
of being excellent."[36]

The following year also brought new translations in Italy of Mann's
works. Bruno Arzeni's Italian version of the Joseph tetralogy, a truly
remarkable accomplishment, appeared in 1954 through Mondadori as Volumes 6 and 7 of the complete edition. How great Mann's popularity had
now become with Italian readers is clearly proven by the fact that at this
time works of the German writer were also issued by a series of other
publishers, such as the Florentine press Sansoni, which brought out
Giuseppe Zamboni's translation of *Tristan,* and the Biblioteca Universale
Rizzoli with its editions of *Padrone e cane (A Man and his Dog)* and *Tonio
Kröger,* executed by Remo Costanzi. In the same year Einaudi issued an

entirely new translation of *Death in Venice (La morte a Venezia)*, by Anita Rho.

Not only the newspapers and journals but also the Italian radio became more intensely occupied with the personality and work of Thomas Mann. During his stay in Rome the writer, at the microphone himself, had spoken to the Italian public, and since that time radio broadcasts, which were primarily transmitted on the intellectually fastidious "terzo programma" ("third program"), had increased about him and his work: thus in February 1954 the Italian radio carried a commentary arranged by the Germanist Ferruccio Amoroso, "La famiglia Mann allo specchio autobiografico," which brought the author of the program a letter of appreciation from Thomas Mann:

> You have given me true pleasure with your kind letter and with the text of your Roman radio discourse: a delightful conversation and almost a kind of little family novel. I was astonished to see how well informed you are with regard to 'us.' I do not often think in the first person singular, but I gladly think in the first person plural.[37]

In the same year (1954) the young Neapolitan critic Franco Rizzo wrote an article in the journal *Letterature Moderne* on Mann's story *The Holy Sinner*, "L'eletto di Thomas Mann," which so greatly impressed the writer that with heartfelt words of thanks he invited Rizzo to visit him in Zürich, in order to hold a long discussion with him about his work:

> I am afraid that I have not yet thanked you for sending your fine study on the *Eletto*, which I enjoyed so much. In general I am very happy about the extraordinarily intelligent interest which for some time now has been shown in my work in Italy. But I confess that I have a particular personal weakness for that little *curiosum* which *The Holy Sinner* represents, and I must say that I know of perhaps no other critical review, in any language, which captures its character with more fineness and certainty than yours.[38]

7. The Year of Death, 1955

In Spring 1955 in the Trieste publishing house Eugenio Borsatti, a detailed and exhaustive study by the Germanist Guido Devescovi on Thomas Mann's *Doctor Faustus* appeared under the title *Il Doktor Faustus di Thomas Mann*. In his book, Devescovi analyzed the individual and, in this work of Mann's, important motifs such as disease, music, magic, politics; occupied himself critically with the various characters; and came to grips with the other more important critics of the same work, above all with Walter Boehlich, Georg Lukács, Erich Heller, Hans Mayer, and especially Hans Egon Holthusen, who had arrived at a very negative judgment with regard to the novel. Although Devescovi did not agree with *Doctor Faustus* in every particular, after careful investigation and interpretation he nevertheless came to the conclusion that the stirring work, representing a confession of the author, ought to deeply impress every reader with its atmosphere of a "despairing hope" for a moral purification of the German people. Devescovi was convinced that Thomas Mann wished, in his novel, to condemn Faustian pride, quite immaterial as to whether it is manifest in the character of a man or of an entire nation. The thought stated at the end of the work that through Grace death is overcome expressed—according to Devescovi—Thomas Mann's view that redemption, the return to pure humanity, lay within the realm of possibility for the German people. In addition to his moral sense of responsibility, Devescovi admired in Thomas Mann his poetical sensitivity and artistry of presentation, in which the German writer was indeed not surpassed by any of his contemporaries.[39]

Thomas Mann was very grateful to the Italian scholar for his thorough interpretation, and from his written reply it becomes apparent how very much this critical response to his last great novel touched him:

> What above all became clear to me from your penetrating study is your enormous Germanistic education, which I, in particular, have every reason to admire. How much you have absorbed of German thought, how much you have read, indeed just by me and about me—fifteen things on 'Faustus' which I myself never saw—fortunately, I probably ought to say; for there is of course much which is hostile and negative among them, and it is almost astounding that all the adverse material which you had to digest was unable to completely smother your sympathy with the novel, your feeling for its curious and radical directness. For me the book still has something of a Leyden jar, which one cannot touch without receiving an electric shock. But admittedly, stupidity and fundamental antipathy are immune against it.[40]

In the same letter Thomas Mann also made some interesting remarks about his own knowledge of Italian. Although he had forgotten much of the language with which he was once quite familiar, especially in his youth, it was not too difficult for him to read it if it concerned a critique of his work, and in this case a novel so close to his heart as *Doctor Faustus*.

> To my shame I must confess that I read Italian only imperfectly and was not always able to follow your thoughts exactly. But it is remarkable how much one nevertheless understands when it concerns oneself and one's work; and if a study is concerned entirely with this book, which has remained closer to my heart than all the others, probably because it has cost me the most, then I can suddenly fancy myself to be a good and alert reader even of languages which are more foreign to me than Italian, still halfway familiar to me and much heard from youth onwards.[41]

Among his Italian translators Thomas Mann had always had a special liking for Lavinia Mazzucchetti, and therefore he was particularly happy that at the beginning of 1955 she declared herself ready to translate the just-finished novel *Felix Krull* into her mother tongue. In a letter to her he expressed his pleasure, at the same time drawing her attention to some difficulties of the text:

Just two words today to express my *real pleasure* over the news that you
would like to translate Krull. 'Was will ich mehr, ich bin geborgen—nun
braucht sich Beckmesser nicht mehr zu sorgen,' "What would I more? I'm
quite protected; Beckmesser now need be no more dejected" as it says in *Die
Meistersinger.** Be assured I am happy on my account and that of the book,
but likewise be assured also for *you,* who are therewith offered an exercise
not without charm and binding you to life—at the same time not too difficult,
but amusing. Difficulties for any translator are really only presented in the
Mme Houpflé chapter with the Alexandrine improvisations in French and
German, in connection with which I call attention that the good woman
begins with Victor Hugo: 'Pourquoi, quand l'heure vous appelle, N'es-tu pas
encore prêt pour la chapelle,' which is from *Hernani.†* Naturally, she then
says instead of 'Habille-toi, vite!', 'Déshabille-toi!' rendered in the reference
edition as 'Déshabillez-vous vite!'[42]

For Thomas Mann's eightieth birthday Lavinia Mazzucchetti had
planned a book which, under the title *Dialogo con Goethe (Dialogue with
Goethe),* was to include all the essays and other works which in the course
of his life Thomas Mann had written about Goethe. In a letter to Thomas
Mann the Italian scholar mentioned her partiality for his essay *Phantasy on
Goethe (Phantasie über Goethe),* which first appeared in English in 1948 as
the introduction to the American anthology *The Permanent Goethe,* and
not until some months later was published in the German language in the
volume *Neue Studien.* In his letter of reply Thomas Mann confessed his
own weakness for the little work:

> As for the *Fantasia su Goethe,* I actually share your sympathy for this little
> work, which is the lightest and at the same time most comprehensive that I
> have ever written about Goethe, and the partiality is not harmed by the fact
> that there are places in which I repeat a little what I have said in other of my
> Goethe essays. I believe that you are right in considering it particularly
> indicated for a public which has not become familiar with Goethe, and your
> idea of making from it a little volume on its own has, for me, something
> exceedingly attractive.[43]

The book *Dialogo con Goethe,* until now appearing only in Italian, also
contains, in addition to works which Thomas Mann wrote in various
epochs about Goethe, the seventh chapter of the novel *The Beloved Returns (Lotte in Weimar)* under the title "Una mattina di Goethe" (A
Morning in the Life of Goethe). In a lengthy introduction the editor analyzed
the gradual change in Mann's attitude towards Goethe and the deposition

---

*The quotation from *Die Meistersinger* is Englished by Ernest Newman in
the Breitkopf & Härtel score published in Leipzig, 1911, p. 425.
†Trans. note: The reference edition of *Felix Krull,* see bibliography, has
the following French: 'Comment, à ce propos, quand l'heure nous appelle,
n'êtes-vous pas encore prêt pour la chapelle?'

which Goethe's ideas had found in his work; she ended with affectionate congratulations upon the writer's eightieth birthday: "In celebration of his eightieth year the Casa Editrice Mondadori presents to its greatest living author, instead of the usual garland of critical eulogies, the gift of a book which is already entirely his . . . Not praise, but affectionate gratitude must be offered to the one who, while we were forced to live in this, our difficult time, has liberally given us the vigorous comfort of his thought and of his example."[44] Because of a delay in publication it was, however, not possible to complete the book in time for the eightieth birthday of the writer; it was only in October 1955, after his death, that it could be published.

In 1955 three further volumes of the *opera omnia* came out in Italy: Volume 4, under the title *Romanzi brevi*, contained the collected stories in translation by Bruno Arzeni, Emilio Castellani, Lavinia Mazzucchetti, Mario Merlini, Ervino Pocar, and Giorgio Zampa; Volume 5 contained *Carlotta a Weimar (The Beloved Returns)* and *Confessioni del cavaliere d'industria Felix Krull (Confessions of Felix Krull, Confidence Man)*, the Goethe novel, as well as *Felix Krull*, in Lavinia Mazzucchetti's translation; and Volume 11, *Scritti storici e politici*, contained the political and historical essays, whose Italian versions came from various translators (Bruno Arzeni, C. Baseggio, Mirella Battaglia, Lavinia Mazzucchetti, Ervino Pocar, and Liliana Scalero).

As late as May 1955, a few months before his death, Thomas Mann accepted an invitation from Paolo Grassi and Giorgio Strehler, the directors of the famous avant-garde "Piccolo teatro della Città di Milano," to go to Milan to read in German from his writings before a group of young people and to take part in a symposium on his work. Thomas Mann took the greatest interest in the fate of the "Piccolo teatro," which had been founded in 1947 by the then twenty-six-year-old Giorgio Strehler, who had the courage to offer the public—for Italy indeed unique at that time—an avant-garde repertoire by bringing many ultra-modern Italian and foreign plays to the stage. In spite of his frail health Thomas Mann was prepared to follow up the invitation, but the plan was not pursued any further.

The great interest of the Italian public and of the Italian press in Thomas Mann's personality and in his work was particularly demonstrated, however, on the occasion of his eightieth birthday. There was hardly an Italian newspaper or journal which did not commemorate the anniversary with appreciative words. Thus Piero Calamandrei, the publisher of the Florentine monthly literary magazine *Il Ponte*, dedicated a special issue (June 1955) to Thomas Mann with contributions by leading Germanists and critics of Italy and abroad. In his "Saluto a Thomas Mann," he himself lauded the literary and human greatness of the eighty-year-old man, who in his opinion had much in common with Benedetto Croce: although their languages were different, they still represented the same views and ideals and thereby proved the unity of European thought. Calamandrei hoped that

Mann's longing for world peace might come true, since at bottom it is not the politicians but the great philosophers who mould and guide the history of the world. He concluded his "Salute to Thomas Mann" with the thought that Thomas Mann belonged to these spiritual leaders and that views such as those about the possibility of a "co prehensive financing of peace" (expressed in his address *The Years of My Life*) were of historical significance.

> In the journey of humanity one sees that at bottom the politicians are only the recorders of history: but its true authors, those who mark the stages through which must pass the advance of the peoples who are on the march towards their peaceful unification, are the great universal spirits whom Thomas Mann calls to mind today and among whom he converses as equal to equal.[45]

Calamandrei was grateful to Thomas Mann for permission to publish in *Il Ponte* a heretofore unpublished manuscript, a portion of the essay *Versuch über Schiller,* which Thomas Mann had read in shortened form at the Schiller ceremonies in Stuttgart and Weimar. This segment appearing in *Il Ponte* dealt with the friendship between Schiller and Goethe, under the title "Spirito e Natura, ovvero Schiller e Goethe" ("Spirit and Nature, or Schiller and Goethe").

In addition to an article by Hermann Stresau, the *Il Ponte* special issue contained an article by Ferruccio Amoroso, "Appunti sulla poesia di Thomas Mann" ("Notes on the poetry of Thomas Mann"), which discussed various motifs in Mann's work such as irony, music, and politics. With great understanding Amoroso pointed to two important characteristics of Thomas Mann: intelligence and goodness work together and prevent a one-sidedness in the work of the writer, who understands in order to love, and loves in order to understand. And finally we find two biographical works: an essay from the pen of Lavinia Mazzucchetti dealt with the man, the personality of the writer and its reflection in his work ("L'uomo Thomas Mann"), while the writer's youngest daughter, Elisabeth Mann Borgese, told about her childhood and her relationship to her father in the reminiscences "Infanzia con mio padre."

Even a popular weekly journal such as *Il Contemporaneo,* appearing in Rome, dedicated the entire issue of 4 June 1955 to the German author. It let Thomas Mann himself speak with his address on Schiller, delivered in Stuttgart and Weimar, "Discorso su Schiller," and presented a number of little-known photographs of the writer. On the title page appeared a congratulatory article, signed with "Il Contemporaneo," in which Mann's concept of humanism, whose goal was reconciliation and peace, was examined.

In addition to a clear listing of the most significant dates in the life and work of the writer, the newspaper published an article by Georg Lukács, translated by Cordelia Gundolf, as well as Ranuccio Bianchi Bandinelli's description of Thomas Mann's visit to Rome in the year 1953 and their talks together about problems of archaeology.

In his article "Il grande gioco" ("The Great Game") the critic Giacomo Debenedetti, who had interviewed Thomas Mann a few times, endeavored an analysis of the novel *Doctor Faustus* and of the problems of the Devil, whereby he raised the question whether mankind of today could be saved through art. According to Debenedetti's opinion, Thomas Mann had replied to this question very evasively and spiced with romantic irony. Only a contradictory salvation was possible, whose necessary consequence must be a loss of self. Artwork could be created, yet life, even the everlasting life, was lost: that, so concluded the author, was the Devil's game. "In brief: if salvation is possible, it is very similar to the famous victory in which the victor falls exhausted upon the body of the conquered."[46] Debenedetti saw as a paradox the fact that Thomas Mann could not believe in a salvation through art and yet wanted to create a masterpiece:

> The matter is complicated by a further paradox: in order to place in doubt the possibility of salvation through art, Thomas Mann has written a novel, that is to say, a work of art, no doubt undertaken with that hope for a masterpiece, which his Devil denies to the conscious writer. The true Faust is Thomas Mann, who endeavors to play a joke on the Devil. For this great game, also useful to all as an example, we here and on this occasion, wish to thank him.[47]

While in his article "La selva ironica" ("The Ironic Forest") Franco Fortini concerned himself with the rôle of irony in Thomas Mann's work, in the article "Amor Fati," Galvano Della Volpe investigated the relation of the artist to his surroundings and to life in general.

Of special significance, however, was the article "Manniano all'incontrario" ("Mannian, but Headed in the Opposite Direction") by the young Italo Calvino, born in 1923 in Cuba and brought up in Liguria, who with novels such as *Il sentiero dei nidi di ragno,* 1947 (*The Path to the Nest of Spiders*) and *Ultimo viene il corvo,* 1946 (*Last Comes the Raven*) had quite early made a name for himself. He analyzed the importance of Thomas Mann for the generation of young writers, hence that group which aspired to an objective, "spoken" story and which saw its models in Tolstoi and Flaubert. In his search for a writer who stood closer to the generation of today, the people of the present, Calvino came upon Thomas Mann, who in the synthesis of middle class and decadence had given literature a new direction:

> And in his view of the classic and realistic burgher, fixed to stubbornly scrutinize the meanderings of decadentism and of irrationalism, almost to the point of losing himself in them, but then always remaining 'above' them, interposing between them and himself the lens of historical distance, of the classicism of language, of the irony of the great narrator, we found a contemporary example of how the writer of an epoch of transition and drama can live

the old and the new at the same time, can participate in the totality of the
drama yet remaining himself, judge and supreme orchestrator.[48]

In this potentiality of Mann's to convey the traditional and the modern at
the same time Calvino saw a basis for admiration and for rejection of the
writer: "Mann wants to dominate and at the same time encompass the
crisis of contemporary culture in the channel of his Goethian classicism."[49]

Italo Calvino, the writer of a new generation, saw Thomas Mann with
new eyes, yet was convinced that he and his young colleagues could learn
much from the German writer:

> Old and new: for him the bourgeois rationalism is the 'old,' where his
> nostalgia as enlightened conservative extends, while the weak Hanno Bud-
> denbrook or the demoniacal Leverkühn are the 'new,' concerning which,
> however, he feels one must recognize a necessity and a truth. For us, quite to
> the contrary: the 'old' is that which to him seems new, the 'new' is something
> much more solid and rational than the good merchants of Lübeck. And from
> the 'old' we want to extract all the refined sharpness which it contains in order
> to make use of it ourselves and to arrive at the 'new.' Mannians, but headed in
> the opposite direction—that is, forward—in this way could one define a
> proper and new relationship with Mann.[50]

The special issue of *Il Contemporaneo* also contained an article "Mann
'e' noi" by the journalist Carlo Bernari, born in Naples in 1909 and editor of
Tempo, who declared that already in his early work Mann recognized and
dealt with problems which are also of importance to the younger generation. While Jorge Amado commemorated Thomas Mann's Brazilian
mother in an illustrated article ("La madre brasiliana"), the Germanist
Cesare Cases occupied himself with Thomas Mann's novel *Confessions of
Felix Krull, Confidence Man* in the article "Un romanzo picaresco" ("A
picaresque novel"). After a review of the origin and diffusion of the
species, Cases compared the fragment already published in 1922 and the
final version of the novel. The division between spirit and life, between
artist and burgher, which Mann early perceived and presented in his works
ever anew, extending to the grotesque in *Felix Krull,* was seen by Cases as a
characteristic of the modern world. At the same time, he saw in *Felix Krull*
a developmental novel laid out very similarly to the Joseph tetralogy, only
with the difference that in *Krull* the development proceeds negatively,
which is already indicated by the hero's necessity for constant mas-
querade. If Thomas Mann is also regarded as the representative of decadence, then in Cases' opinion he had, by means of a deep, objective
analysis, contributed a great deal towards explaining and evaluating this
phenomenon.

The news of Thomas Mann's death on 12 August 1955 found an even
stronger echo in the Italian press than his eightieth birthday. He was
mourned as if he were a writer in his own land and with profound emotion

he was named "L'ultimo grande tedesco" ("The last great German"). In its issue of 23 August the widely circulated weekly newspaper *Il Mondo* honored the deceased writer with a photographic reportage from the various stages of his long life and let him speak through some essays (with the "Lübecker Ansprache" ["Lübeck Address"] and with his treatise on André Gide). In his article "Parodia e verità" ("Parody and Truth") the critic Giorgio Zampa concerned himself with the reaction of various nations to Thomas Mann's work, whose egoistical and political goals frequently produced an incorrect official judgment, and he was convinced that Mann himself was aware of this and therefore could no longer feel at home anywhere: "Mann has gone, conscious of no longer belonging to any country, to any party, to any social class."[51]

In spite of the many honors from all over the world and the great demands which were made upon him from all sides, Thomas Mann preserved to the end his incredible creative power and strict self-discipline, a fact which aroused Giorgio Zampa's admiration:

> What other writer, having in advanced age completed a work of the bulk and of the strain of *Faustus,* with an immense labor behind him, set in order and, by general opinion, concluded: what other would have found strength and will to set himself new tasks, not secondary, incidental, but such as to engage all energies, to demand great concentration, employment of all the spiritual faculties: to play, once again, for all or nothing?[52]

Also in Federico Gozzi's article "Il liberale Thomas Mann" ("The Liberal Thomas Mann") unrestricted admiration was expressed for the German writer, who above all in his political attitude had gone through a great process of gradual maturation into liberal humanism and thus found recognition by the most prominent people of his time: "Certainly not by chance could Benedetto Croce dedicate precisely to him the *Storia d'Europa nel secolo decimonono (History of Europe in the Nineteenth Century)* which remains the most noble document of the liberal doctrine during the Fascist oppression."[53]

Another important Italian contribution in the year of Thomas Mann's death was the special edition which the publisher of the Milanese journal *aut aut,* Enzo Paci, dedicated to the personality and work of the German writer. In his article "L'ironia di Thomas Mann" ("The Irony of Thomas Mann") Paci showed, by means of many examples from Mann's work, the latter's partiality for the ironic antithesis between life and spirit, love for life and longing for death, and in his investigation came to the conclusion that even in death Thomas Mann's figure was crowned and glorified with a smile which Paci defined with the words: "It is the smile of human dignity which entrusts to our responsibility the triumph of life over dissolution, the work and the struggle for a more just and more free future."[54]

In his study "Felix Krull si confessa" ("Felix Krull confesses") the critic Glauco Cambon investigated the character of this picaresque hero and some motifs important to the novel, such as that of ambiguity and that of alienation. Cambon regarded the novel as a parody of the educational novel, and saw a return of the writer to the cultural sphere of his mother in the fact that in his old age Thomas Mann turned once again to the type of picaresque novel originating in Spain.

It would lead too far afield to explore the essays on Thomas Mann by the other literary historians of the time, such as Roberto Sanesi, Gianantonio De Toni, and Giacomo Cives, but in summary one may say that, particularly in the commemorative year 1955, the Italian press thoroughly and very seriously discussed the complete work of the writer. The outlook of the critics who once, especially prior to 1914, were occupied almost solely with the literature of their own country, had now become worldwide: Thomas Mann was compared with figures such as Flaubert, James Joyce, and T. S. Eliot, and perhaps not wrongly one can say that, after the Second World War, Italian literary research surveyed and judged the literature of the world with a cosmopolitanism earlier uncommon.

8. Mann and Italy after 1955

In carefully examining the Italian critics who concerned themselves with the work of Thomas Mann, one perceives that their judgment with regard to his artistic qualities proves to be altogether positive after 1945; indeed, in his last years of life and after his death, occasionally even enthusiastically praiseful. The only work of Thomas Mann which met with rejection in Italy immediately after its appearance and still into the fifties was his novella *Mario and the Magician.* In the Fascist period many Italians who did not wish to see or to recognize the political undertones felt the description of conditions in Torre di Venere to be an attack upon their homeland. The Fascist government very quickly became aware that Thomas Mann had really exercised a severe and scathing criticism on its methods and placed the short piece on the Index without hesitation.

Immediately after the war, in the year 1945, a new translation of the novella finally appeared which, however, even then still did not meet with an unclouded response. Although the Italians, apart from a few exceptions, were now also clearly aware of Thomas Mann's political intent, this work was nevertheless still regarded by a few critics as anti-Italian.

Hence, as late as 1956 the influential Germanist Giovanni Necco wrote in an article about the novella:

> The dark and tense atmosphere of *Mario and the Magician* is intimated from the first measures of the story. Cipolla is a hypnotist who on a sultry summer evening puts all of his suggestive magical forces at work before the public of a bathing resort. The author concentrates his unconcealed antipathy on the ominous figure of the 'magician,' who with demoniac power, accompanied by

a sardonic smile, frightens and disturbs his spectators. The novella is enveloped in an aura of sorcery and magic. The artistic objectivity is impaired by a certain ill-concealed prejudice of Mann against our people, their customs, and their basic honesty. This lack of understanding and this intolerance, which clearly appear in other Mannian pages as well (see, for example, *Death in Venice*), could displease us Italians owing to so much of the unfounded and purely subjective that is always connected with prejudices. But, on the other hand, no one can deny the artist the reactions of his sensibility in relation to the world surrounding him, and one knows that Goethe himself, in addition to his *Italienische Reise* and the *Römische Elegien,* overflowing with enthusiasm, wrote the rather bitter and venomous *Venezianische Epigramme.* The political thesis of Lukács, who sees in Cipolla, transferred and varied, the figure of the 'Duce,' is unquestionably arbitrary and is of no use to the legitimate interpretation of the story.[55]

Actually the novella *Mario and the Magician* never became a popular success in Italy, which is proven by the fact that since 1947 it never again appeared as a separate edition. If one wishes to read *Mario and the Magician* in Italy today, one must turn to the volume of short novels ("romanzi brevi") in the *opera omnia* series where—in the words of Lavinia Mazzucchetti—". . .the little waiter, so to speak, becomes supported by personalities who enjoy a much longer and more substantial fame, such as Tonio Kröger, Spinell, Gustav Aschenbach, and Professor Cornelius."[56]

In spite of this, in 1956 the much-disputed novella experienced a temporary rediscovery by means of an experiment by the Scala of Milan. The Italian producer Luchino Visconti, known chiefly through his films, was primarily responsible for the success of this ballet staging of *Mario and the Magician* since through the medium of the dance and music he knew how to mold anew an artwork which was so strongly defined by the intellectual. In order to do as much justice as possible to the essence of Thomas Mann's work, Visconti also made use of dialogue and a chorus (the rôle of the Magician, for example, is purely a spoken part). The composer Franco Mannini had discussed the plan for the "danced melodrama" (as he called it) with Thomas Mann during the author's visit in Rome and had met with complete understanding, even sympathy from him concerning this project. To be sure, his music played only a background rôle, while the décor had an important function. Here the discrepancy between the realism of the first scene and Mario's dream world in the second part could be effectively contrasted. Judging by the good, occasionally even enthusiastic reviews in the Italian press, the Milan Scala's ballet was a great success and the question is obvious: why were other theaters not also prepared to present *Mario e il mago?*

If one intends to examine the reception of Thomas Mann in Italy, then one must not fail to mention the "Centro Thomas Mann," founded in Rome in 1957, which, however, bears his name quite falsely. It describes itself as a cultural association which regards it as its duty to devote itself to the literature, history, and politics of both parts of present-day Germany. But in reality this so-called "Thomas Mann Center" created by Italian intellectual leftists is financed by the Italian Communist Party and is possibly supported by the government of the German Democratic Republic (concerning this, admittedly, opinions differ). The association has nothing to do with Thomas Mann himself; because of the high regard in Italy for this German writer, his name was given preference over that of Bertolt Brecht, who had been considered for a while.

The work of Thomas Mann remained alive in Italian critical circles also. The anthology *L'arte di Thomas Mann (The Art of Thomas Mann)*, published for the first time in 1956 with a lengthy introduction by the editor, Bonaventura Tecchi, for many years the leading Germanist at the University of Rome, has received several reprints in the course of the years. In 1958 Mondadori issued the collected essays of G. A. Borgese, who had died in 1952, under the title *Da Dante a Thomas Mann (From Dante to Thomas Mann)*. To examine here the profusion of lesser articles on Thomas Mann in Italian newspapers and journals in the years following his death would go beyond the limitations of this chapter. The deep interest of the Italian public in the life and work of the German writer, in particular, is clearly proven by the crowds of visitors to the travelling exhibition on Thomas Mann which, arranged by the government in Bonn, was displayed in various Italian cities in 1962 and universally met with the greatest attention. Within the framework of this event, Italian critics and Germanists such as Guido Devescovi, Lavinia Mazzucchetti, and Emilio Castellani had the opportunity to deliver reports upon the latest state of their Thomas Mann investigations.

Finally, one should not leave unmentioned here a controversy whose subject was Thomas Mann's political integrity and which in the year 1958 was caused by the writer Ignazio Silone in the Roman journal *Tempo Presente,* which he founded. In the issue of January 1958 he printed the article "Thomas Mann e il dovere civile" ("Thomas Mann and Civic Duty), in which, starting from the volume *Scritti storici e politici* of the *opera omnia,* he analyzed the development of Mann's political attitude. He reproached the German writer with having gone into exile only late, but above all with not having rejected Fascism more decisively:

> But the most telling example of the prevalence in him of prejudice against any other political or moral consideration still remains, however, his constant silence with regard to Italian Fascism, although he was not lacking in information about its oppressive character and in spite of his friendship with many anti-Fascists, among whom first of all was Benedetto Croce.[57]

This harsh, in no way provoked, attack by Silone on the German writer, who had already left Germany prior to Hitler's seizure of power and thereby had become one of the first emigrants, caused a spirited echo from among the readers of the journal, which was published in articles in the March issue. Silone was most convincingly refuted through a letter from the writer's youngest daughter, Elisabeth Mann Borgese, who once again presented the circumstances of her father's emigration and by means of various examples from his political writings showed that he had early and with all clarity recognized the danger of Fascism and had warned against it in works such as *Mario and the Magician*. In her opinion it was nevertheless understandable that the German situation was closer to him than the Italian and that he devoted his greatest attention and criticism to National Socialism in Germany:

> It was the German Fascism which destroyed him, the tragedy of Germany was his personal tragedy. To reproach him for not having written an entire book against Mussolini would be the same as reproaching Salvemini, Borgese, or you for not having done the same against Hitler. But it would not enter the mind of any honest man to deduce from this that the Italian emigrants have been supporters of Nazism; and your reproach in regard to my father remains absolutely incomprehensible.[58]

In his reply to this letter Silone admitted that his judgment had been too harsh and above all hasty, since he had not looked enough into the pertinent literature. At the same time, he stressed that, nevertheless, in his personal relations with Thomas Mann in Zürich, where before the war they had both stayed as emigrants, he had been disappointed by his reserve with regard to the expression of his political opposition and by his lack of practical initiative. It appears that this impression of the Italian can be attributed to differences in age and temperament. Whoever was acquainted with Thomas Mann knows that in conversation he was seldom able to overcome a certain reserve. It is clearly apparent from his work that in the course of time his political convictions underwent changes (which can be very easily defined by origin, influences, development, and experiences), but there is no doubt at all that from the very beginning he took a rejecting, indeed occasionally bellicose, attitude with regard to Fascism as well as to National Socialism.

9. Summary

When one surveys the reception and spread of Thomas Mann's work in Italy from the beginnings to the present day, one is obliged to state that at first the interest of public and critic developed only very hesitantly. While in Scandinavia and Russia the writings of the German author, especially in the intellectual circles, were very early a part of the preferred reading material, in Italy occupation with his work set in only substantially later.[59] After bestowal of the Nobel Prize to Thomas Mann in the year 1929, the attention of the Italian public was gradually attracted to him and his work. From that time on his books appeared in ever greater number, and young Italian intellectuals such as Emilio Castellani, but also the working-class youth of Italy, found in the books of Thomas Mann a counterbalance to Fascist propaganda.

In the early years of the thirties the Italian critics also began to seriously concern themselves with Thomas Mann's thought. Literary journals such as *Il Convegno* brought out articles about Mann's work, and Germanists such as Italo Maione and Lavinia Mazzucchetti dedicated extensive studies to him. In Italy, Thomas Mann was admired above all for his objectivity, his irony, and the almost classic lucidity of his presentation.

In 1936 appeared the first Italian monograph devoted exclusively to the work of the German writer, *L'opera di Thomas Mann,* by Ladislao Mittner, who attributed Mann's clarity and elegance to French influences. At the same time the Italian Germanist emphasized the importance of the autobiographical elements as well as the self-discipline with which Thomas Mann created his works.

After the German-Italian cultural agreement and the establishment of the so-called Berlin-Rome Axis in the year 1938, though, a lengthy interruption commenced as soon as Mann's works appeared on the blacklist and could be neither printed nor read in Fascist Italy. After the end of the war, however, interest set in all the stronger: the Italian public felt an affinity to Thomas Mann as to hardly any other contemporary writer.

In the year 1947 the Milanese press Mondadori decided to bring out a ten-volume Italian edition of Thomas Mann's entire works, which would be editorially supervised by Italy's leading Thomas Mann scholar, Lavinia Mazzucchetti. In the same year Thomas Mann was elected as foreign member of the venerable Accademia dei Lincei, which five years later, in 1952, awarded him the international literary prize, the Premio Feltrinelli.

During his visit to Rome in the spring of 1953, the writer received the honor bestowed upon him by the Accademia and thereby had the opportunity to become personally acquainted with the most prominent representatives of Italian literature of his day. By this time his popularity in Italy had unquestionably reached its zenith. How great the enthusiasm of public and critic had become for him is shown by the strong response which his eightieth birthday, and shortly thereafter the news of his death, aroused in the Italian press. The spread of Thomas Mann's work and concern with his ideas not only in the circles of literary criticism but also in the Italian public prove that Mann's artistic concepts found deep understanding among his Italian readers.

IV
Mann's Influence on Italian Literature

1. Introduction

Italian Literature of the twentieth century is characterized by various currents and tendencies which to some extent run side by side. While one group of writers, such as D'Annunzio and Fogazzaro, is still entirely bound up with the nineteenth century, in another the new spirit of the twentieth century makes itself noticeable. For the adherents of this second tendency who were sometimes older in years, the ideals of Benedetto Croce, directed against convention and rhetoric, are of great significance. Although in the thirties Fascism put a temporary end to many of these avant-garde tendencies and experiments in Italy, nevertheless, precisely during this period there came, from the ranks of emigrant writers such as Giuseppe Antonio Borgese and Ignazio Silone, or the members of the *resistenza* who remained in Italy, important, trend-setting works such as the novels by Cesare Pavese, Natalia Ginzburg, and Alberto Moravia.

Italian literature did not experience a new blossoming until the *Neorealismo* in the years after the Second World War. Although this trend, which developed as a reaction to the rhetoric of Fascism, frequently suffers from a disregard of language, Italian writers are quickly finding their way back to a lyrical interpretation of reality, to a form of expression which as early as the thirties had its Italian representatives in Corrado Alvaro and Elio Vittorini.

The novella form, flourishing in Italy since Boccaccio and, because of its conciseness, extensively promoted by Fascism, was now abandoned in favor of a longer story form, since only the novel or the long story offered enough space to explore painstakingly the ambit of an individual's life and to present his problems sufficiently. The novel form, which in Italy—apart from a few exceptions—previously had never really been able to gain acceptance, became in the years after the Second World War an important form of its literature, as proven by the works of Alberto Moravia, Carlo Emilio Gadda, and Tomasi di Lampedusa.

While before the war Italian literature had traditionally oriented itself to the French and Russian, from 1945 it turned to a new model, American literature. Cesare Pavese, as well as Elio Vittorini, both prime movers of modern Italian literature, rendered pioneer duty in this respect in that as early as the thirties they began to translate American writers such as

Melville, Dos Passos, Faulkner, Hemingway, Steinbeck, and many others into their mother tongue, and consequently gained a home for them in Italy.

As was stated in the previous chapter, because of its strong intellectual-philosophical character, German literature only slowly found a certain degree of approval in Italy; hence at first its effect on Italian creativity remained of limited significance.

In the following expositions, we investigate whether and to what extent the German writer Thomas Mann exercised an influence on Italian literature. Since Mann's works, as was discussed in detail in Chapter III, did not appear in Italian translation until relatively late, it was at the outset reserved for the Germanistic experts to interpret his world of ideas in Italy and to make it familiar to a relatively small circle of students. Only after the distinction conveyed by his winning the Nobel Prize in the year 1929 did Mann's work become known to wider circles in Italy. Yet the political situation in Fascist Italy and later also in National Socialist Germany—above all since the founding of the "Berlin-Rome Axis" (1938)—prevented an expansion and deepening of the significance of Thomas Mann for Italian literature. During the Second World War, Mann's work was completely suppressed in Italy. After the war ended, however, no further hindrances stood in the way of his popularity in Italy, the *opera omnia* began to appear, and within a few years his entire works were accessible to the Italian public in excellent translations.

If one therefore wishes to investigate the influence of Thomas Mann on the Italian literature of our day, one must naturally concern oneself with the younger and youngest Italian writers, since among the older generation hardly any influence can be possible. The only exception is perhaps Giuseppe Antonio Borgese, who as a Germanist in Milan came into contact with Mann's work quite early.

The selection of representatives of the more recent Italian literature, who are discussed here, is therefore restricted to some of the most important writers of the younger and youngest generation, who either—like Pavese and Vittorini—have themselves expressed an opinion on Thomas Mann's art, or—like Lampedusa and Bettiza—show distinct traces in their work of the German writer's influence.

2. Giuseppe Antonio Borgese (1882–1952)

Borgese, born in Sicily in 1882, was not only a prominent Germanist and cultural philosopher but also a gifted writer. His work *Tempesta nel nulla* (1931) exhibits strong reminiscences of Mann's idyll *Song of the Little Child* (1919) and of his novella *Disorder and Early Sorrow* (1926). In both of these tales, Mann revealed his partiality for his youngest daughter Elisabeth, which with north German restraint he elevated to works of art. Borgese also made his deep love for his daughter the theme of a poem, and when with southern exuberance and Italian rhetoric he glorifies the strong bond which unites father and daughter, then his motifs and declarations are indeed extraordinarily similar to those of Thomas Mann.

In his *Tempesta nel nulla* Borgese describes a mountain climb in the Engadine with his daughter Nanni. During this walking tour, impaired by bad weather, and which leads across a dangerous, narrow ridge where the peril of a sudden fall is all too great, the father reproaches himself severely. He has the feeling that in his egoism he had led his child astray into this danger-filled excursion, especially since both he, himself, as well as Nanni had been warned by a dream the preceding night. During the ascent the two actually are caught in a storm. Therewith, however, the ominous atmosphere is cleared and the father is then in the position to ease his conscience through a candid discussion. In the knowledge that the child is very well aware of the great tension, but is worried only about the wellbeing of the father, Borgese confesses his almost mythical love for his daughter, which strongly resembles that in Mann's *Gesang vom Kindchen:*

> Little tree which really walks beside me! living!
> Thou, so green!
> I may then lead thee back into the valley, thou who art my Isaac, my lamb.
> God was not the monster of the jaws of the precipice into which thou shouldst plunge.
> Thy hand is in mine.
> The delicate odor of plants, which flows from thy temples, from thy long gown, all green, with the pattern of flowers, this odor of childhood which the breath of the forests recognizes and makes its own, is not the crushing odor of Death.[1]

Thomas Mann also made use of biblical, Old Testament images to elevate his deep love for his daughter into the realm of the mythical:

> And so all at once then
> My dreaming emotion embraces the most precious living thing
> To me on earth: my little child, thou, and the most sacred possession besides,
> That I acquired and preserve, consolation in life and in death,
> I sit by the basket of the Nile, on guard, and hold thy little hand,
> Contemplating thy little face and its special form.[2]

In contrast to Thomas Mann, for Borgese nature and its diverse manifestations are of great significance as a reflection of human moods and emotions. Common to both, however, is fatherly love for the youngest daughter, in whom the old family tradition is embodied and in whom the revered ancestors live on:

> I looked her in the eyes and became confused in them. In her, charmed, I loved her mother, with the virginal voice; I loved my mother, with the gentle eyes, who was so far away.

And I was sorry that she had not known her, that she had never again seen her
since she was just a little baby, with her few blond hairs on her feeble head,
which were so soft and fine that they evoked tenderness, almost evoked pity,
to look at them![3]

In his daughter's features Thomas Mann discovered a mixture of Nordic
and oriental characteristics, from the "Low- and Eastern lands" ("Nieder-
und Morgenland"*)[4] and interpreted it as inheritance from the two groups
of forefathers coming from different cultural spheres:

Do thine eyes smile upon me kindly?
Indeed blue they shine as Nordic ice, yet sometimes barely perceptible
To my searching mind, from their depths it darkens
Somehow sweet and exotic, in unaccustomed melancholy—while yet
Thy brows are blond, just like your Hanseatic forefathers
(Smile I must, in truth, so well I know the feature),
Who dignified and with sober disposition strode to the Rathaus
And in the council chamber offered the snuff box to their neighbors—
Merchants chiefly, round-bearded, and owners of far-voyaging ships.[5]

Just as in Thomas Mann for whom the days of his youth in Lübeck rise
before his mind's eye at the sight of his small daughter, so in Borgese
memories of his own childhood in Sicily awaken during the descent from
the Engadine mountains:

Thus, mists of visions rising up from all sides, I no longer saw the Valley of
Fedoz, the Engadine; but my mountains, the valley
where I was born. . .
I was born on the night of San Martino, which has as many shooting
stars as that of San Lorenzo.
My father stepped out onto the balcony, and in those messages of light
read a prophecy, a destiny.
I grew up facing the great horizons; and I heard distant sounds.
The rivers, descending in the night among the forests, had voices
of love; the lights went out in the farmhouses on the hills to let
the stars draw near.[6]

In Borgese and Thomas Mann the motif of their sister emerges in connection with their youngest daughter:

We walked, holding hands; I forgot the years; from all the relatives, the living
and those who were under the earth, there grew, I don't know how, a single
entity; and my daughter was one of my blood, a sister.[7]

The name "Schwesterchen" ("Little Sister"), which the members of the
family used in addressing the little girl, evoked in the German writer

---

*Trans. note: "Morgenland" normally is rendered as "Orient"; however, it
might be rendered here "Eastern" to follow Mann's word rhythm.

through association memories of his childhood in Lübeck. The nuns who came to his family home to care for the sick and dying and were loved and respected by all, were likewise called "Schwestern" ("Sisters"):

> 'Little sister' thou art called at home, and the name sounds strange.
> 'Sisters' once, in the gabled home land, were called the gray
> Brides of the Savior with cowl and rosary, who lived together
> Somewhere in the crooked street, obedient to a Mother Superior,
> Where the boy visited them, to see the golden chapel,
> And from among them the gentlest nursed the father until death,
> Also often looked after us children, when we fell feverishly sick.[8]

For both writers the figure of the youngest daughter is the continuation and preservation, directed towards the future, of a long chain of people and traditions, and at the same time the object of a deep love which inspired the Italian as well as the German writer to profoundly felt poetical works:

> Then I will speak and sing of the little child, the youngest of mine,
> Who appeared to me in the most difficult time, when I was no longer young.
> And what no craving of the soul, no higher ambition could do,
> Fatherly feeling brings about: it makes me a metrical poet.[9]

In Borgese's *Tempesta nel nulla* motifs emerged which exhibited strong reminiscences of Thomas Mann's *Song of the Little Child:* love for the youngest daughter and the close ties with her became for both writers an intense experience bordering on the mythical. Looking at the child, not only memories of revered ancestors came alive, but also those of the Sicilian and Hanseatic writers' own youth. The figure of the daughter, who was also regarded as the beloved sister, was at the same time a link with the future and a symbol for the continuation of the family with its traditions and handed-down idiosyncrasies.

In the basic mood as well as in the individual motifs, such strong parallels are shown in both writers that one may probably safely assume that the Italian was very familiar with Thomas Mann's work and in addition must have been extraordinarily impressed by it. Hence it seems a handsome and appropriate decree of Fate that many years later he fell in love with the heroine of the *Song of the Little Child* on their first meeting and after a short time, in spite of all opposition, brought her home as his wife.

3. Cesare Pavese (1908–1950)

Cesare Pavese, born in the Piedmont in 1908, belonged to a younger generation than Borgese. He was active politically as a convinced anti-Fascist and with others, such as Elio Vittorini and Carlo Levi, was exiled to south Italy in the early thirties. For Pavese, American literature, whose masterpieces he translated into Italian, was the important model for his own literary activity. Yet for him the work of Thomas Mann was also an educational experience with which he had to come to grips.

In a radio interview Pavese declared that for him the greatest contemporary narrator was Thomas Mann and, among the Italians, Vittorio De Sica.[10] Also in his diary *The Burning Brand (Il mestiere di vivere)*, Pavese discussed the work of Thomas Mann several times, above all his tetralogy *Joseph and his Brothers*, in which he especially admired the fashioning of the myth. The Italian writer, who in his work again and again dealt with psychological and mythical problems and ideas, here saw in Thomas Mann a master who was capable of showing him a new path:

> The travelling over one's own ruts which everyone does, you discover today, has vexed you for some time (4 April '41, II); and then (12 April '41) it appeared to you as a happy reward of the effort of living and in fact since then you have no longer complained about it, but ('42, '43) have investigated with pleasure how in childhood these ruts engrave themselves. Still prior to rereading Thomas Mann's *Jacob* (December 42). You have ended (September '43) with the discovery of the myth-uniqueness, which thus fuses all of your old psychological frenzies and your most lively mythical-creative interests. It is established that the *need for construction* is born for you out of this law of return.[11]

Pavese sees realized in the work of Thomas Mann a perfection of structure which is characterized by the reiteration of events in modified form. In the novel *The Tales of Jacob*, for example, the events are manifestations of the will of God, which is recognized and comprehended by mankind. In Mann's treatment of the mythical material, Pavese sees influences of Kant and Vico:

> The *return of events* in Thomas Mann (in the chapter *Ruben goes to the well*) is in essence an evolutionist conception. Events try to happen, and each time they happen more satisfactorily, more perfectly. The *mythical stamps* are like the *forms of the species*. That which appears to separate this conception from naturalistic determinism is the fact that its factors are not sexual selection or the struggle for existence, but a constant will of God that a certain plan be realized. For the rest, Mann's way of expression seems to cause one to understand that what determines events one-by-one is the human spirit which, according to its laws, perceives them *and makes them happen* each time substantially the same but richer. A Kantian formalism, lowered into mythological material, in order to interpret it in a unitarian manner. Behind this, is Vico.[12]

Just as the problem of time exercised a particular power of attraction on Thomas Mann, so it also affected Pavese. In his novel *The Magic Mountain*, Mann had devoted his special attention to this motif and emphasized that in this work it was a case of a "time novel," "because pure time itself is its subject, which it deals with not only as the experience of its hero, but also in and through itself."[13] Like Thomas Mann, Pavese endeavored to shorten or to lengthen it by means of his narrative style:

The true story (*Primo amore* and *Campo di grano*) treats time as matter, not as a boundary, and masters it, shortening it or slowing it down, and it tolerates no didactic segments which are the time and the vision of real life; rather, it resolves the temporal environment in an impulse (fundamental synthesis or generative idea) of construction (perspective distance or reconsideration).[14]

Yet if one surveys the work of Cesare Pavese, terminated all too early through the writers suicide in the year 1950, one perceives that here the influence of Thomas Mann played a rôle only in isolated instances. As the Italian writer himself often admitted, it was chiefly the American and French models which were in his mind, and although he also greatly admired Mann's work, he nevertheless appears to have taken it up as a model for his own creative work only to a limited extent.

4. Elio Vittorini (1908–1966)

The Sicilian Elio Vittorini, born in the same year as Pavese, also concerned himself with Thomas Mann and his work, though—in contrast to Pavese—with an entirely negative result: Vittorini was convinced that his art had not in the slightest to do with that of the German writer; indeed, he declared that Thomas Mann's work was completely incomprehensible to him.

There are writers, and even great writers, whom I find myself absolutely unfit to enjoy and even to understand, to comprehend. Thomas Mann for example. It is in fact a whole vein of literature which is inexplicable to me: the one in which one perceives, purposely, the speculative action of the intellect as when in an X-ray we observe the barium running through the viscera which it wants to reveal to us. Especially then if it deals with the subspecies which likes to demonize, I plunge into a state of allergy and do not even know how to distinguish between creatures and abortions—in their proliferation.[15]

With this rejecting criticism Vittorini at the same time turned against all writers of speculative intellect for whom, as a champion of simple, easily grasped prose, he was incapable of mustering any appreciation. Vittorini's artistic concern was the presentation of people, not those degraded by civilization, but those who are close to nature and myth, such as he believed he could still find in the villages of his Sicilian homeland.

5. Tomasi di Lampedusa (1896–1957)

While the Sicilian Elio Vittorini abruptly turned away from the literary art of Thomas Mann, his twelve-year-senior countryman Tomasi di Lampedusa unquestionably stood much closer to the views of the German writer. For several reasons, his novel *The Leopard (Il gattopardo)* was a sensation soon after its publication in the year 1958. The author, descended from old aristocratic stock, was completely unknown in literary circles until, in the last years of his life, during 1955 and 1956, he completed his only novel. For years he had occupied himself with drafts and plans for it, yet the manuscript was sent back by various publishers to whom it had been submitted. When the book finally appeared a short time after the death of its author, it quickly became an international success.

Similar to Thomas Mann's *Buddenbrooks,* the theme here is the decline and destruction of a family; and exactly like Thomas Mann, Lampedusa had also leaned upon handed-down events in the history of his own family, just as the figures portrayed in the novel were modelled after definite personalities in his own family. In their works both the North German Thomas Mann and the Sicilian Tomasi di Lampedusa were rooted in the tradition of the great European novel, for which the French and the Russians set the course; and both writers were conscious of this tradition which was of such great importance for them.

The question now arises, if and how much Lampedusa was influenced by Thomas Mann's work. The possibility quite exists—indeed, the probability—that the Sicilian was acquainted with Mann's works and might even have read them in German, since he commanded that and several other European languages.

If one compares the novel *The Leopard* with Mann's *Felix Krull,* then some obvious parallels appear in the characterization. Tancredi Falconeri, the nephew of the Prince and beloved by all, in his boyish charm and his cleverness unquestionably resembles the captivating hero of Thomas Mann. Even the Prince, severe in his judgment, loves Tancredi, who in every situation knows the correct thing to do and wins all hearts with his youthful high spirits and his natural tact. After a long journey in an open carriage through hot Sicily, the relatives are welcomed by Tancredi: "He helped the Princess to descend from the carriage, dusted off the Prince's top hat with his shirt, distributed sweets to his girl cousins and jokes to the male cousins, almost genuflected before the Jesuit, returned the passionate outbursts of Bendicò, consoled Mademoiselle Dombreuil, teased all, enchanted all."[16]*

Thomas Mann's Felix Krull is also provided with the same joy of life and the same intuition, and a spiritual kinship seems to exist between the two figures. Yet according to his own declaration, Lampedusa had especially admired the accomplished dancer Fabrice del Dongo in Stendhal's *La Chartreuse de Parme,* whom he may have had in mind in creating his youthful hero Tancredi.[17]

In an episode in the Sicilian palace Donnafugata, parallels are found to another novel of Thomas Mann, *Royal Highness (Königliche Hoheit).* Tancredi and his fiancée Angelica undertake expeditions through the long uninhabited wings of the enormous princely palace, just like Klaus Hein-

---

*Lampedusa, *The Leopard,* tr. Archibald Colquhoun (New York: Pantheon Books, 1960), p. 67.

rich and his sister Ditlind, the children of the Grand Duke in *Royal High-ness,* whose "voyages of exploration into uninhabited regions of the Old Palace" were due to Klaus Heinrich's "roving curiosity."[18] On their trips of discovery or their "rummages,"[19] as Klaus Heinrich calls it, the Italian lovers and the German brother and sister stumble upon bleak rooms and forlorn halls with old, tattered furniture, and at the same time find objects of ambiguous nature from which the young people disconcertedly shrink back. Thus in a detached little Rococo salon Tancredi and Angelica find a cupboard which contains strange objects:

> It was very deep, but empty save for a roll of dirty material, upright in a corner; in it was a bundle of little whips, switches of ox sinews, some with silver handles, others covered halfway up with a charming, very old silk, white with little blue stripes, upon which one could discern three rows of small blackish spots: and little metal instruments, inexplicable. Tancredi was afraid.[20]*

Klaus Heinrich and Ditlind have a very similar experience which likewise frightens and makes them uneasy. After climbing a spiral staircase they come into an isolated room "where there were several strange objects. There were some awkwardly large, broken muskets with thickly rusted locks, which indeed had been too bad for the museum, and a retired throne with torn red velvet cushions, short, wide-swung lion's legs and hovering little children above the chair back, who supported a crown. But then there was a badly bent and dusty, cage-like and ghastly-seeming thing which long and greatly occupied them. If they were not deceived by appearances, then it was a rat trap, for one recognized the iron spike upon which the bacon was to be fixed, and frightful to think how the trap-door had fallen down behind the big and hostile, biting beast . . ."[21]

By means of these somewhat sinister discoveries, a more serious and a deeper meaning is added to the childish delight in "rummaging": through the disquieting impressions the attention of the Italian lovers and also the German brother and sister is drawn to the dark, doubtful side of life and they are prepared for the abysses that Fate still holds in readiness for them.

The fact that Klaus Heinrich and Ditlind are presented as naive children, and Tancredi and Angelica, on the other hand, as adult lovers, understandably indicates differences in the atmosphere of the "rummaging." For the lovers the explorations are full of sensual rapture and erotic temptations, and their adventures therefore have a more particular signficance than those of the characters of Thomas Mann. Consequently, when in Lampedusa, in the motif of the "rummaging" or, as it states in his novel, "the dreamy wanderings,"[22]* reminiscences are found of the novel *Royal Highness,* the Italian writer then went far beyond Thomas Mann in his treatment and gave the motif a more stratified meaning.

---

*Lampedusa, *The Leopard,* tr. Colquhoun, p. 185.

Unquestionably, similarities and parallels can be established in connection with Thomas Mann and Lampedusa, which however probably rest more on their mutual literary models—the great tradition of the Russian and French novel of the nineteenth century—than on a direct influence of Thomas Mann on the Sicilian author.

6. Enzo Bettiza (b. 1927)

The novel *Il fantasma di Trieste* (1958) by Enzo Bettiza, who comes from Spalato, is also a work which—like Lampedusa's *The Leopard* and Thomas Mann's *Buddenbrooks*—has the decline of a family for its theme. The hero of this novel, Daniele Solospin, longs to discover more about his own family in order to understand himself better: "Then what was I," he asks himself, "from where did I come, where did I put down my roots?"[23] His deep search into the world of his forefathers, whose character and actions he fashions with unsparing frankness, reminds one of Thomas Mann's preoccupation with the history of his family in Lübeck and their portrayal in *Buddenbrooks*.

Yet in contrast to Mann, Enzo Bettiza's hero Daniele comes to the realization that it can be dangerous to inquire too much into the past in order to investigate one's own origins. "Unfortunately, I know today with the same assurance that it is very dangerous to lead a boy, an adolescent, into a premature contact with the mystery of his own origins, especially if they are confused and dark."[24]

Daniele's longing for death grows out of the feeling of being lost; exactly like Hanno Buddenbrook he also has the feeling that life is not worth living and that one must offer it passive resistance:

> Thus, in a still dark and confused way, he had begun to perceive that he, in affliction, behaved like a thirsty man with a glass of fire. More than from thirst, he suffered from the impossibility of quenching it in the flames. The world burning from pain attracted him like a gaping volcano, rich in all those hellish burns which his instinct of preservation sought to resist passively, with drowsiness and listlessness.[25]

Also in Hanno Buddenbrook's character a certain indifference regarding life becomes apparent early, which is noticeable to the father, Thomas Buddenbrook, and disturbs him, especially since the latter has a presentiment of his own early death and longs for an energetic successor as director of his firm: "I can die earlier than we think, my son. You must be here! . . . Try to understand that your indifference distresses me!"[26]

Hanno's indifference and passivity, however, are still stronger than the father fears, and when the youth must choose between life and death, he offers no resistance to the temptation of death. While in spite of his loneliness and his despair Daniele endures his difficult life, Hanno is willingly ready to obey the voice of Death. He can no longer turn back and follow the summons of life, he jerks back "out of fear and aversion," and in response to the voice of Life "he shakes his head and stretches his hand out behind him in repulse and flees forward upon the way which has opened to him to escape."[27]

Just as Hanno is a child of his home city of Lübeck, Daniele Solospin's destiny is also closely interwoven with the people and history of his native city Trieste, that often-fought-over city, upon which three different cultures have imprinted their mark: the German-Austrian, the Italian, and the Slavic. For hundreds of years these features have determined the life of the people, and the character of the city is governed by representatives of the various nationalities. So already as a child Daniele was exposed to distinct types of people, and his upbringing in the period before the First World War was defined by these manifold influences.

Daniele's development unquestionably reminds one of that of Hans Castorp, who transcends his averageness in the international atmosphere of the magic mountain. Daniele is very early fascinated by the color and diversity of life in his native city, where he is especially drawn by the harbor as a center of international trade. "Trieste was in those days a lively and gay city. The harbor, where ships, goods, riches from the remotest corners of the world landed, seemed a swaying forest of masts interwoven by skeins of rigging, from which, whipped by the bora, waved the flags of all the peoples of the earth. The harbor was Daniele's favorite walk."[28]

As in Trieste the East and West thrust against one another, so in the restless, simmering period before the First World War new conflicts arose repeatedly among the races, nationalities, and classes. The evolution of the well-to-do merchant's son into a revolutionary does not seem to be an unusual occurrence in that epoch of political and social crises.

In addition to parallels with Thomas Mann's novels *Buddenbrooks* and *The Magic Mountain,* in Bettiza's *Il fantasma di Trieste* similarities to Mann's *Doctor Faustus,* as well, should not be overlooked. The life and destiny of Daniele Solospin are reported by a chronicler who relies in part upon Daniele's own diary. Thomas Mann had employed the same method in order to obtain a certain distance from the events which indeed strongly affected him personally. Since Bettiza's novel also appears to contain much that is autobiographical, he may have inserted the chronicler for the same reasons.

Daniele's fate is just as tragic as that of Adrian Leverkühn. Both are incapable of loving anyone, and above all a woman; by visiting a brothel both strive for a certain substitute for their lack of the ability to love, yet the attempts of both to master their lack of contact by this means end, although in different ways, disastrously. For both, the final alternative seems to be devotion and admiration, bordering on the homosexual, for a man of the same age, yet the shadow of disaster and destruction lies over this association as well. The fate of the hero is loneliness, since all those with whom they come into more intimate contact are sacrificed to destruction. Already as a small child Daniele experienced the death of his mother; as a boy, that of his beloved Slavic nanny. The fact that normal human contacts are denied to him is the price he must pay for his development as a man of modern times. This state of affairs becomes clear in Bettiza's novel in a crucial discussion: Daniele's conversation with the Devil in the semidarkness between day and night, which strongly calls to mind Adrian Leverkühn's encounter with the Devil in Palestrina. Adrian first of all feels the icy cold which streams out against him from the area, from the sofa, and makes him shudder. "Then of a sudden I feel struck by a cutting cold, as if one sat in a winter-warm room and all at once a window came open outward towards the frost. But came not from behind me, where the windows are, but falls on me from the front."[29] Daniele, also, is first aware of the presence of the Devil through the emanation of a cold which benumbs him. "Then he noticed that his feet and hands were ice-cold."[30]

This numbness quickly spreads over his entire body, so that the terrifying feeling becomes ever stronger in Daniele that he can no longer move, that he cannot flee from this sinister happening. "And yet he could no longer move, now that he was sweating ice, now that he felt confined, imprisoned within his own body as in a piece of meat suddenly deprived of elasticity, cold and heavy."[31] Just as the German composer Adrian Leverkühn is not sure whether he is awake or dreaming, the Italian is also in doubt whether his uncanny experience can be attributed to a state of exhaustion and sleep: "Or was he sleeping? Was not this humming in his ears perhaps the humming of sleep? But how can one imagine sleep without dreaming? Only by dreaming can one succeed, sometimes, in suspecting being submerged in sleep; and he was not dreaming. And therefore he was not sleeping."[32]

Yet just as with Adrian, in the case of Daniele as well, the sense of hearing is sharpened, he also records the words of the Devil accurately and in full alertness. "The only sense-organ which remained awake, indeed, too awake, in Daniele's cold body, was his hearing, whose sensitiveness, extraordinarily redoubled, amplified each tiniest nocturnal noise into a deep vibration."[33]

In Bettiza's novel also, as in *Doctor Faustus,* we find the Devil in the dark of the room sitting on a sofa, where—interrupted only by a cold and sinister laugh—he begins to unfold his ideas with diabolical cynicism. At the same time, again reminding one of *Doctor Faustus, Il fantasma di Trieste* is concerned with a discussion and clarification of social, artistic, and political problems. Daniele Solospin, like the heroes of many of Mann's tales, is an outsider to society, but while in the case of Mann the problem of the outsider, the alienation, the isolation, is generally symbolized by means of the fate of an artist, Bettiza presents it rather through a young man, who as the representative of a new age must overcome the bourgeois world of the nineteenth century in order to be fit for the new century. Indeed, all of Mann's ideals are contradicted by the evolution of Daniele, who in order to fight for a better future is prepared, as a Communistic functionary, to destroy the old traditions.

Although in Enzo Bettiza's novel many thoughts and events are wholly other than in the spirit of Thomas Mann; on the other hand, many motifs and incidents appear to point to an influence of the German writer on this young Italian author.

As a kind of homage by Bettiza to the writer from Lübeck may be considered the fact that concerning the grandfather of his hero Daniele, the Italian author reported that he had been a Consul in Bremen and Hamburg, which, like Mann's home, are Hanseatic cities. A friend of the Solospin family tells about the respect which from all sides had been shown to this forefather of Daniele. "Who does not remember the son of your great-grandfather, that is, your grandfather, Daniele, the famous Pier Paolo Solospin, Consul in Bremen and Hamburg, of whom even my father, in moments of lucidity, speaks as of a saint!"[34]

The motif of the hero who endeavors to find and understand himself also occurs in Italo Svevo's novel *Confessions of Zeno (La coscienza di Zeno)*. The Trieste-born Ettore Schmitz—who in protest against his German surname assumed the pseudonym Italo Svevo—also came, as did Enzo Bettiza, from the northeastern part of Italy, which is defined by Slavic and German influence. In his novel *Confessions of Zeno*, Svevo describes, similarly to Thomas Mann in *The Magic Mountain*, the development of a young man of the bourgeoisie, a development which reaches its conclusion with the beginning of the First World War. Through experiencing sickness and death, through encounters with a multitude of contemporaries, and confrontation with the most important intellectual currents of their time, the protagonists of both novels are allotted a maturation process.[35]

7. Mann's Effect in Italy in the Judgment of Contemporary Italian Writers

As was already mentioned in the previous accounts, the presentation of philosophical ideas and problems—preferred by the German writers—is traditionally incompatible with Italian literature. Hence it is hardly surprising that present-day German literature, and consequently also its great representative Thomas Mann, exercised no influence worth mentioning on the literary creativity of Italy.

In Vasco Pratolini's journal *Diario Sentimentale* is an entry from November 1935, from which it is evident that this important Italian writer rejected Thomas Mann's works as too philosophical and too intellectual. With the exception of the novel *Buddenbrooks*, the heroes of Mann's novels, and in particular of *The Magic Mountain*, appear sickly to Pratolini and therefore lacking true persuasive power.[36]

But when, nevertheless, certain traces or reminiscences of Thomas Mann's ideas can be detected in the works of some Italian authors such as Borgese, Lampedusa, Bettiza, and Svevo, then this evidence seems to rest on the fact that the same basic attitude towards the life of modern man is inherent to these Italians, namely, the feeling of isolation of the individual in society and the danger to man which is bound up with it. This view is also championed by Cesare Cases, who in an unpublished letter declared: "In reality the success of Thomas Mann in Italy is independent of a possible influence on Italian narrative, generally averse to the problematic element; rather, one could think that admiration for this author is due to the consciousness of estrangement."[37]

Modern Italian writers such as Ignazio Silone and Italo A. Chiusano confirmed in verbal and written statements to the author of this book that their work was not influenced by Thomas Mann, although both proffered unreserved admiration for the writings of Thomas Mann. Chiusano attributed this phenomenon to the fact that Mann, whose thought and writing is unquestionably European—indeed actually universally oriented—is yet basically so strongly bound to German tradition that to a certain degree he must remain foreign to Italian writers. "Mann, although a European, and in the final analysis a citizen of the world, still always remained in spirit, style, way of facing problems, cultural interests, personality, etc., a man profoundly, characteristically German. We Italians are much different, and even there where we admire in him the excellence of a sovereign spirit and art, we still face the world in a completely different way, with a completely different cast and sound and color."[38]

The critic Carlo Bernari mentioned a still further reason for the fact that Thomas Mann exercised such a slight influence on modern Italian literature. In Bernari's opinion the work of the German writer is so polymorphic and rich in content and style that it can be imitated only with difficulty: "The narrative of Mann is not like that of a Proust or a Joyce—nor even of a (Virginia) Woolf—which, limited as they are and unified by style and inspiration, lend themselves even to the flattest kind of imitation; but it is of a sort so manifold and varied, by language and by content, as to lend itself with difficulty to duplication."[39]

Without exception, the Italian writers and critics are convinced that Thomas Mann's work is much read and admired, to be sure, but is not regarded as a model for their own creative work. A further reason for this singular circumstance is seen by the critic Sergio Checconi in the fact that today Thomas Mann is regarded by many Italians as outmoded, since he appears to them to be too strongly bound to the nineteenth century. Checconi, however, is of the opinion that this attitude is due to a feeling of envy and awareness of their own shortcomings on the part of modern Italian writers: "In reality, even if very unjustly, today Mann is generally regarded in Italy as an antiquated, nineteenth-century writer; and my conviction that it is a matter of envy and of inability to attain the Mannian ideal of 'greatness' cannot, naturally, change things.''[40]

Not only in Italy, but also in the rest of the world, the following fact may be established: however little Thomas Mann's work exerted an effect on the creative work of other writers, the critics took an enthusiastic interest in his work and with the appearance of each new book alluded to the significance and greatness of its author.

8. Summary

The preceding investigation showed that the influences of Thomas Mann's works on Italian literature were felt only in isolated cases. Thus, in a work by Giuseppe Antonio Borgese, distinct parallels are found to Mann's *Song of the Little Child:* in the story *Tempesta nel nulla,* just as in Mann's piece, the motif of the boundless love of a father for his daughter, a love raised into the mythical, plays the leading rôle. Looking at the child, who is also called sister, brings back in both writers the memory of their forefathers, of family tradition. One is probably not wrong when, in a comparison of both works, one infers an apparent influence of Thomas Mann on the Italian writer.

Cesare Pavese, who belonged to the younger generation of Italian writers, shared with Thomas Mann a preference for the poetical moulding of mythological material and above all of the problem of time. Although Pavese saw in Mann a guide whom he admired and respected, nevertheless only very slight influences on his work may be discerned.

In contrast to Pavese, Elio Vittorini's attitude regarding Thomas Mann is entirely negative. His rejection is based on an intense antipathy against all speculative-intellectual writers, in whom he misses a closeness to nature and to the soul of the people.

In the novel *The Leopard,* by Prince Tomasi di Lampedusa, there are obvious parallels to Mann's *Buddenbrooks* and above all to *Royal Highness.* Although direct influence from the German writer is not excluded, one must attribute certain mutualities primarily to an affinity of both writers for the Russian and French novelists of the nineteenth century, to whom they both were deeply indebted.

The novel *Il fantasma di Trieste,* by the Italian novelist Enzo Bettiza, shows intensely striking similarities to Mann's *Buddenbrooks* and *Doctor Faustus.* In the treatment of the theme of the decline and destruction of a family and in connection with the appearance of the Devil, Bettiza was obviously strongly inspired by Thomas Mann. But beyond that, his novel is defined by the same basic mood as *Doctor Faustus:* Daniele Solospin and Adrian Leverkühn both suffer from lack of contact and isolation, which arise from a lack of the ability to love and whose result is a flight into the homosexual.

The fact that Thomas Mann's effect on Italian literature remained so limited can be attributed to various phenomena: the German writer was unquestionably very strongly rooted in the traditions of his country, and his way of thinking often remained alien to the Italian writers. Because of his close spiritual bond with the narrative art of the nineteenth century, he was further regarded by many modern Italian authors as "outmoded."

Although Thomas Mann found no direct imitators in Italy, one must at the same time bear in mind that, in the rest of Europe and above all in Germany, he had "created no school." On the other hand, Italian critics had repeatedly thoroughly occupied themselves with the work of Thomas Mann, for whom, from the beginning of his literary activity, the North-South tension was a "fascinating subject," and whose life and creative work were profoundly imbued with the longing of the northerner for Italy.

V
Results of the Investigation of Mann's Relationship with Italy

From earliest times, longing for the south has been inherent in the German's character. Favorable climate, refined culture, and also religious reasons induce him again and again to cross the Alps in order to partake of the wonders of Italy and there to receive stimulation and inspiration for his own intellectual and artistic creativity. If one traveller to Italy discovers the gateway to antiquity at the sight of the ancient ruins, for another it is the atmosphere of the south which he seeks: beauty of landscape, magic of Italian cities such as Venice, and idiosyncrasies of the people signify the true "Arcadia" to the German. Even in his youth, Thomas Mann felt an inclination for the south. As a twenty-year-old he set out upon his first journey to Italy and in the course of his life often returned there.

At first, Mann unquestionably was somewhat reserved as regards the Italian atmosphere. Although the intense colors, the noise, and the hot, dazzling sun fascinated him to a certain extent, he could at first find no close personal relationship to this "ambiente" so in contrast with his north German home. During his first sojourns in Rome and Palestrina, he was intensely conscious of his belonging to the northern world. And yet these early encounters with the Latin cultural sphere, to which Mann was basically linked by inheritance from his mother, left behind a deep impression, much deeper and more significant than he could at first suspect. Indeed, throughout his entire work, a registering of these encounters with the Italian world and its people became, in time, increasingly more noticeable, naturally often defined through the character of a particular figure, and consequently not to be unconditionally regarded as an expression of the writer's own views.

Already in Thomas Mann's early novellas, a part of the action was transferred to Italy. The youthful heroes of these works, lonesome in their north German environment and not understood by it, hope—although in vain—to find themselves in the south and to overcome their alienation from society. Thus, precisely owing to his immersion in the southern world, Tonio Kröger becomes aware of his belonging to the north.

In the novella *Gladius Dei*, Thomas Mann for the first time occupied himself with the Italian Renaissance: Although the action takes place in the

Munich of the turn of the century, the figure of the monk Hieronymus was modelled after the historical Savonarola. A few years later, in the drama *Fiorenza,* the author once more concerned himself with the epoch of Lorenzo il Magnifico; and here, too, the preacher from Florence plays the leading rôle.

Whereas *Fiorenza* centers about the religious and moral arguments between Savonarola and Lorenzo de' Medici, in *The Magic Mountain* and in his novella *Mario and the Magician* Mann gave political significance to the Italian element. While the figure of Settembrini embodied the concepts of freedom, liberalism, and humanism, the dangers of Fascism were symbolically pointed out through the magician Cipolla.

In *Doctor Faustus,* also, Italy became the setting of a sinister occurrence: It is in Palestrina that the Devil appears, to whom the German composer Adrian Leverkühn sells his soul. In this work, just as in *Mario and the Magician,* contemporary Italy was described. On the other hand, in the essay *Die Erotik Michelangelos* and also in the novel *The Holy Sinner,* characters and events from Italy's past come alive.

Hence in the work of Thomas Mann from the very beginnings to the end, one can trace his preoccupation with the land south of the Alps, with its history, its people, and its thought. The writer became increasingly aware of the close relationship between North and South and ever more strongly perceived it as one of the most important motifs in his creative work. At the same time he knew that with his love for Italy he shared in a long tradition, in the longing of the northerner for the south. In this ancient yearning Mann saw "the insufficiency in oneself, the need for completion and deliverance through the completely other, the south, the brightness, clarity and lightness, the *gift* of the beautiful . . . We know the rôle which Mantegna and Venice played in Dürer's life; and it is and remains symbolic that, for Goethe, the classical Walpurgisnacht stands next to the romantic one."[1]

In spite of the gradually strengthening spiritual bond with Italy, of which Thomas Mann himself was aware, it took a considerable time before the Italian critics began fully to appreciate his work. Not until after the bestowal of the Nobel Prize in 1929 was the attention of the Italian reader drawn towards Thomas Mann; however, during the thirties, Italian literary historians occupied themselves ever more thoroughly with his work. To be sure, after the conclusion of the Nazi-Fascist cultural agreement, the writer's name was very soon placed on the Black List, so that from 1938 to 1945 his works were no longer accessible in Italy. Yet after the ending of the Second World War, interest in Thomas Mann set in all the more strongly. In the year 1947 he was elected a member of the Accademia dei Lincei, and at the same time the publishing house Arnoldo Mondadori decided to bring out a complete edition of Mann's works in Italian translation. In 1952 the highly endowed Premio Feltrinelli was awarded to him, which demonstrated the love and great veneration which was now tendered to Mann's work.

On the basis of his high esteem in Italy, one could assume that the German writer had also exerted a strong effect on contemporary Italian literature. Through closer inspection of the works of modern Italian writers one can, however, determine only slight traces of influence from Mann's work. This fact can be explained variously. Traditionally, Italian literature has in general turned away from the subject matter treated by Thomas Mann. For another thing, it is almost impossible, for Latin writers above all, to rework inspirations gained from the work of Thomas Mann because it is so multiform in content and style. Unquestionably, Thomas Mann is also so strongly bound to the nineteenth century that to many of the modern Italian writers he seems outdated and no longer unconditionally representative. Nevertheless, in modern Italian novels various themes recur which Thomas Mann treated in his works: loneliness and isolation of the hero, alienation of man in a mechanized world, decline and destruction of an old family.

In general Italian literature takes the French, Russian, and in more recent times the American writers above all as models; nevertheless, in the case of some Italian authors, one can discern the same basic attitude towards modern life that Thomas Mann represented.

Mann's work has had only a limited influence on modern Italian literature; on the other hand, his contact with the land beyond the Alps was of inestimable value for his own human and artistic development. Thomas Mann was convinced that, through contact with the south, German writing and thought acquired a supranational dimension. Thus, in Mann's opinion, the "yearning attachment to the Mediterranean, its sun, its character" had "created German classicism." The significance of a synthesis of North and South is demonstrated not only in the case of Goethe, but also of Nietzsche, who grafted "the old antithesis of North and South, of Romantic and Classic" onto the antithesis "of National and European."[2]

Through overcoming his own conservative-nationalistic attitude and through contact with the Latin world, Thomas Mann became first of all European in the best sense of the word. Later the sphere of his life and creative work extended to the New World, to America, whose citizenship he pridefully embraced in order at last to feel like and prove to be a mediator between peoples and cultures, a true citizen of the world.

CHRONOLOGICAL TABLE

Thomas Mann's Trips to Italy

Year	Month	Place	Nature or Purpose of the Trip	Personal testimony
1895	July-October	Rome-Palestrina	First Italian sojourn - holiday with brother Heinrich	"Last year, then, I stayed in Italy, in Rome and environs. I passed the hot months in the mountains, at the end of September returned to the city." (*The Will to Happiness*)
1896	October (3 weeks)	Venice	Holiday stay	
1896	November	Naples, Via S. Lucia 28 II	Probably setting down the novella *Disillusionment*	"I live here . . . far too expensively, but with a very beautiful view of the sea and Vesuvius. I spent about 3 weeks in Venice, then went by ship to Ancona and from there via Rome directly here. I am very happy here. Only now, I discover, am I really in the south, the eminent proximity of the Orient which chimes in here causes this. It is very amusing." (To Kor-

Year	Month	Place	Nature or Purpose of the Trip	Personal testimony
				fiz Holm, Naples, 6.XI.1896.)
1896	From December	Rome, Via del Pantheon 57 II	Sojourn together with brother Heinrich—Extensive reading—Preparation of the novella volume *Little Herr Friedemann*	"I devoured, in the dense smoke of countless 3-Centesimi cigarettes, Scandinavian and Russian literature and wrote." *(A Sketch of my Life)*
1897	Summer	Rome	In collaboration with Heinrich the *Bilderbuch für artige Kinder,* with satirical poems and caricatures, was produced.—Plan for *Buddenbrooks,* first conceived of as a joint work of the brothers.	"Being used to having the Pantheon before my front door and to be able to look from the Pincio over the majestic city toward St. Peter's, I am apprehensive—as if of an evil destiny—to return to Munich's Schwanthal-desert next year." (To Otto Grautoff, Rome, 13.I.1897.)
				"In the summer one has to leave the city for a few months; we shall probably be going to Palestrina again, perhaps also to Naples and its environs." (To Otto Grautoff, Rome, 13.I.1897.)
1897	Summer	Palestrina, "Casa Bernardini"	Preparatory work for *Buddenbrooks*	"The real Europe and the most intensive culture are found

Year	Month	Place	Nature or Purpose of the Trip	Personal testimony
				only in the Latin countries, France, Italy, Spain—that is Europe." (To Otto Grautoff, Palestrina, 20.VIII.1897.)
1897	Fall	Rome, Via Torre Argentina 34 III	Beginning of writing of the novel. The first page of the original manuscript is dated "End October 1897."	"When I began to write *Buddenbrooks* I sat in Rome . . . three years I wrote on the book, with pains and faithfulness." *(Bilse und ich)*
1898	To the end of April	Rome		"Still in the course of my Roman sojourn my first little book appeared . . . I was allowed to see 'me' lying in the display windows of the Roman 'Librerie'." *(A Sketch of my Life)*
1901	May	Florence	Holiday stay. Friendship with the English girl Mary Smith, to whom Thomas Mann dedicated the novella *Gladius Dei:* "To M. S. in remembrance of our days in Florence."	"She is so very clever, and I am so stupid, to always love those who are clever, although for all that I cannot keep up in the long run." (To Heinrich Mann, 7.V.1901.) "The affair with the little English girl who looked as if she were created by Botticelli, only much merrier, was in the beginning a harmless flirt; eventually, however, it

Year	Month	Place	Nature or Purpose of the Trip	Personal testimony
				took on a strangely serious character, and indeed—believe it or not—mutually. The farewell was almost worthy of a stage performance." (To Paul Ehrenberg, Munich, 26.V.1901.)
1901	June July	Venice Mitter-bad near Merano	Holiday stay	"The publication of *Buddenbrooks* is coming closer to its end, thank Goodness. It was for me and for the printers a repulsive piece of work." (To Paul Ehrenberg, Mitterbad, 18.VII.1901.)
1901	5 November to 19 December	Riva on the Lago di Garda, Villa Cristoforo	Curative stay	
1902	2 October to 15 November	Riva on the Lago di Garda	Work on *Tonio Kröger*	"It is beautiful here and I am recovering markedly. In the morning I always row several hours on the lake and especially at the beginning was again completely enchanted." "I even work, although very prudently and even more line by line than usual, since what I have in mind (a lengthy novella) is again something so 'difficile' that it abso-

Year	Month	Place	Nature or Purpose of the Trip	Personal testimony
				lutely must have some time." (To Kurt Martens, 16.X.1902.)
1904	16 April to 6 May	Riva on the Lago di Garda	Curative stay	"Although I usually will not admit it, I will nevertheless confess it to you just once, that I am really a little jealous of the sciences and secretly would have a fiendish delight if you would quite thoroughly neglect them. This is old-fashioned, sentimental and mean, I know!" (To his future wife, Katja Pringsheim, Riva, end of April 1904.)
1907	May	Venice	Holidays on the Lido	"At the time of the premiere (of *Fiorenza*) I was bathing on the Lido and the sea held me fast. But tomorrow I travel with my wife to the (ought one to believe it?) sixth performance." (To Hilde Diestel, Munich, 22.V.1907.)
1909	Spring	Livorno	Holiday with brother Heinrich. Work on an essay critical of culture and the times, which was not completed.	

Year	Month	Place	Nature or Purpose of the Trip	Personal testimony
1911	Mid-May	Brioni, off Istria	Holiday stay with wife Katja	
1911	26 May to 2 June	Lido at Venice, Hôtel des Bains	Holiday with wife Katja	"Yesterday we moved in here, after having spent a wonderful vacation at the Lido. (For Brioni was nothing for any length of time)." (To Hans von Hülsen, Bad Tölz, 15.VI.1911.)
1913	19 June to 12 July	Viareggio	Holiday	
1923	October	Bolzano, Hotel Austria	Holiday. Numerous meetings with Gerhart Hauptmann	"Every night we have drinks with Hauptmann, who is a rather good old man." (To Heinrich Mann, Bolzano, 17.X.1923.)
1924	October	Sestri Levante	Holiday stay. The first ten days with Ernst Bertram	*The Magic Mountain* is completed—a triumph of stubbornness, even if nothing more. Here I am getting a rest." (To Hans von Hülsen, Sestri Levante, 17.X.1924.) "My wife and I have been here for one week or two, respectively, with the two little ones, Michele and Elisabetha—for I went ahead of them after the completion

Year	Month	Place	Nature or Purpose of the Trip	Personal testimony
				of my novel." (To Georg Martin Richter, Sestri-Levante, 17.X.1924.)
1925	2 March	Venice-Cattaro	To commence a Mediterranean cruise with wife Katja to Egypt	"I am going on a journey at the beginning of March: Mediterranean voyage of five weeks." (To Julius Bab, Munich, 22.II.1925.)
1925	25 March May	Naples Florence Venice	Participation in "International Culture Week" Holiday stay	
1925	September October	Casamicciola on Ischia, Hotel Pithaecusa	Holiday with wife and youngest children Michael and Elisabeth	"Many thanks for your good offices on my behalf with the *Nouvelle Revue Française*. I am impatiently expecting the next issues, especially in connection with your article on *The Magic Mountain*." (To Félix Bertaux, Casamicciola, 27.X.1925.)
1926	31 August to 13 September	Forte dei Marmi	Holiday with wife and the two youngest children. Episode with the magician, which found its recording in *Mario and the Magician*.	"We must send you our warm greetings from this beautiful place where we are spending some weeks with our children. I am now fully recovered, and we are enjoying sea, mountains, and sunshine. Nevertheless, this

Year	Month	Place	Nature or Purpose of the Trip	Personal testimony
				time we are not fully satisfied in the south, next summer we shall return to the Baltic Sea full of repentance." (To Ida Boy-Ed, Forte dei Marmi, 8.IX.1926.)
1930	Mid-February	Genoa	Start of Mediterranean trip to Egypt and Palestine	"It was a significant trip, far up the Nile into Nubia, then slowly via Aswan,
	8 April	Genoa	End of the trip	Luxor, Cairo, into the Near East. Was I careful!" (To Maximilian Brantl, Munich, 29.IV.1930.)
1934	July	Venice	Participation in an "International Art Congress"	"The profit was the reunion with the city and its beach island, always loved for profound and complex reasons, where a certain story, now already twenty years old, took place." (To Karl Kerényi, Zürich, 4.VIII.1934.)
1947	30 July to 3 August	Meina on the Lago Maggiore	With wife Katja, houseguest of the publisher Arnoldo Mondadori. Press conference with Italian and German journalists.	"From there (Zürich) one has in addition all kinds of excursions, also into Italy to Mondadori and to Lucerne for a meeting with Hesse." (To Kitty and Alfred Neumann, Flims, 14.VII.1947.)
1952	September	Venice	Address at the UNESCO	

Year	Month	Place	Nature or Purpose of the Trip	Personal testimony
			Congress on *The Artist and Society*.	
1953	20 to 30 April	Rome	Reception by the "Accademia Nazionale dei Lincei," to express thanks for the Antonio Feltrinelli Prize.	"So tomorrow we are flying, then. Of course I am pleased, to some extent, about seeing Rome again, but nevertheless, as usual, I am travelling unwillingly. At the end of the month we want to be back." (To Lavinia Mazzucchetti, Zürich, 19.IV.1953.)
1953	29 April	Rome	Private audience with Pope Pius XII.	"Kind regards from Rome just at the moment of our departure. The card shows you St. Peter's. Yesterday I visited the Pope, His Holiness Pius XII. He was very friendly." (To Frido and Toni Mann, Rome, 30.IV.1953.)
1953	End of April	Palestrina	Seeing again the little mountain town where he spent the summer of 1896 with his brother Heinrich.	"They were exceedingly rich days, filled with impressions (in Rome and Palestrina) upon which I reflect with emotion." (To R. Bianchi Bandinelli, Zürich, 3.V.1953.)
1954	4 and 5 February	Rome	First stop on the trip Zürich-Sicily	"In a few days we are supposed to travel to Sicily—why and for

Year	Month	Place	Nature or Purpose of the Trip	Personal testimony
				what purpose I do not quite understand. In Morocco there is snow, and in Taormina it will also be bitter cold. . ." (To Erika Mann, Zürich, 27.I.1954.)
1954	6 to 21 February	Taormina, Hotel San Domenico Palace	Holiday stay with wife Katja	"Here we are, after two days in Rome . . . it is mild and we think, amichevolmente (what is that in German?) about the 'Paver of the Way.' The journey was far, and from Milan to Rome we had an unheated sleeping-car, so that one spent the night as if in the open air. By no means salubrious. Now we are taking care of ourselves and the Ionian Sea glitters." (To Richard Schweizer, Taormina, 8.II.1954).
1954	22 February to 1 March	Florence Rome—	Meeting with daughter Elisabeth Mann Borgese	"A double visit to Rome, the reunion with the Bargello in Florence, a few pleasant days with Medi, and finally, together with her, an excellent performance of Verdi's *Otello* at the Scala in Milan have, however, compensated

Year	Month	Place	Nature or Purpose of the Trip	Personal testimony
				us so much in the end that we do not regret undertaking the trip." (To Bruno Walter, Zürich, 12.III.1954.) "The city (Rome) is, as are all today, over-motorized, and one can hardly go for a stroll anymore on the Pincio. But it still enraptures me again and again by the perspective of the millennia that it offers, and when I see San Pietro again or the Foro Romano, then my heart beats faster." (To Klaus Mampell, Zürich, 17.V.1954.)

NOTES

Chapter I

1 Thomas Mann, *Gesammelte Werke* (Frankfurt, 1960), Vol. XI, 103. Subsequently cited as *Werke* with Roman volume numbers and Arabic page numbers.

2 Thomas Mann, *Briefe I* (Frankfurt, 1961), 7. The three volumes of letters (ed. Erika Mann) (Frankfurt, 1961, 1963, 1965) are subsequently cited as *Briefe, I, II* and *III,* followed by Arabic page numbers.

3 *Werke XI,* 103

4 *Ibid.*

5 Thomas Mann spoke of these mountains somewhat carelessly as the "Sabine Mountains."

6 The question of whether the writing of the novel *Buddenbrooks* was actually begun in Palestrina is still disputed. Even Thomas Mann appeared not to have been clear about it, yet in his *Lebensabriss,* completed in February 1930, he maintained: "Already in Palestrina I had, after zealous preparations, begun to write *Buddenbrooks (Werke XI,* 104). But in the *Lebenslauf,* written at almost the same time for the book *Les Prix Nobel en 1929,* he described it differently: "It was also in Rome, where I began writing the novel *Buddenbrooks" (Werke XI,* 414).

In a third *Lebenslauf,* written in 1936 for America, on the other hand, he reported: "And it was also in this year of my Italian hideaway, in Palestrina, the birthplace of the great composer, in the Sabine Mountains, that I began to write the novel *Buddenbrooks, Verfall einer Familie,* which I then, a twenty-five-year-old, completed in Munich and which was destined to become one of the greatest German literary successes ever, a true German book of family devotions." *(Werke XI,* 451)

On the first sheet of the *Buddenbrooks* manuscript, in the Thomas Mann Archive in Zürich, we find the dating which one may probably consider as accurate: "Rome, end of October 1897." It is thus to be assumed that Thomas Mann only began the actual setting down of his novel in Rome after his return to the Eternal City in Autumn of 1897, but that the most important preparations go back as early as the summer weeks previously spent in Palestrina. When he returned to Munich in April 1898, the manuscript begun in Rome—in the writer's own words—"is already dangerously swollen." *(Werke XI,* 117)

7 As if by a miracle, following the destruction of the hotel "Casa Bernardini" through the bombs of the Second World War, the guest book with the entry "Thomas Mann, poeta di Monaco," was recovered, and in memory of the great German writer's stay the little street of steps in Palestrina was christened "Via Thomas Mann."

8 Heinrich Mann, "Mein Bruder." *Ein Zeitalter wird besichtigt* (Berlin, 1947), 232

9 Details in Chapter II, Section 8: *Doctor Faustus*

10 *Werke XI*, 117

11 *Briefe I*, 70

12 Letter to Hans von Hülsen, quoted in Herbert Lehnert, *Thomas Mann— Fiktion, Mythos, Religion* (Stuttgart, 1965), 121

13 *Werke XI*, 123

14 Naturally *Felix Krull* is meant.

15 Inge Jens, ed., *Thomas Mann an Ernst Bertram* (Pfullingen, 1960), 18. (Mann had first planned a novella by the title of "Zauberberg.")

16 Jens, *Mann an Bertram*, 130

17 *Werke XI*, 357

18 *Ibid.*

19 Jens, *Mann an Bertram*, 139

20 Cf. Thomas Mann, *Lebensabriss, Werke XI*, 124: "The significant, that is nothing more than what is rich in association, and I remember well the grateful understanding with which, as Ernst Bertram read to us out of the manuscript the profound Venetian chapter of his Nietzsche mythology, I heard mentioned the title of my story."

21 Jens, *Mann an Bertram*, 140

22 Jens, *Mann an Bertram*, 145

23 Jens, *Mann an Bertram*, 152

24 Details in Chapter II, Section 7: *Mario and the Magician*

25 Jens, *Mann an Bertram*, 152

26 Lavinia Mazzucchetti, "Thomas Mann und der Zauberer." *Die Zeit*, No. 32 (6 August 1965), 10

27 *Briefe I*, 369

28 *Briefe I*, 317–318

29 Cf. Klaus Schröter, *Thomas Mann in Selbstzeugnissen und Dokumenten* (Reinbek, 1964), 138, 140

30 *Briefe III*, 264

31 *Briefe III*, 294

32 *Briefe III*, 295

33 *Briefe III*, 294

34 *Briefe III*, 295–296

35 *Briefe III*, 296

36 *Briefe III*, 294–295

37 *Briefe III*, 324

38 *Briefe III*, 331

39 Thomas Mann—Karl Kerényi, *Gespräch in Briefen* (Zürich, 1960), 198–199

40 *Werke XII*, 577

41 *Ibid.*

42 *Ibid.*

43 *Werke XII*, 576–577

44 Herbert Wegener, ed. Thomas Mann, *Briefe an Paul Amann* (Lübeck, 1959), 54

45 "Über Dante," *Jugend* (Munich), No. 24 (September 1921), 622

46 *Ibid.*

47 Lavinia Mazzuchetti, born in Milan in 1889, was, after student days in her native city, already prominent in 1911 with her first book, *Schiller e l'Italia*. After earning her Doctorate of Philosophy, she spent the years from 1912 to 1913 in Germany, which, for most of her countrymen, was at that time still more or less *terra incognita* as to its literature. She wished to experience it for herself, in order then to use her practical knowledge and encounters in the capacity of a mediator between German and Italian literature.

From 1917 to 1924 she was employed as a lecturer; thereafter, until 1929 as Professor at the University of Milan, from which she was removed on account of her anti-Fascist attitude. Professionally, this was the hardest blow of her life; yet henceforth all of her energies were applied to activity as a free-lance writer, literary historian, translator, and critic. In the Milan publishing house Mondadori, she became the editor of the works of Goethe, Gottfried Keller, Thomas Mann, Stefan Zweig, Hans Carossa, Ernst Wiechert; and, in 1962 after the death of Hermann Hesse, she was commissioned to prepare a five-volume Italian edition of his works. In innumerable newspaper and magazine articles, in essays, and in forewords to her editions appearing at the Mondadori press, to the end of her life she introduced her countrymen to the writings of Kafka, Döblin, Rilke, Hofmannsthal, Schnitzler, Werfel, Gerhart Hauptmann, and many others, with most of whom she was linked in friendship.

If one looks at the titles of her works, one then becomes aware of the breadth of her interests and realizes that she was capable of interpreting the entire evolution of German literature from the earliest times up to expressionism and the present: *August Wilhelm Schlegel und die italienische Literatur* (1917); *Il nuovo secolo della letteratura tedesca* (1926); *I Nibelunghi* (1927); *La vita di Goethe* (1932; 1949); *Goethe e il 'Cenacolo' di Leonardo* (1939); *Die Schweiz und Italien* (1941); she was the editor of the great, twelve-volume, complete edition of the works of Thomas Mann; and, finally, in 1962, his *Lettere a italiani* were selected, translated, and annotated by her.

Lavinia Mazzucchetti dedicated the greatest part of her life's work to the writings of Thomas Mann, whose trailblazer and leading interpreter she became in Italy. To be sure, the beginning, in the twenties, was made everything but easy for her. Hence, for example, in 1927 a leading Milanese press rejected her offer to let them publish a translation of his novella *Disorder and Early Sorrow (Unordnung und frühes Leid)*, even though she had placed at their disposal the rights without license fees, granted to her by the author.

48 Jens, *Mann an Bertram*, 93

49 Jens, *Mann an Bertram*, 120

50 Unpublished letter from Lavinia Mazzucchetti to Thomas Mann. Copy in the possession of the author of this work:

> Ich habe den Ausschnitt aus der *NZZ* tüchtig herumgehen lassen und viele haben sich gefreut, und ich muss sogar Ihre Worte schnell übersetzen, um sie einigen Sie verehrenden, aber nicht deutschkundigen Freunden zu übermitteln. Es ist ein grosser Trost, dass Sie überhaupt da sind, nicht nur als Künstler, auch als Mensch, und es gehört zu den vielen guten Dingen dieser Jahre, dass

man einige menschlich sichere Anhaltspunkte in dem Wirbelsturz behält, und auch, dass man nie an Ihnen irre zu werden braucht. Also: haben Sie Dank! Und wenn wir es auch nicht so bald erleben: Ihre Worte leben und bleiben und tun dem Deutschtum gut. Ich habe beinahe mit Erstaunen beim Lesen Ihres Briefes an meiner Bewegung und Erschütterung festgestellt, wie sehr ich durch zwanzig Jahre Kulturverbindung an dem echten Deutschland noch hänge . . ., obwohl ich es so oft leichtsinnig mit dem unechten verwechsle und beschimpfe. Und so wie mir geht's vielen, und allen haben Sie in der richtigen Stunde geholfen. Grazie.

51 In summer 1935 at the Salzburg Festival, Thomas Mann became personally acquainted with Arturo Toscanini, whom he had long admired as a great artist and person.

52 "Mia cara e buona amica. Lei è un tesoro. La ringrazio infinitamente d'avermi mandato la traduzione della risposta di Thomas Mann al 'sehr geehrter Herr Dekan ecc. ecc. di Bonn . . .' Magnifica—commovente—profonda e umana. Grazie ancora per la Sua nobile fatica a mio riguardo." Quoted after L. Mazzucchetti, *Lettere a italiani* (Milan, 1962), 34

53 *Briefe II*, 15

54 Borgese, who was born in 1882 in the province of Palermo on Sicily, was the founder of the journals *Medusa* and *Hermes* and contributor to many other important Italian publications. From 1907 to 1908 he was the Berlin correspondent of the newspapers *La Stampa* and *Il Corriere della Sera*. In 1921 appeared his major novel *Rubè*, which dealt with the dilemma of a young Italian intellectual who, by means of continual merciless self-analysis, alienates himself from life and loses all hold thereon.

In American exile, in the years 1935 to 1937, Borgese wrote a first detailed study of the essence and history of Fascism in order thereby to bring the dangers of this movement before the eyes of the American public above all. In the first part of this book written in English, *Goliath, the March of Fascism,* Borgese concerned himself with the mythos which prepared the way for Fascism. He regarded Dante, Petrarch, and Machiavelli as the creators of this mythos, which is based on belief in the Roman Empire and the cult of antiquity. The result of this glorification was the desire to rule the world and therewith the foundation for the nationalism represented by d'Annunzio and Mussolini and their concepts regarding race. Borgese was convinced that the rise of Fascism could have been stemmed, however, through the intervention of the leading Italian classes, the officer corps, and even of the Vatican. In the last analysis, he therefore concludes, the tragedy of his homeland came about through the collective fault of the Italian people.

55 *Briefe II*, 124

56 *Briefe II*, 378

57 *Briefe II*, 183

58 *Briefe II*, 172

59 "For Thomas Mann—the renowned German who does not allow one to despair of the future—cordially Sforza."

60 "Mon cher Comte, C'est avec un plaisir intense que j'ai lu votre livre sur l'Italie et les Italiens. Je vous remercie sincèrement de me l'avoir envoyé et encore avec une si flatteuse dédication. On ne saurait traîter avec plus d'esprit, de compréhension, d'élégance et d'autorité un sujet sur lequel le monde ne pourra jamais

être assez éclairé—et qu'il est tellement curieux de connaître." *(Briefe II, 204)*

61 "Vous êtes heureux! Vous pouvez déclarer que, pour votre pays, le fascisme est quelque chose d'étranger et contre nature. Ce serait difficile de prouver que le national-socialisme joue le même rôle en Allemagne . . . Votre conviction que 'la longue formation historique des Italiens leur permettra de se trouver prêts pour le cadre plus large que l'avenir créera pour tous les peuples de l'Europe' est beaucoup mieux fondée que les espérances analogues que notre pays et notre peuple peuvent nous inspirer. Et pourtant il est peut-être permis de croire que l'Allemagne de Dürer, de Bach, de Kant et de Goethe, l'Allemagne qui a créé 'l'Iphigénie,' 'le Fidelio' et la 'Neuvième Symphonie' a un souffle historique qui ira plus loin que celui du nazisme et du racisme. Après tout l'on pourrait même dire que le peuple des Allemands, essentiellement non-politiques comme ils sont, est d'une certaine façon prédestiné pour le monde unifié et dépolitisé qui doit se former après l'abolition des autonomies nationales et que, dans une pareille situation, il aurait l'occasion de déployer ses meilleures qualités." *(Briefe II, 204–205)*

62 *Briefe II*, 294

63 *Briefe II*, 177

64 *Werke XI*, 182–183

65 *Briefe II*, 195

66 The philosopher-historian Benedetto Croce (1866–1952), from the Abruzzi, was the chief representative of Neo-Idealism against the predominance of Positivism. In his internationally renowned literary journal *La Critica,* appearing since 1903, and whose editor he was for over fifty years, he championed his ideas and applied them in his interpretations of Italian and foreign writings. At that time he held the view that literature and art were created intuitively without any influence from the intellect, and accordingly contained no moral or philosophical aims at all. Form and content must constitute a unity. The critic has the duty of judging a work of art *in se* and *per se,* independent of social and political stipulations of the time. Because of his theories Croce soon became the most influential personality in the field of Italian literature for the first half of the twentieth century. From 1920 to 1921 he held the post of Minister of Education and Cultural affairs of his country. Although a convinced opponent of Mussolini, even after the latter's seizure of power in October 1922 he continued to remain in Italy where, however, he lived completely withdrawn on his estate. Owing to his high international repute the government did not dare to undertake any steps whatsoever against him, although it was no secret that he was gathering an ever greater band of followers, "i crociani," around him. With increasing age Croce became ever more strongly aware of his political responsibility; he recognized that the purely aesthetic must be supplemented by taking an active position regarding the questions of the day as well as by a practical realization of his ideas.

67 "Pur mo venian li tuoi pensier tra i miei
   con simile alto e con simile faccia,
   si che d'entrambi un sol consiglio fei."

68 *Briefe II,* 570

69 Werke XI, 211–212

70 Cf. Lienhard Bergel, "Thomas Mann and Benedetto Croce," in Charles Neider, ed., *The Stature of Thomas Mann* (New York, 1947), 235–241

71 "Lo giorno se n'andava, e l'aer bruno

> toglieva gli animai che sono in terra
> dalle fatiche loro, ed io sol uno
> m'apparecchiava a sostener la guerra
> sì del cammino e sì della pietate,
> che ritrarrà la mente che non erra.
> O Muse, o alto ingegno, or m'aiutate,
> o mente che scrivesti ciò ch'io vidi,
> qui si parrà la tua nobilitate.''

72 "Per quanto è nelle mie possibilità (materiali e di preparazione intellettuale) sto seguendo con un interesse veramente nuovo per me, l'opera di quello ch'io giudico (e Dio mi correga se sbaglio) il più geniale e completo artista del nostro tempo, Thomas Mann. Già risale a molto tempo fa il mio incontro con esso nella storia delle mie letture, e fu con la 'Montagna Incantata,' romanzo che a mio parere è di una perfezione stilistica e narrativa rarissima. Più tardi la mia conoscenza si arricchì, e quello che mi era sembrato uno degli scrittori più difficili a comprendersi (i colloqui nel su citato romanzo fra il signor Settembrini e Naphta, e lo stesso Hans Castorp, e il finale, così struggente ed impreveduto, e tutta quell'atmosfera di malattia, di decadenza, di ambiguità del libro) ebbene, nelle opere ch'io lessi in seguito, Thomas Mann mi si rivelò sempre più affascinante e comprensible.'' (Undated letter from Daniele Manini to Lavinia Mazzucchetti. Original in the possession of the author of this work.)

73 The Milanese press A. Mondadori without doubt ranks today among the largest and most important publishing houses of Italy. Arnoldo Mondadori, born in a small village near Mantua in 1889 as the son of an artisan, could with good reason call himself a self-made man: he once began as an apprentice in a little printing-works, until in 1912 in Verona he acquired his own printing shop and therewith began his successful career as a publisher. Arnoldo Mondadori died in the spring of 1971. His son Alberto, born in 1914, joined his father's firm quite early, soon rose to Publishing Consultant and Literary Director and today is Vice-President of the important publishing enterprise, into which in 1958 was incorporated the cultural press "Il Saggiatore.'' Two extremely popular weekly journals, *Tempo* and *Epoca,* were also founded by him, and as their editor he has personal responsibility for them. Finally, he occupied himself with film work as a hobby, and in 1935 won the international prize for 8mm film in Venice for his film "I ragazzi della Via Paal.'' Alberto Mondadori has also made a name for himself as a lyric poet: in 1959 *Canto d'ira e d'amore per l'Ungheria* appeared, an epic poem, which treats with the tragedy of the Hungarian revolt. His works of biography and contemporary history, *Figure nel tempo* and *Il conto della vita,* came out in book form in 1963 and 1965, respectively. Alberto Mondadori died in 1976.

74 L. Mazzucchetti, *Lettere a italiani* (Milan, 1962), 65–66. Subsequently cited as *Lettere,* followed by Arabic page numbers.

75 Although Lavinia Mazzucchetti unreservedly recommended Bacchelli's novel for reading and publication, it was no longer mentioned by Thomas Mann in later correspondence. Several years went by before the appearance of the book in English translation in New York; however, not in the Alfred A. Knopf press.

76 Luigi Dallapiccola, born in Istria in 1904, became internationally renowned chiefly through chamber music compositions, two operas "Volo di Notte'' (1940)

and ''Il Prigioniero'' (1949), as well as a ballet ''Marsia'' (1948). As early as 1934 Dallapiccola, who at that time taught in the conservatory in Florence, had given piano instruction to the writer's second eldest daughter, Monika Mann, and as a token of gratitude from her father, received his works with a handwritten dedication. But not until 1952 in New York did the two men become personally acquainted. Luigi Dallapiccola died in 1975.

77 *Lettere*, 74

78 ''Mi sono annotato molti punti della Sua lettera, specie dove Lei parla del giovane amico che le regalò la 'Melancolia' di Dürer e che si sottrasse alla vita. Divido il Suo dolore per lui. Non sono passati ancora due anni da quando perdetti il mio figlio maggiore Klaus, uno scrittore molto dotato che si è dato volontariamente la morte. Non poteva vivere in un mondo come quello di cui Lei parla nella Sua lettera dicendo cose molto vere.'' *(Lettere, 85–86)*

79 Bianchi Bandinelli (born 1900 in Siena, died 1975) is the author of many standard works and, not only because of his excellent knowledge of the German language, was a welcome Cicerone for the visiting couple. His great energy made it possible for him to combine the profession of a University professor with that of a politican.

80 R. Bianchi Bandinelli, ''Un incontro a Roma,'' *Il Contemporaneo*, II (4 June 1955), 4

81 *Briefe* III, 297

82 *Ibid.*

83 *Briefe III*, 297–298

84 *Briefe III*, 418–419

Chapter II

1 Cf. Chapter I, Note 4

2 *Werke VIII*, 56

3 Further details in Chapter II, Part 4: *Death in Venice*

4 *Werke VIII*, 56

5 *Werke VIII*, 62

6 *Werke VIII*, 135–136

7 *Werke VIII*, 275

8 *Werke VIII*, 337

9 *Werke VIII*, 290

10 *Werke VIII*, 290–291

11 *Werke VIII*, 305–306

12 *Werke VIII*, 198

13 Alfred Teichmann, *Savonarola in der deutschen Dichtung (Berlin, 1937)*, 42

14 *Werke VIII*, 197

15 *Werke VIII*, 200–201

16 Th. C. van Stockum, *Von Friedrich Nicolai bis Thomas Mann* (Groningen, 1962), 326

17 *Werke VIII*, 214–215

18 *Briefe I*, 18

19 *Briefe I*, 19

20 *Briefe I*, 19

21 *Briefe I*, 17
22 *Briefe I*, 23
23 *Briefe I*, 25
24 *Briefe I*, 20
25 *Briefe I*, 20
26 Ernst Steinmann, *Ghirlandaio* (Bielefeld, 1897), 47
27 *Briefe III*, 408
28 *Werke VIII*, 1064
29 *Werke VIII*, 1018
30 *Werke VIII*, 1018
31 *Werke XII*, 94
32 *Werke VIII*, 1066
33 *Werke XII*, 96
34 *Werke VIII*, 990
35 *Werke VIII*, 988–989
36 *Werke XI*, 561
37 *Werke XI*, 561
38 *Werke VIII*, 987
39 *Werke VIII*, 447
40 *Werke VIII*, 461
41 *Werke VIII*, 463
42 *Werke VIII*, 464
43 *Werke VIII*, 474
44 *Werke VIII*, 480
45 *Werke VIII*, 480
46 *Werke VIII*, 480–481
47 *Werke VIII*, 483
48 *Werke VIII*, 483
49 *Werke VIII*, 484
50 *Werke VIII*, 488
51 *Werke VIII*, 487
52 *Werke VIII*, 490
53 *Werke VIII*, 491
54 *Werke VIII*, 499
55 *Werke VIII*, 501
56 *Werke VIII*, 503
57 *Werke VIII*, 506
58 *Werke XI*, 394
59 *Hans Kasdorff, Der Todesgedanke im Werke Thomas Manns* (Leipzig, 1932), 95–96
60 *Werke XI*, 850
61 August Graf von Platen, *Sämtliche Werke in vier Bänden* (Stuttgart, 1882), I, 130:
    Wer die Schönheit angeschaut mit Augen
    Ist dem Tode schon anheimgegeben.
62 von Platen, 131:
    Wen der Pfeil des Schönen je getroffen
    Ewig währt für ihn der Schmerz der Liebe.

63 Cf. Gerhart Hauptmann, *Und Pippa tanzt*
64 *Werke VIII*, 450
65 *Werke VIII*, 62
66 *Werke VIII*, 446
67 *Werke VIII*, 1087:
    Wisse, du bist im Osten gezeugt. Es zeugte im Märchen
    Nordisches Seefahrerblut dich, nach Abenteuern begierig,
    Doppelt ist deine Heimat, niederdeutsch und exotisch.
68 *Werke VIII*, 1087:
    Wie meinem Sinn die Vaterstadt zwiefach stehet: am Hafen
    Einmal der Ostsee, gotisch und grau, doch als Wunder des Aufgangs
    Noch einmal, entrückt, die Spitzbögen maurisch verzaubert,
    In der Lagune,—vertrautestes Kindheitserbe und dennoch
    Fabelfremd, ein ausschweifender Traum.
69 *Werke VIII*, 1088:
    Fand er nicht, heimischen Wasserruch witternd, die Rathaus-Arkaden,
    Wie sie Börse hielten, die wichtigen Bürger der Freistadt,
    Wieder am Dogenpalast, mit seiner gedrungenen Bogen-
    Halle, worüber die leichtere schwebet in zierlichen Lauben?
    Nein, nicht leugne man mir geheimnisvolle Beziehung
    Zwischen den Handelshäfen, den adligen Stadtrepubliken,
    Zwischen der Heimat nicht und dem Märchen, dem östlichen Traume!
70 *Ibid.:*
    Naschte nicht weihnachtlich der Knabe die wonnige Speise,
    Weit berühmt durch das Land, die die heimischen Zuckerbäcker
    Formten in Tortengestalt, aufprägend des türmigen Stadttors
    Bild der Masse, indes sie gewiss doch, die klebrige Manna,
    Aus dem Orient stammt, ein Haremsnaschwerk aus Mandeln,
    Rosenwasser and Zucker, und, getauft auf Sankt Markus,
    Über Venedig kam in die Heimat. Mazapan heisst sie. . .
71 Thomas Mann, *Briefe an Paul Amann* (Lübeck, 1959), 43
72 *Werke XI*, 392
73 Jens, *Mann an Bertram*, 139
74 *Werke III*, 143
75 *Werke III*, 89
76 Hans M. Wolff, *Thomas Mann, Werk und Bekenntnis* (Bern, 1957), 67
77 See the investigation on pp. 66–72 regarding the connection of Lodovico
    Settembrini with the historical Luigi Settembrini.
78 *Werke III*, 221
79 *Werke III*, 222
80 *Werke III*, 136
81 *Werke III*, 136
82 *Werke III*, 136
83 *Werke III*, 563
84 *Werke III*, 215
85 Wolff, *Thomas Mann*, 65
86 *Werke III*, 216
87 *Werke III*, 216

88 *Werke III,* 216

89 Wolff, *Thomas Mann,* 65

90 *Werke III,* 341

91 *Werke III,* 710

92 *Werke III,* 714

93 *Werke III,* 967

94 Hans Mayer, *Thomas Mann, Werk und Entwicklung* (Berlin, 1950), 141

95 *Ibid.*

96 *Werke III,* 969

97 "Infelice! Che cosa fai per l'amor di Dio!", *Werke III,* 980

98 "Gli italiani per colpa loro e della fortuna perderono libertà, indipendenza, costume ed ogni cosa più diletta all'uomo; e ritennero soltanto ciò che non potevano perdere, la loro natura, che è un'armonia di concetti e un'assennatezza nell'arte. Quest'armonia ed assennatezza divenne abito della mente, ed applicata alle credenze, alle scienze, alla politica e alle varie parti della vita, ci fece risorgere. Se noi smetteremo questo abito, saremo perduti per sempre; se lo serberemo, adoperandolo nelle cose della vita, acquisteremo importanza molta fra le nazioni. Da tanti anni abbiamo lavorato con l'arte, e siamo riusciti a dare unità alla patria nostra: con l'arte ancora lavoreremo per dare libertà e pace alla coscienza di tutti i cristiani." Luigi Settembrini, *Lezioni di letteratura italiana* (Florence, 1964), II, 1182–1183

99 Pasquale Villari, *Studies Historical and Critical* (London, 1907), 154

100 Villari, *Studies,* 143

101 "Nel mondo non vi sono che due soli partiti, gli uomini onesti, ed i birbanti. Io mi sono sforzato sempre di appartenere agli onesti, e non mi sono brigato mai dei nomi, perchè ho veduto molte opere nefande commesse da uomini detti o realisti, o liberali, o assolutisti, o repubblicani, o costituzionali. Io amo la libertà, la quale per me significa l'esercizio dei propri diritti senza offendere nessuno, significa giustizia severa, significa ordine, significa rispetto ed obbedienza alle leggi ed alle autorità. Questa libertà io amo caldamente, questa è la libertà desiderata dagli uomini onesti: e se amarla è delitto, mi confesso reo, e ne accetto la pena." Luigi Settembrini, "Difesa," in *Opere Scelte* (Turin, 1955), 265.

102 "Vi si trova, insieme con molti bozzetti, ritratti e aneddoti, resi con grande maestria d'arte, la manifestazione quanto mai sincera d'un'anima costantemente e quasi naturalmente limpida e sicura nella visione e nell'attuazione del bene." *Enciclopedia Italiana* (Rome, 1936), XXXI, 542.

103 *Briefe III,* 51

104 Harry W. Rudman, "A Possible Prototype of Mann's 'Settembrini,' " *Germanic Review,* 25 (December 1950), 299

105 Unpublished letter from Cesare Cases to Heinz Saueressig, 17 March 1966. Photocopy in possession of the author of this work.

106 "Un corpo d'esercito, sotto il generale Raffaele Cadorna, marciò, con molte cautele d'ordine politico, su Roma, dopo che erano riuscite vane le trattative col papa iniziate dal re. Dopo una breve resistenza, le artiglierie italiane apersero una brescia presso Porta Pia. Il Papa fece sospendere le ostilità (20 settembre 1870)." Adolfo Omodeo, *L'Età del Risorgimento Italiano* (Naples, 1960), 458.

107 "A me (che contrariamente a Lei sono—come Lei sa—un ideologo pervicace ed inguaribile, sia pure con rimorsi) Settembrini interessa proprio come personaggio porta-idee: mi interessa cioè vedere perchè per incarnare le idee di

Settembrini Mann abbia preso proprio un italiano (mentre la logica avrebbe voluto che prendesse piuttosto un francese essendo il francese il tipico 'Zivilisationsliterat' bollato nelle *Betrachtungen eines Unpolitischen* e almeno parzialmente riabilitato nello *Zauberberg*)." Unpublished letter from Cesare Cases to Lavinia Mazzucchetti, 23 February 1956. Copy in the possession of the author of this work.

108 Helmut Koopmann, *Die Entwicklung des 'intellektualen' Romans bei Thomas Mann*, (Bonn, 1962), 160.

109 Thomas Mann, Karl Kerényi, *Gespräch in Briefen*. (Zürich, 1960), 199–200.

110 *Briefe I*, 350–351

111 Giosuè Carducci, *Edizione Nazionale delle Opere* (Bologna, 1939), 385

112 *Werke III*, 86

113 *Werke III*, 223

114 Herman Meyer, *Das Zitat in der Erzählkunst* (Stuttgart, 1961), 215

115 *Werke III*, 85

116 *Werke III*, 85

117 "Bisogna fare l'arte realistica: rappresentare quel che è reale, in termini più naturali, con la verità. Bisogna cacciar via l'ideale, il metafisico, a rappresentare l'uomo, la natura, la realità, la ragione, la libertà. A ciò accoppiare lo studio degli antichi, che sono realistici e liberi, Omero, Eschilo, Dante, e della poesia popolare, col sentimento moderno e con l'arte." Quoted from G. L. Bickerstath, *Carducci* (New York, 1913), 23–24

118 *Werke III*, 348

119 *Werke III*, 223

120 Ernest Hatch Wilkins, *A History of Italian Literature* (Cambridge, Mass., 1961), 421

121 *Werke XII*, 393–394

122 *Werke III*, 496

123 *Werke III*, 717

124 *Werke III*, 90

125 *Werke III*, 223

126 In *Reflections of a Non-Political Man*, in the chapter "Vom Glauben," Thomas Mann had already admiringly emphasized this side of Petrarch: "Petrarch, Erasmus, Voltaire,—the world of humanity opens up, the kingdom of fanaticism closes at the sound of these names." *Werke XII*, 499.

127 Meyer, *Das Zitat*, 222

128 *Werke III*, 224

129 *Werke III*, 224

130 "He was terrible in the viciousness of his life and of his writing, especially in the extraordinary system of blackmail that underlies his voluminous correspondence. He was called 'the scourge of princes': even the Emperor was among his victims." Wilkins, *History*, 240

131 *Werke III*, 518

132 *Werke III*, 141

133 *Werke III*, 141

134 *Werke III*, 141

135 "He was of a deeply loving spirit, and craved love; he was immediately sensitive to beauty, especially to beauty of nature and to musical and poetic beauty; his imagination was constantly alert and endlessly resourceful; he had an insatiable

thirst for knowledge, especially for philological knowledge; and he was driven by an incessant urge toward literary and scholarly creativity." Wilkins, *History*, 399

136 *Werke XI*, 316.

137 Lavinia Mazzucchetti, "Thomas Mann und der Zauberer," *Die Zeit*, Nr. 32 (6 August 1965), 11

138 Thomas Mann, "Demokratie und Leben," *Vossische Zeitung*, Nr. 245 (23 May 1924)

139 *Werke XI*, 313

140 *Werke XI*, 140

141 *Briefe I*, 299–300

142 *Werke XI*, 879

143 Thomas Mann gave this so-called *Deutsche Ansprache* in the Beethovensaal in Berlin.

144 *Werke XI*, 880

145 *Werke XI*, 672

146 *Werke VIII*, 658

147 *Werke VIII*, 658

148 Thomas Mann appears to be relating his experiences to one or more friends. Occasionally he interrupts himself with direct remarks to his listeners, as "you are right," "you must admit," "you understand our nervousness," and in this way he arouses the feeling of direct participation in the event.

149 *Werke VIII*, 666

150 *Werke VIII*, 666–667

151 *Werke VIII*, 666

152 *Werke VIII*, 711

153 *Briefe I*, 315

154 Thus Thomas Mann wrote to the Freiburg critic Otto Hoerth: "I am especially grateful to you for recognizing my wish to be just and find in the story no animosity towards Italy or that which is Italian. I admit that in the course of the story there grew out of the personal and chiefly unimportant events something of critical idealism and political morality, which permits a definite antipathy to be recognized and gives the atmosphere, at the outset only irritating, its final sinister and explosive character." *Briefe I*, 299

155 Further details appear in the book review published in 1928 in the journal *Das Tagebuch*, in which, to a certain extent, Thomas Mann kept his distance from the harsh criticism which Bruno Frank leveled against Italian Fascism and its adherents, yet on the other hand added a not very flattering characterization of the régime as such, to which the good-natured Italians had fallen victim. "Is this menacing narcotic puffing up of a healthy, naive and charming people, this charlatanism about honor, morality and superiority, this brutal and perfidious revolutionary renunciation of European qualities and achievements, which in the long run are nevertheless inalienable, is all this violence and excessive abnormality, this self-glorification and bullying, this entirely unpleasant and compromising uproar absolutely necessary in order to achieve the state of energy to make oneself fit for the times? Is all of that also only truly popular down there and to the pick of the land is it something besides a grievous shame? It might be coincidence, but I still have not spoken with any educated Italian who has not shrugged his shoulders over it." *Werke X*, 695

156 *Werke III*, 980
157 *Werke VIII*, 665
158 *Werke VIII*, 665
159 *Werke VIII*, 665
160 *Werke VIII*, 676
161 *Werke VIII*, 702
162 *Werke VIII*, 703
163 *Werke VIII*, 679
164 *Werke VIII*, 684
165 *Werke VIII*, 684
166 *Werke VIII*, 670
167 *Werke VIII*, 670
168 *Werke VIII*, 678
169 *Werke VIII*, 676
170 *Werke VIII*, 696
171 *Werke VIII*, 684
172 *Werke VIII*, 707
173 *Werke VIII*, 658
174 *Werke VIII*, 659
175 *Werke VIII*, 663
176 *Werke VIII*, 672
177 *Werke VIII*, 709
178 *Werke VIII*, 664
179 *Werke VIII*, 664
180 *Werke VIII*, 659
181 *Werke VIII*, 679
182 *Werke VIII*, 667
183 *Werke VIII*, 687. The German expression "null null" is a euphemism for the word "toilet."
184 *Werke VIII*, 706
185 "Era questo frate Cipolla di persona piccolo, di pelo rosso e lieto nel viso, e il miglior brigante del mondo; e oltre a questo, niuna scienza avendo, sì ottimo parlatore e pronto era, che chi conosciuto non l'avesse, non solamente un gran rettorico l'avrebbe stimato, ma avrebbe detto esser Tulio medesimo o forse Quintiliano: e quasi di tutti quegli della contrada era compare o amico o benvogliente." Giovanni Boccaccio, *Il Decamerone* (Milan, 1942), 398.
186 Characteristics, which Thomas Mann has also assigned to Settembrini and other Italian figures of earlier works.
187 Some of these findings I owe to the valuable study by Erwin Koppen: "Quest' idioma celeste . . ." in *Arcadia* 1 (1966), 192–209.
188 *Werke VI*, 280
189 *Werke VI*, 280
190 *Werke XI*, 155
191 *Werke XI*, 156
192 *Werke XI*, 213
193 *Werke VI*, 281
194 *Werke VI*, 291
195 *Werke VI*, 291

196 *Werke VI*, 281
197 Heinrich Mann, "Mein Bruder," in *Ein Zeitalter wird besichtigt* (Berlin, 1947), 232
198 *Werke VI*, 282
199 Heinrich Mann, "Mein Bruder," 232
200 *Werke VI*, 282
201 Karl Kerényi, *Tessiner Schreibtisch* (Stuttgart, 1963), 99
202 *Werke VI*, 285
203 *Werke VI*, 285
204 *Werke VI*, 286
205 *Heinrich Mann, "Mein Bruder,"* 232
206 *Werke VI*, 286
207 *Werke VI*, 298
208 *Werke VIII*, 465
209 *Werke VIII*, 465
210 *Werke VI*, 298
211 *Werke VI*, 644
212 *Werke VI*, 647
213 *Werke VI*, 215
214 *Werke VI*, 216
215 *Werke VI*, 217
216 "Ed egli a lui: 'Tu prima m'inviasti
    Verso Parnasso a ber nelle sue grotte,
    E prima appresso Dio m'alluminasti.

    Facesti come quei che va di notte,
    Che porta il lume dietro e sè non giova,
    Ma dopo sè fa le persone dotte."

    Dante Alighieri, *La Divina Commedia* (Florence, 1938), 339. German translation by Karl Vossler, *Die Göttliche Komödie* (Zürich, 1945), 354

    [Drauf er zu ihm: 'Du wiesest mir zuerst
    Den Weg zum Felsenquell auf dem Parnass,
    Und dann zu Gott den Weg erhelltest mir.

    Du schrittest wie der Wandrer durch die Nacht
    Mit seinem Licht am Rücken, das nicht ihm,
    Doch hinter ihm den Menschen Klarheit spendet.']
217 *Werke VI*, 217
218 In his book *Romanische Dichter*, Karl Vossler had placed this "tornata," without a statement regarding a source, under the title "Allegorie" at the head of his translations of selected portions of the *Divina Commedia*, so that Thomas Mann could easily have considered this nine-line strophe to be a part of the *Divina Commedia*.
219 "Voi che intendendo il terzo ciel movete."
220 "Canzone, i' credo che saranno radi
    Color che tua ragione intendan bene,
    Tanto la parli faticosa e forte.
    Onde se per ventura egli addiviene

Che tu dinanzi da persone vadi,
Che non ti paian d'essa bene accorte;
Allor ti priego che ti riconforte,
Dicendo lor, diletta mia novella:
Ponete mente almen com'io son bella!''
Quoted by Erich Berger, "Eine Dantestelle in Thomas Manns *Doktor Faustus*," *Monatshefte*, XLIV, 4 (April-May 1957), 213

221 *Werke VI*, 475

222 *Werke XI*, 103

223 Perhaps the reason for the absence of Michelangelo's name is to be looked for in Thomas Mann's endeavor not to let the two great main characters of his drama be overshadowed by a prominent historical figure from the ranks of the creative artists.

224 "Leverkühn's tone-painting possesses much of Dante's poem, still more from that crowded wall swarming with bodies, upon which here angels blow into the trumpets of destruction, there Charon's barge discharges its cargo, the dead rise, saints pray, demon masks await the beckoning of the serpent-wreathed Minos, the damned man, voluptuous in flesh, clutched, pulled, by grinning sons of the pit, makes hideous descent, while he covers one eye with his hand and with the other stares full of horror into eternal doom, yet not far from him Grace still pulls two sinning souls up from ruin into salvation,—in short, from the structure of groups and scenes of the Last Judgment." *Werke VI*, 476

225 *Werke VIII*, 808

226 *Briefe II*, 388

227 *Werke XI*, 154–155

228 *Werke VIII*, 815

229 *Werke VIII*, 817

230 *Werke VIII*, 854

231 *Briefe III*, 165

232 *Werke IX*, 783

233 *Werke IX*, 785

234 *Werke IX*, 789

235 *Werke IX*, 789

236 *Werke IX*, 790

237 *Werke IX*, 790

238 *Werke XI*, 687

239 *Werke VII*, 9

240 *Werke VII*, 9

241 *Werke VII*, 234

242 *Werke VII*, 234

243 *Werke VII*, 196–197

244 Hermann J. Weigand, "Thomas Mann's Gregorius," *Germanic Review*, XXVII (February-April 1952), 10–30; 83–93

245 *Werke VII*, 197

246 *Werke VII*, 198

247 *Werke VII*, 203

248 *Werke VII*, 197

249 *Werke VII*, 197–198
250 *Werke VII*, 236
251 Quoted in Weigand, "Mann's Gregorius," 28
252 Hans Wysling, "Die Technik der Montage," *Euphorion*, LVII (1963), 162
253 Jens, *Mann an Bertram*, 139

Chapter III

1 "Per mia parte, l'ho letto, sottolineando con continue approvazioni." Benedetto Croce, "Thomas Mann: "Betrachtungen eines Unpolitischen'," *La Critica*, 18 (May 1920), 183
2 "Oggi ho ricevuto la Sua cortese lettera e il fascicolo di 'Convegno' contenente *Disordine*, e ho ancora appena il tempo di ringraziarLa di cuore . . . Così, per questa volta, mi è negata la possibilità, innanzi tutto, di verderLa, e poi, in particolare, di stringerLe la mano per la Sua traduzione, un prodotto della massima accuratezza e di doppia padronanza linguistica. Un fatto che apprezzo tanto più ora che il medesimo racconto, di cui amo il tocco leggero, in Francia è stato completamente snaturato. Quanta pena Ella dev'essersi data soltanto per le canzoncine! Anche Saverio e Anna Viola mi sembrano ben riusciti. Sono lieto che il Suo talento abbia presentato il mio ai Suoi compatrioti sotto una luce più favorevole di quella in cui i Francesi l'hanno veduto in quest'occasione." *Lettere*, 18–19
3 Hans Bürgin, *Das Werk Thomas Manns* (Frankfurt a. M., 1959), 83
4 Lavinia Mazzucchetti, *Die andere Achse* (Hamburg, 1964), 31–32
5 "La sua arte è tutta autobiografia: quelle storie d'artisti, di famiglie—sono il ritratto suo e della sua famiglia. Ma egli con una sorveglianza attenta sa rendersi indipendente dalla sua stessa vita:—elaborando impressioni e ricordi della sua infanzia o della giovinezza sa spogliarli d'ogni ombra di tenero sentimentalismo e oggettivarli nella forma essenziale d'un organismo plastico." Italo Maione, *Contemporanei di Germania* (Turin, 1931), 96
6 "La sua arte, cosciente e coscienziosa, è lavoro di cesellatore e perciò arte, sopratutto, della parola. Egli ama la parola di un amore appassionato e maniaco: ogni frase deve avere il giusto peso, il giusto volume, la giusta vibrazione. È creatore, ma anche osservatore della parola appropriata ed insostituibile, che riassume, un po' come il *Leitmotiv*, il segreto di un'anima." Ladislao Mittner, *L'opera di Thomas Mann* (Milan, 1936), 155
7 "La radice dell'umanità e quindi anche dell'arte manniana è in quell'inconfondibile e vigoroso senso di autodisciplina attiva che trasforma l'estetismo in un valore morale." Mittner, *L'opera*, 162
8 "Per noi amici suoi italiani . . . è motivo di particolare commozione ed orgoglio potergli dare un segno di devoto omaggio all'inizio del nostro non meno tormentoso crepuscolo, e proprio nel giorno in cui egli raggiunge in vegeta ed operosa vigoria il suo settantesimo anno. Lo facciamo ristampando in degna vesta questi caratteristici piccoli capolavori già cari al nostro pubblico, riprendendo così nel modo migliore l'antica serie dei Narratori nordici, senza ventilazione.
Noi sappiamo e ricordiamo quanto Thomas Mann abbia sempre rispettata e seguita la vera Italia sotterranea degli ultimi decenni, respingendo invece sin dal principio ogni illusione od indulgenza per l'Italia fascista e siamo quindi ben certi che al grande europeo sarà grato il ritorno ai suoi più fidi lettori italiani." Lavinia

Mazzucchetti, Foreword to Thomas Mann, *Disordine e dolore precoce* (Milan, 1945)

9 "Voglio informarLa che la Sua gentile missiva del 10 novembre, con gl'interessanti allegati, la lettera aperta in italiano e l'articolo su *Mario,* sono felicemente arrivati. Tutto questo mi ha molto interessato, specialmente la notizia che Lei, ora, è ufficialmente nominata curatrice delle mie opere. Sarà certo un onere, per Lei, ma Ella lo porta di pieno diritto." *Lettere,* 50

10 "Oggi ho ricevuto le due copie di *Moniti all'Europa,* un bellissimo libro, trascelto bene e di cui mi compiaccio vivamente." *Lettere,* 54

11 "Oltre a ringraziarLa, voglio rispondere alla Sua lunga relazione, giuntami poco tempo fa, circa l'edizione completa delle mie opere, che dovrà essere sorvegliata e curata dalla nostra amica Lavinia Mazzucchetti. È questa, per me, una gioia e una soddisfazione particolare, dato che ho piena fiducia non solo nelle generali capacità letterarie di Lavinia, ma anche nella sua specifica simpatia per la mia opera personale e nella sua eccelente attitudine a questo lavoro." *Lettere,* 54

12 "Non posso chiudere questa lettera senza esprimere ancora una volta la mia sincera soddisfazione per il suo bel progetto di un'edizione in dieci volumi delle mie 'opera omnia.' Da quando l'editore S. Fischer di Berlino pubblicò un'edizione, anch'essa in dieci volumi, delle mie opere, la cosa non è più stata fatta in nessun paese e che ora ciò avvenga proprio in Italia, un paese cui fin da giovane mi son sentito così strettamente legato, dove ho vissuto spesso in qualità di ospite riconoscente e che anche nelle mie opere è un elemento che ricorre così spesso, rappresenta, per me, una gioia particolare." *Lettere,* 54–55.

13 The Accademia dei Lincei, which in the beginning was mainly instituted for the natural sciences and then also made archaeology, ancient history, and Oriental studies its special fields of interest, was founded in Rome as early as 1603, hence twenty-one years after the Accademia della Crusca. After an existence of twenty-seven years it was started again in 1745 in Rimini, where after ten years it once more came to an end. In 1801 it was founded anew in Rome and now, as the possessor of a vast library as well as important collections of manuscripts and incunabula, plays a prominent rôle in the cultural life of Italy. Of late the Academy has administered the international literary prize of the Feltrinelli Foundation, established in 1947, and possesses the right to choose, on its behalf, the respective prize-winners.

14 "Illustre Presidente,
mi duole fortemente di rispondere con così grave ritardo alla Sua lettera del 7 ottobre. Indirizzata a Zurigo, donde io era già partito, essa ha percorso vie lunghe e traverse prima di giungere alla mia casa di California.

So quanto veneranda e gloriosa sia l'Accademia dei Lincei. Vedo dunque, con grato orgoglio, quanto onore si rifletta su me dalla nomina che me ne fa Socio.

Socio Straniero, com'Ella mi scrive; ma solo in quanto si possa essere stranieri all'Italia. Del pensiero e dell'arte italiana fui sempre, quanto mi fu concesso, cultore e devoto amante; né questi legami si sono attenuati, anzi si sono rafforzati con la distanza e gli anni. Godo vivamente della nuova opportunità che ora mi si offre di sentirmi fraterno, e quasi direi, non ospite ma consanguineo, agli spiriti eminenti che, ricordati o presenti, abitano le stanze dove spero di salutarLa personalmente." *Lettere,* 59

15 "Sono stupito che con la *Carlotta* Lei sia già così innanzi da mancarLe solo più un capitolo. Suppongo che sia 'il settimo,' e credo quasi ch'Ella non lo troverà così difficile come Le sembra." *Lettere,* 53

16 "Ora è arrivata anche *Carlotta a Weimar,* e resto stupefatto dell'esatezza della traduzione che, a quel che vedo, non perde una sola sfumatura dell'originale . . . E le illustrazioni? Lei che ne dice? Io non vorrei dir nulla. Penso che nessun narratore sia mai stato soddisfatto di come hanno illustrato i suoi libri. La mia perplessità, pertanto, non vorrebbe dir molto. Eppure, eppure . . ." *Lettere,* 67

17 "Ma so essere abbastanza oggettivo per riconoscere il talento che si esprime nelle illustrazioni di *Carlotta a Weimar,* tra le quali mi piace sopratutto l'ultima, la scena nella carrozza, dove l'elemento immaginario o sognante di quell'incontro è ridato dallo artista con molta comprensione." *Lettere,* 69

18 "È arrivato il *Faustus,* con la Sua intelligente e brillante prefazione, che lumeggia diversi rapporti e che sarà di grandissimo aiuto in Italia a quel mio libro così poco familiare. È una bella edizione, nonostante la ridicola sovracoperta, da cui ho subito liberato la mia copia. La legatura è molto dignitosa e i caratteri grandi e piacevoli. Tutti quanti hanno veramente fatto il possibile per alleggerire al lettore il suo duro compito!" *Lettere,* 77

19 "Nell'opera di questo grande scrittore si possono segnare due periodi . . . Al primo, che va su per giù dal 1901 al 1928, e che ebbe insigni riconoscimenti, segue l'altro che da quella data va fino ad oggi, e risponde a una sostanziale evoluzione del Mann (e fu infatti chiamata da alcuni una conversione), che da un individualismo romantico e magari decadente, il cui emblema fu una Germania orgogliosa e solitaria . . . passò a un umanesimo europeo, ove la tragica e grande sua patria non debba attendere a soggiogare il mondo ma a farsi europea." Francesco Flora, "Il Premio dell'Accademia dei Lincei a Thomas Mann nel 1952." *Letteratura Moderna,* 6 (1956), 343

20 "Di questo primo periodo un'esplicita coscienza è in quelle *Considerazioni di un apolitico,* che, apparse nel 1918, furono l'interpretazione di molta parte della sua opera di narratore in germanica torre d'avorio e un programma che durò, sebbene già inquieto di qualche dubbio, molti anni ancora; ed egli stesso ebbe a scrivere più tardi che l'aver fissata in una strenua analisi quella sua posizione, fu già un primo stimolo a rinnovarsi sulla raggiunta chiarezza. I terribili eventi che l'Europa e il mondo vissero, quando la sua patria faceva il suo 'patto col diavolo,' delirando contro presunte razze inferiori di instaurare l'astratta supernazione (riscontro al male inteso superuomo), aiutarono Thomas Mann a intendere la necessità sociale a cui nessuno scrittore che non sia vano può sottrarsi. Questa carità sociale approfondì l'anima e l'arte del Mann e trasse in piena luce l'umanesimo che vi era ancora latente. Ormai egli poteva affermare che tutto quanto è separatista, antiromano, antieuropeo—e cioè, tutto quanto, per questa parte, il Mann dichiarava estremamente tedesco—lo sconcertava e sgomentava anche quando si presenta come la libertà evangelica di un Lutero." Flora, *Letteratura Moderna;* 343-344

21 "Anche l'opera posteriore di Thomas Mann compreso *L'Eletto,* pur con la sua materia medioevale ed edipica, è illuminata dall'esperienza in cui egli comprese la verità dell'arte come spiritualizzazione della materia e totale umanesimo. A questo rinnovato scrittore, che invoca al mondo una nuova speranza in pagine ove l'arte sua grande si è approfondita per più umana verità, si volge la nostra grata ammirazione d'oggi e l'attesa del domani." Flora, *Letteratura Moderna,* 345

22 "Le confesso che ne godo moltissimo. Con tutto il rispetto per Stoccolma, ma 'Roma eterna' e l'incoronazione petrarchesca mi fa ancora più impressione. Notizie dirette non ne ho sinora avute. Forse dovrò venirlo a sapere quando la cosa verrà

resa pubblica, cioè in giugno. Sarebbe un guaio perché devo fissare il mio viaggio in base a quella data e sapere molte cose per tempo, oltre che prepararmi al discorso che ci si aspetta da me (in che lingua? tedesco? francese? italiano?), ecc. *Readiness is all!* Di sotto mano, poi, dovrei raccogliere informazioni, e sapere anche qualcosa sulla storia dell'Accademia." *Lettere,* 90-91

23 "Sono presente con loro in ispirito orgoglioso dello insolito onore che loro hanno conferito su di me. Spero poter esprimere personalmente la mia profonda gratitudine durante il mio proposto soggiorno in Roma la prossima estate. Con ossequi alla gloriosa Accademia i miei più distinti saluti." *Lettere,* 91

24 *Briefe III,* 264

25 "Egregio signor Professore,
Accolga i miei ringraziamenti per la Sua lettera del 1° luglio, che giunse a Zurigo il 10 e mi raggiunse qui ieri. Gran valore hanno per me anche gli allegati, e sopratutto la motivazione del conferimento al premio che è particolarmente bella. Anche l'Annuario dell'Accademia Nazionale dei Lincei mi ha molto interessato." *Lettere,* 92–93

26 *Briefe III,* 287

27 "L'accoglienza della società intellettuale di Roma—così cordiale da sgomentare—mi fece l'effetto di un bel sogno e non potevo non ricordare il tempo in cui, giovanissimo, passavo per le vie della città: nessuno sapeva allora di me e nessuno di me si occupava. Ora ho avuto onori su onori e la visita a Pio XII è stata per me il miscredente e l'allievo della cultura protestante un avvenimento profondamente singolare e commovente." *Lettere,* 98

28 "Abbia i miei ringraziamenti per la Sua cortese lettera del 24 settembre. Aggiungo l'espressione del mio compiacimento per l'edizione nella 'Medusa' del *Romanzo di un romanzo,* edizione che mi sembra riuscitissima. Comprendo che *Romanzo di un romanzo* non poteva rappresentare un volume completo e trovo molto abile l'aggiunta dei due altri pezzi autobiografici." *Lettere,* 93–94

29 "La bella edizione dei *Saggi* mi ha procurato una vera gioia e spero di arrivare a vedere davanti a me, compiuta, *l'opera omnia* nella vostra meravigliosa lingua." *Lettere,* 98–99

30 "Mi ha fatto molto piacere leggere nel 'Corriere della Sera' il simpatico articolo che ha scritto sul nostro incontro privato, e quello così intenso e vivo sul *Dottor Faustus." Lettere,* 103

31 "Quando ho ricevuto la Sua cara lettera del 2 maggio, stavo proprio accingendomi a scriverLe: sentivo il bisogno di dirLe quanto fossi felice di averLa conosciuta, e ringraziarLa per i colloqui che abbiamo avuti insieme. Tra tutte le centinaia di persone incontrate a Roma, Ella è senz'altro da annoverarsi tra le due o tre figure più autorevoli e importanti. Le sono inoltre molto grato per i chiarimenti e gli incitamenti che ho avuto dai Suoi interessanti scritti." *Lettere,* 103

32 "Ed ora mi permetta di dirLe che mi sento molto onorato per la proposta fattami dal 'Corriere della Sera.' Se io riuscissi a lavorare più velocemente, e non temessi le scadenze, sarei lietissimo di accettare questa offerta, e felice di diventare un regolare collaboratore di un giornale di così larga diffusione, e che La annovera tra i suoi collaboratori. Ma come stanno le cose, ed essendo io quasi sempre impegnato in lavori che assorbono tutte le mie forze, e obbligato a piccole consegne giornaliere, mi sentirei spaventato ed oppresso dall'impegno di consegnare ogni mese un articolo nuovo, senza contare che il mio talento è—dopo tutto—volto

essenzialmente a un certo genere di narrativa, e che la saggistica resta—più o meno—un'attività marginale." *Lettere,* 104

33 "Questo naturalmente non è un rifiuto di massima all'invito del 'Corriere.' Infatti non potrò impedirmi di interrompere ancora con un saggio—riflessioni sui problemi dell'arte e della vita—il mio lavoro letterario. E in questa occasione mi ricorderò certamente del 'Corriere della Sera,' ed offrirò loro il mio articolo. Le sarò quindi molto grato di informare, in questo sense, il Dottor Mario Missiroli." *Lettere,* 104

34 "EccoLe la prefazione richiesta, che spero risponda in certo qual modo alle Sue aspettative. È un'espressione, comunque, della commozione provocata in me da questa raccolta di lettere, che certo farà una forte impressione." *Lettere,* 109

35 "A causa di un equivoco, di una sbadataggine, i due volumi a me inviati sono finiti in una biblioteca contenente doppioni e copie omaggio, e così non li ho firmati. Me ne dispiace davvero e chiedo mille scuse. Può ben credermi che avrei esaudito senza indugio il desiderio così semplice e pur commovente delle due persone che si sono rese benemerite di questa così toccante pubblicazione. È *Lei* che dev'essere ringraziato, non io. Se le mie parole d'introduzione dovessero contribuire un poco ad aprire al libro la via che porta al cuore dei lettori, ciò costituirebbe, per me, una grande soddisfazione." *Lettere,* 110.

36 "La traduzione mi fa l'effetto di essere eccellente." *Lettere,* 112.

37 "Lei mi ha procurato una vera gioia con la Sua cortese lettera e col testo del Suo radiodiscorso romano: una conversazione deliziosa e quasi una specie di piccolo romanzo famigliare. Sono rimasto stupefatto al vedere quanto bene Ella sia informata sul conto 'nostro.' Non penso molto in prima persona singolare, ma in prima persona plurale penso volentieri." *Lettere,* 114

38 "Temo di non averLa ancora ringraziata per l'invio del Suo bello studio sull'*Eletto,* la cui lettura mi ha pure fatto tanto piacere. In generale sono felicissimo dell'interesse oltremodo intelligente che la mia opera, già da qualche tempo, riscuote in Italia. Ma confesso che ho una particolare debolezza personale per quel piccolo *curiosum* che è *L'Eletto,* e debbo dire che forse non conosco alcuna recensione critica, in nessuna lingua, che ne colga il carattere con più finezza e sicurezza della Sua." *Lettere,* 116

39 Guido Devescovi, *Il Doktor Faustus di Thomas Mann* (Trieste, 1955), 148

40 *Briefe III,* 395

41 *Briefe III,* 395

42 Here Thomas Mann's own, unpublished letter to Lavinia Mazzucchetti of 8 March 1955 is quoted, which was shown in the original to the author of this work.

43 "Quanto alla *Fantasia su Goethe,* condivido in realtà la Sua simpatia per questo lavoretto, che è la cosa più leggera e insieme più riassuntiva ch'io abbia mai scritto su Goethe, e non nuoce alla predilezione che ho per esso il fatto che ci siano dei punti in cui ripeto un po' quel che ho detto in altri miei saggi goethiani. Credo che Lei abbia ragione nel ritenerlo particolarmente indicato per un pubblico che non abbia dimestichezza con Goethe, e la Sua idea di farne un volumetto a parte ha, per me, qualcosa di oltremodo allettante." *Lettere,* 117

44 "Per il giubileo degli ottant'anni la Casa Editrice Mondadori offre al suo più grande autore vivente, invece della consueta ghirlanda di critici omaggi, il dono di un libro che è già tutto suo . . . Non lode ma affettuosa gratitudine conviene offrire a chi, mentre ci toccava vivere in questo duro nostro tempo, ci ha largito il valido

conforto del suo pensiero e del suo esempio." Lavinia Mazzucchetti in Thomas Mann, *Dialogo con Goethe* (Milan, 1955), 29–30

45 "Nel cammino dell'umanità si vede che in fondo i politici non sono che i registratori della storia: ma i veri artefici di essa, coloro che segnano le tappe attraverso le quali deve passare l'avanzata dei popoli in marcia verso la loro pacifica unificazione, sono i grandi spiriti universali, che oggi Thomas Mann rievoca, e tra i quali da pari a pari conversa." Piero Calamandrei, "Saluto a Thomas Mann," *Il Ponte*, 11 (June 1955), 867

46 "Insomma se salvezza può darsi, essa è molto simile alla famosa vittoria, in cui il vincitore cade prostrato sul corpo del vinto." Giacomo Debenedetti, "Il grande gioco," *Il Contemporaneo*, II, 23 (June 1955), 6

47 "La faccenda si complica di un ulteriore paradosso: per mettere in dubbio la possibilità di salvazione attraverso l'arte, Thomas Mann ha scritto un romanzo, cioè un'opera d'arte, intrapresa senz'altro con quella speranza nel capolavoro, che il suo diavolo contesta allo scrittore cosciente. Il vero Faust è Thomas Mann che cerca di giocarsi il diavolo.

Di questo grande gioco, utile a tutti anche come esempio, qui e in questa occasione, lo vogliamo ringraziare." Debenedetti, 6

48 "E nel suo sguardo di borghese classico e razionale fisso a scrutare ostinatamente i meandri del decadentismo e dell'irrazionalismo, quasi fino al punto di immedesimarsi in essi, ma poi sempre restando 'altro' da essi, frapponendo fra quelli e sé la lente del distacco storico, della classicità di linguaggio, dell'ironia del grande narratore, trovammo un esempio contemporaneo di come lo scrittore d'un'epoca di transizione e dramma può vivere il vecchio e il nuovo insieme, può partecipare della totalità del dramma pur restando se stesso, giudice e orchestratore supremo." Italo Calvino, "Manniano all'incontrario," 7

49 "Mann vuole dominare e nello stesso tempo inglobare la crisi della cultura contemporanea nell'alveo della sua classicità goethiana." Calvino, 7

50 "Vecchio e nuovo: per lui la razionalità borghese è il 'vecchio', cui vanno le sue nostalgie di conservatore illuminato; mentre l'estenuato Hanno Buddenbrook o il demoniaco Leverkùhn sono il 'nuovo' di cui comunque egli sente di dover riconoscere una necessità e una verità. Per noi, tutto il contrario: il 'vecchio' è quel che a lui parve nuovo, il 'nuovo' è qualcosa di solido e razionale molto più che i buoni mercanti di Lubecca. E dal 'vecchio' noi vogliamo trarre tutta l'affinata acutezza che contiene per servircene e raggiungere il 'nuovo'. Manniani all'incontrario, cioè in avanti, così potrebbe essere definito un giusto e nuovo rapporto con Mann." Calvino, 7

51 "Mann se ne è andato, consapevole di non appartenere più a nessun paese, a nessun partito, a nessuna classe sociale." Giorgio Zampa, "Parodia e verità," *Il Mondo*, VII, 34 (August 1955), 3

52 "Quale altro scrittore, portata a termine in avanzata vecchiezza un'opera della mole e della tensione del *Faustus*, con un immenso lavoro dietro di sè, ordinato e, per opinione generale, concluso: quale altro avrebbe trovato forza e volontà per accingersi a nuovi compiti, non secondari, accessori, ma tali da impegnare ogni energia, da richiedere alta concentrazione, impiego di tutte le facoltà spirituali: per giocare, ancora una volta, a tutto o nulla?" Zampa, 3

53 "Non certo a caso Benedetto Croce poteva dedicare proprio a lui quella *Storia d'Europa nel secolo decimonono* che resta il documento più alto della

dottrina liberale durante l'oppressione fascista." Federico Gozzi, "Il liberale Thomas Mann," *Il Mondo,* VIII, 34 (August 1955), 2

54 "È il sorriso della dignità umana che affida alla nostra responsabilità il trionfo della vita sulla dissoluzione, il lavoro e la lotta per un futuro più giusto e più libero." Enzo Paci, "L'ironia di Thomas Mann", *aut aut,* XXIX (September 1955), 375

55 "L'atmosfera cupa e tesa di *Mario e il mago* è accennata fin dalle prime battute del racconto. Cipolla è un ipnotizzatore che in una afosa serata estiva mette in opera tutte le sue suggestive forze magiche dinanzi al pubblico di una stazione balneare. L'autore concentra la sua non dissimulata antipatia sulla sinistra figura del 'mago' che con demoniaca potenza, accompagnata da un sorriso sardonico, sgomenta e conturba i suoi spettatori. La novella è avvolta in un'aura di malefizio e sortilegio. Incrina l'obiettività artistica una certa maldissimulata prevenzione del Mann contro la nostra gente, i suoi costumi e la sua fondamentale onestà. Questa incomprensione e questa insofferenza, che traspaiono chiaramente anche da altre pagine manniane (vedi, per esempio, *La morte a Venezia*) possono spiacere a noi italiani per quel che di immotivato e puramente soggettivo che è sempre insito nei pregiudizi, ma, d'altra parte, nessuno può inibire all'artista le reazioni della sua sensibilità di fronte al mondo che lo circonda, e si sa che Goethe stesso accanto al *Viaggio in Italia* e alle *Elegie romane,* ribboccanti di entusiasmo, ha scritto gli *Epigrammi veneziani,* piuttosto acri e velenosi. La tesi politica del Lukács che vede trasposta e deviata in Cipolla la figura del 'Duce', è certamente arbitraria, né giova alla legittima interpretazione del racconto." Giovanni Necco, "Thomas Mann in italiano," *Gazzetta del Mezzogiorno,* 16 March 1956, 4

56 Lavinia Mazzucchetti, "Thomas Mann al Forte dei Marmi," *La Provincia di Lucca,* IV, 2 (April-June 1964), 54

57 "Ma l'esempio più rilevante della prevalenza in lui del guidizio di casta su ogni altra considerazione politica o morale resta pur sempre la sua costante reticenza nei riguardi del fascismo italiano, sebbene non gli mancassero informazioni sul suo carattere oppressivo e malgrado l'amicizia con molti antifascisti, tra i quali in primo luogo Benedetto Croce." Ignazio Silone, "Thomas Mann e il dovere civile," *Tempo Presente,* III, 1 (January 1958), 5

58 "Era il fascismo tedesco che gli bruciava, era la tragedia della Germania la sua tragedia personale. Rimproverarlo per non aver scritto un libro intero contro Mussolini sarebbe come rimproverare Salvemini, Borgese o te per non aver fatto altrettanto contro Hitler. Ma non salterebbe in mente a nessun galantuomo di dedurre da ciò che i fuorusciti italiani siano stati filonazisti; e il tuo rimprovero a mio padre rimane del tutto incomprensibile." Elisabeth Mann Borgese, Letter to Ignazio Silone (1900–1978), *Tempo Presente,* III, 3 (March 1958), 220

59 In Sweden a translation of the novel *Buddenbrooks* appeared in 1940, and in 1910 in Russia the first of a five-volume complete edition of Mann's works was published.

Chapter IV

1 "Arboscello che cammini davvero accanto a me! vivente!
Tu, verde!
Mi è stato dunque permesso ch'io ti riconducessi a valle, tu che sei il mio Isacco, il mio agnello.

Dio non era il mostro dalle fauci di rupe dove dovevi cadere.

La tua mano è nella mia.

L'odore fino, vegetale, che parte dalle tue tempie, dal tuo vestito lungo, tutto verde, a mazzetti di fiori, quest'odore d'infanzia che il respiro dei boschi riconosce e fa suo, non è l'odore schiacciante della morte."

G. A. Borgese, *Tempesta nel nulla* (Milan, 1950), 44

2 *Werke VIII*, 1089

Und so umschliesst denn

Auf einmal mein träumend Gefühl das Liebste auf Erden

Menschlich mir: mein Kindchen, dich, und das geistigste Gut noch,

Das ich erwarb und bewahre, im Leben Trost und im Tode,

Sitz'ich beim Korbe des Nils, wachthabend, und halte dein Händchen,

Dein Gesichtchen betrachtend und seine besondere Bildung.

3 "Io la guardai negli occhi, e in essi mi smarrii. In lei, rapito, amai sua madre, dalla voce virginea; amai mia madre, dagli occhi mansueti, ch'era tanto lontana. E mi rincrebbe ch'essa non la conoscesse, che non l'avesse mai più vista da quando era proprio una piccola bimba, coi suoi pochi capelli biondi sul debole capo, cosí teneri e fini che facevano dolcezza, quasi facevano pietà, a guardarli." Borgese, *Tempesta*, 46–47

4 *Werke VIII*, 1087

5 *Werke VIII*, 1087

Lächelt mir freundlich dein Auge?

Blau zwar strahlt es wie nordisch Eis, doch zuweilen, kaum fassbar

Meinem prüfenden Sinn, aus seiner Tiefe erdunkelt's

Irgendwie süss und exotisch, in fremder Schwermut,—indes doch

Blond die Braue dir steht, ganz wie den hansischen Vätern

(Lächeln muss ich fürwahr, so wohl erkenn' ich das Merkmal),

Welche mit nüchternem Sinn und würdig schritten zum Rathaus

Und im Sitzungssaale die Dose boten dem Nachbarn,—

Kaufherrn zumal, rundbärtig, und Reeder fernreisender Schiffe . . .

6 "Cosí, sorgendo da ogni parte brume di visione, non vedevo più la valle di Fedoz, l'Engadina; ma i monti miei, la valle su cui nacqui . . .

Io nacqui la notte di San Martino, che ha tante stelle filanti quante quella di San Lorenzo.

Mio padre uscí sul balcone, e in quei messaggi di luce lesse un presagio, un destino.

Io crebbi davanti ai grandi orizzonti; e udivo suoni remoti.

I fiumi, scendendo la notte fra i boschi, avevano voci d'amore; i lumi delle case coloniche si spengevano sui clivi per lasciare accostare le stelle." Borgese, *Tempesta*, 47–48

7 "Camminavamo tenendoci per mano; dimenticavo gli anni; di tutte le parentele, le vive e quelle che erano sotterra, si fece, non so come, una cosa sola; e mia figlia fu una del mio sangue, una sorella." Borgese, *Tempesta*, 47

8 *Werke VIII*, 1080

"Schwesterchen" heisst du im Hause, und wunderlich lautet der Name.

"Schwestern" hiessen dereinst in der giebligen Heimat die grauen

Bräute des Heilands mit Haube und Rosenkranz, die beieinander

Irgendwo wohnten im Winkligen, einer Ob'rin gehorsam,

Wo sie der Knabe besuchte, zu sehen die goldne Kapelle,
Und von denen die Sanfteste pflegte den Vater zu Tode,
Auch uns Kinder oftmals versah, wenn wir fiebrig erkrankten.

9 *Werke VIII*, 1070
Denn ich will sagen und singen vom Kindchen, dem jüngsten der meinen,
Das mir erschien in härtester Zeit, da ich nicht mehr jung war.
Und was kein Drang der Seele, kein höher Befahrnis vermochte,
Das wirke Vatergefühl: es mach' mich zum metrischen Dichter.

10 "... che per Pavese il maggior narratore contemporaneo è Thomas Mann e, tra gli italiani, Vittorio De Sica." Cesare Pavese, *La letteratura americana e altri saggi* (Turin, 1953), 296

11 "Il ripercorrere che fa ciascuno le proprie rotaie scoprì oggi che per un certo tempo ti ha angosciato (4 April '41, II), e poi (12 April '41) ti è apparso premio gioioso dello sforzo vitale e infatti da allora non te ne sei più lagnato, ma ('42, '43) hai indagato con gusto come nell'infanzia si scavino queste rotaie. Prima ancora di rileggere Thomas Mann *Giacobbe* (dicembre '42). Hai concluso (settembre '43) con la scoperta del mito-unicità, che fonde cosí tutti i tuoi antichi rovelli psicologici e i tuoi più vivi interessi mitico-creativi.
È assodato che il *bisogno di costruzione* nasce per te su questa legge del ritorno." Cesare Pavese, *Il mestiere di vivere* (Turin, 1962), 254

12 "*Il ritorno degli eventi* in Th. Mann (cap. Ruben va alla cisterna) è in sostanza una concezione evoluzionista. Gli eventi si provano ad accadere, e ogni volta accadono più soddisfacenti, più perfetti. Gli *stampi mitici* sono come le *forme delle specie*. Ciò che pare staccare questa concezione dal determinismo naturalistico è il fatto che i suoi fattori non sono la scelta sessuale o la lotta per l'esistenza, ma una volontà costante di Dio che un certo progetto si realizzi. Del resto, il modo di enunciare di Mann pare sottintendere che ciò che determina via via gli eventi è lo spirito umano che, secondo le sue leggi, li percepisce *e fa accadere* ogni volta sostanzialmente uguali ma più ricchi. Un formalismo kantiano, calato nella materia mitologica, a interpretarla in modo unitario. C'è, qui dietro, Vico." Pavese, *Il mestiere di vivere*, 282

13 *Werke XI*, 611–612

14 "Il vero racconto (*Primo amore* e il *Campo di grano*) tratta il tempo come materia non come limite e lo domina scorciandolo o rallentandolo e non tollera didascalie che sono il tempo e la visione della vita reale; piuttosto, risolve in impulso (sintesi fondamentale o idea generatrice) di costruzione (distanza prospettica o ripensamento) l'ambiente temporale." Pavese, *Il mestiere di vivere*, 112–113

15 "Vi sono degli scrittori, e anche dei grandi scrittori, che io mi trovo assolutamente negato a gustare e persino a intendere, a capire. Thomas Mann per esempio. È in effetti un intero filone di letteratura che mi riesce inesplicabile: quello in cui si avverte, deliberata, l'azione speculativa dell'intelletto come quando vediamo, a una radioscopia, il bario percorrere i visceri che vuol rivelarci. Specie poi se si tratta della sottospecie che ama *sataneggiare* io precipito in uno stato di allergia e non so nemmeno distinguere tra creature e aborti—nella sua proliferazione." Elio Vittorini, *Diario in pubblico* (Milan, 1957), 368

16 "Aiutò la Principessa a scendere dalla vettura, spolverò con la camicia la tuba del Principe, distribuí caramelle alle cugine e frizzi ai cuginetti, si genuflesse quasi dinanzi al Gesuita, ricambiò gl'impeti passionali di Bendicò, consolò mademoiselle

Dombreuil, prese in giro tutti, incantò tutti." Tomasi di Lampedusa, *Il gattopardo* (Milan, 1963), 39

17 Tomasi di Lampedusa, "Lezioni su Stendhal," *Paragone,* No. 112 (1959), 49 ff.

18 *Werke II,* 64

19 *Werke II,* 64

20 "Era profondissimo ma vuoto, tranne che per un rotolo di stoffa sudicia, ritto in un angolo; dentro vi era un fascio di piccole fruste, di scudisci in nervo di bue, alcuni con manici in argento, altri rivestiti sino a metà da una graziosa seta molto vecchia, bianca a righine azzurre, sulla quale si scorgevano tre file di macchie nerastre: ed attrezzini metallici, inspiegabili. Tancredi ebbe paura." Lampedusa, *Il gattopardo,* 109

21 *Werke II,* 66

22 "vagabondaggi trasognati," Lampedusa, *Il gattopardo,* 110

23 "Cos'ero dunque io, da dove venivo, dove affondavo le mie radici?" Enzo Bettiza, *Il fantasma di Trieste* (Milan, 1958), 55

24 "Purtroppo, con altrettanta precisione io oggi so che è molto pericoloso avviare un ragazzo, un adolescente, a un precoce contatto con il mistero delle proprie origini, specie se queste sono aggrovigliate e oscure." Bettiza, *Il fantasma di Trieste,* 56

25 "Cosí, in modo ancora oscuro e confuso, aveva cominciato ad accorgersi che lui, con la sofferenza, si comportava come un assetato con un bicchiere di fuoco. Più della sete, soffriva l'impossibilità di spegnerla tra le fiamme. Il mondo rovente del dolore lo attirava come un vulcano spalancato, ricco di tutte quelle infernali scottature cui il suo istinto di conservazione cercava di resistere passivamente, con la sonnolenza e la svogliatezza." Bettiza, *Il fantasma di Trieste,* 95

26 *Werke I,* 64

27 *Werke I,* 754

28 "Trieste era allora una città viva e allegra. Il porto, ove approdavano navi, merci, ricchezza dagli angoli più remoti del mondo, pareva un bosco ondeggiante d'alberi intrecciati fra loro dalle matasse di cordame da cui, frustate dalla bora, sventolavano le bandiere di tutti i popoli della terra. Il porto era la passeggiata preferita di Daniele." Bettiza, *If fantasma di Trieste,* 45

29 *Werke VI,* 297

30 "S'accorse,allora, d'avere i piedi e le mani gelate." Bettiza, *Il fantasma di Trieste,* 285

31 "Eppure non poteva più muoversi, ora che sudava ghiaccio, ora che si sentiva chiuso, imprigionato dentro al proprio stesso corpo come in una morsa di carne improvvisamente priva di elasticità, fredda e pesante." Bettiza, *Il fantasma di Trieste,* 286

32 "Oppure stava dormendo? Questo ronzio nelle orecchie non era forse il ronzio del sonno? Ma come si può pensare il sonno senza sognare? Soltanto sognando si riesce, talvolta, a sospettare di essere immersi nel sonno; e lui non sognava. E quindi non dormiva." Bettiza, *Il fantasma di Trieste,* 286

33 "Il solo senso rimasto sveglio, difatti, troppo sveglio, nel corpo freddo di Daniele, era l'udito, la cui sensibilità, straordinariamente raddoppiata, amplificava ogni più piccolo rumore notturno in una vibrazione profonda." Bettiza, *Il fantasma di Trieste,* 287

34 "Chi non ricorda il figlio di suo bisnonno, cioè il nonno di lei Daniele, il famoso Pier Paolo Solospin console di Brema e d'Amburgo di cui persino mio padre nei momenti di lucidità, parla come di un santo?'' Bettiza, *Il fantasma di Trieste*, 305

35 A comprehensive comparison of the two works is found in Lilian A. Furst's article "Italo Svevo's *La coscienza di Zeno* and Thomas Mann's *Der Zauberberg*," *Contemporary Literature*, IX, No. 4 (1968), pp. 492–506

36 "What a great writer is Thomas Mann, but what a sickly amateur is his Castorp. Besides, all the invalids of *The Magic Mountain* are in a certain sense mannered, taken from the textbook. They are real with respect to the illness, to their reactions, to their impulses and the resulting state of the soul, as much as the consumption of the *Lady of the Camellias* (or of Mimì in *Bohème*) is real. *The Magic Mountain* mirrors the intellectual image. With the difference that in Verdi there is the music: a music without artifice, full of health. In Mann there is only philosophy. Perhaps that is why I prefer *Buddenbrooks*." Vasco Pratolini, *Diario Sentimentale*. Florence, 1956, p. 166ff. I wish to thank Johannes Hösle for this reference. Cf. *Arcadia*, 7, No. 2/3 (1972), p. 337

37 "In realtà il successo di Thomas Mann in Italia è indipendente da un eventuale influsso sulla narrativa italiana, generalmente aliena dall'elemento problematico, anzi si potrebbe pensare che l'ammirazione per quest'autore sia dovuta alla consapevolezza dell'estraneità." Unpublished letter from Cesare Cases to the author of this work, 16 May 1966

38 "Mann, benchè europeista e alla fine cittadino del mondo, è pur sempre rimasto, come spirito, stile, modo di affrontare i problemi, interessi culturali, personalità, ecc., un uomo profondamente, caratteristicamente tedesco. Noi italiani siamo molto diversi, e anche là dove ammiriamo in lui l'eccellenza di uno spirito e di un'arte sovrani, affrontiamo però il mondo in tutt'altra maniera, con tutt'altro timbro e suono e colore." Unpublished letter from Italo A. Chiusano to the author of this work, 15 June 1966

39 "La narrativa di Mann non è come quella di un Proust o di un Joyce—e persino di una Woolf—che si prestano, bloccate come sono e unitarie per stile ed ispirazione, anche alla più piatta imitazione; ma è di un genere così composito e vario, per linguaggio e per contenuti, da prestarsi difficilmente ad essere ripetuto." Carlo Bernari, "Mann e noi," *Paragone*, No. 192 (1966), 50

40 "In verità, anche se molto a torto, oggi Mann è generalmente ritenuto in Italia uno scrittore invecchiato, ottocentesco: e la mia convinzione che si tratti d'invidia e d'impotenza ad intendere l'ideale manniano di 'grandezza,' non è in grado, naturalmente, di cambiare le cose." Unpublished letter from Sergio Checconi to the author of this work, 14 June 1966

Chapter V

1 *Werke X*, 311
2 *Werke X*, 312–313

BIBLIOGRAPHY

I. Works by Thomas Mann

Gesammelte Werke. Frankfurt a. M.: S. Fischer, 1960. 12 vols.
Briefe 1889–1936. Frankfurt a. M.: S. Fischer, 1961
Briefe 1937–1947. Frankfurt a. M.: S. Fischer, 1963
Briefe 1948–1955 und Nachlese (and Supplement). Frankfurt a. M.: S. Fischer, 1965
Briefe an Paul Amann. Lübeck: Schmidt-Römhild, 1959
Briefe an Ernst Bertram, 1910–1955. Pfullingen: Neske, 1960
Thomas Mann—Karl Kerényi, *Gespräch in Briefen*. Zürich: Rhein, 1960
"Über Dante," *Jugend* (Munich), No. 24 (September 1921), 622, Dante issue
Michelangelo und seine Dichtungen. Celerina: Quos Ego (n.d.)
Tutte le Opere. Milan: Mondadori, 1949–1966
Disordine e dolore precoce. Milan: Sperling & Kupfer, 1945
Lettere a italiani. Milan: Il Saggiatore, 1962
Dialogo con Goethe. Milan: Mondadori, 1964
"Testimoni della libertà," *Il Mondo*, VI, No. 18 (4 May 1954), p. 1
"Discorso su Schiller," *Il Contemporaneo*, II, No. 23 (4 June 1955), pp. 1–2, 10–11
"Spirito e natura, ovvero Schiller e Goethe," *Il Ponte*, XI, No. 6 (June 1955), pp. 867–877
"Un discorso e un ritratto," *Il Mondo*, VII, No. 34 (23 August 1955), pp. 3–4

II. Thomas Mann Studies

Altenberg, Paul. *Die Romane Thomas Manns*. Bad Homburg: Gentner, 1961
Amado, Jorge. "La madre brasiliana." *Il Contemporaneo*, Vol. 2, No. 23 (June 4, 1955), p. 9
Améry, Jean. "Venezianische Zaubereien: Luchino Visconti und sein *Tod in Venedig*." *Merkur*, Vol. 25, No. 280 (August 1971), pp. 808–812
Amoroso, Ferruccio. "Appunti sulla poesia di Thomas Mann." *Il Ponte*, Vol. 11, No. 6 (June 1955), pp. 878–887
Andersch, Alfred. "Kulturbrief aus Rom." *Konkret*, No. 5 (May 1963), p. 13
———. *Die Blindheit des Kunstwerks und andere Aufsätze*. Frankfurt: Suhrkamp, 1965
Angioletti, G. B. "Thomas Mann a Palestrina." *La Stampa*, February 28, 1959
Barilli, Renato. "Thomas Mann e la tragedia dell'arte moderna." *Convivium*, Vol. 26, No. 1 (January-February 1958), pp. 89–93
Baron, Frank. "Sensuality and Morality in Thomas Mann's *Tod in Venedig*." *Germanic Review*, Vol. 45, No. 2 (March 1970), pp. 115–125
Berendsohn, Walter A. *Thomas Mann; Artist and Partisan in Troubled Times*, University, Alabama: The University of Alabama Press, 1973

Berger, Erich. "Eine Dantestelle in Thomas Manns *Doktor Faustus.*" *Monatshefte,* Vol. 49, No. 4 (April-May 1957), pp. 212–214

Bergsten, Gunilla, *Thomas Manns Doktor Faustus: Untersuchungen zu den Quellen und zur Struktur des Romans.* Tübingen: Max Niemeyer, 1974

Bernari, Carlo. "Mann e noi." *Il Contemporaneo,* Vol. 2, No. 23 (June 4, 1955), p. 8

————. "Mann e noi." *Il Paragone,* No. 192 (1966), pp. 39–52

Bianchi Bandinelli, Ranuccio. "Un incontro a Roma." *Il Contemporaneo,* Vol. 2, No. 23 (June 4, 1955), p. 4

Borgese, Giuseppe Antonio. *Da Dante a Thomas Mann.* Milano: Mondadori, 1958

Braveman, Albert S., and Larry David Nachman. "The Dialectic of Decadence: An Analysis of Thomas Mann's *Death in Venice.*" *Germanic Review,* Vol. 45, No. 4 (October 1970), pp. 289–298

Brennan, Joseph Gerald. *Thomas Mann's World.* New York: Russell & Russell, 1962

Brück, Max von. "Thomas Mann in Italien." *Merkur,* Vol. 18, No. 196 (June 1964), pp. 534–545

Brües, Otto. "Auf römischen Spuren Thomas Manns." *Nürnberger Nachrichten,* August 10/11, 1957

Bürgin, Hans, and Hans-Otto Mayer. *Thomas Mann: A Chronicle of His Life.* University, Alabama: The University of Alabama Press, 1969

Bürgin, Hans, and Hans-Otto Mayer. *Die Briefe Thomas Manns: Regesten und Register.* Band I: *Die Briefe von 1899 bis 1933.* Frankfurt: S. Fischer, 1977

Calamandrei, Piero. "Saluto a Thomas Mann." *Il Ponte,* Vol. 11, No. 6 (June 1955), pp. 865–867

Calvino, Italo. "Manniano all' incontrario." *Il Contemporaneo,* Vol. 2, No. 23 (June 4, 1955), p. 7

Cambon, Glauco. "Felix Krull si confessa." *aut aut,* No. 29 (September 1955), pp. 384–399

Camilucci, Marcello. "Biblismo e razionalismo di Thomas Mann." *Vita e Pensiero,* Vol. 38 (November 1955), pp. 642–647

Campana, Domenico. "Confessioni di un cavaliere d'industria." *Vita e Pensiero,* Vol. 41 (May 1958), pp. 338–344

Cases, Cesare. "Un romanzo picaresco." *Il Contemporaneo,* Vol. 2, No. 23 (June 4, 1955), pp. 8–9

————. *Saggi e note di letteratura tedesca.* Torino: Einaudi, 1961

Cecchi, Emilio. "Thomas Mann." *Accademia Nazionale dei Lincei,* Vol. 3 (1962), pp. 132–136

Checconi, Sergio. *Thomas Mann.* Florence: La Nuova Italia, 1966

Chiusano, Italo A. "Thomas Mann e il realismo critico." *Storia della letteratura tedesca,* Vol. 2, pp. 86–98. Milano: Fabbri, 1969

————. "Thomas Mann e l'Italia." *Settanta,* Vol. 2, No. 18 (November 1971), pp. 72–73

Cives, Giacomo. "Verità, bellezza e psicologia in 'Nobiltà dello spirito.' " *aut aut,* No. 29 (September 1955), pp. 440–457

Cori, Alba. "Il nuovo romanzo di Thomas Mann: La leggenda di Papa Gregorio." *Annali della Scuola Normale Superiore di Pisa,* Vol. 20, No. 1–2 (1951), pp. 1–16

Croce, Benedetto. "Thomas Mann: *Betrachtungen eines Unpolitischen.*" *La Critica,* Vol. 18, No. 5 (May 1920), pp. 182–183

————. *La Corrispondenza Croce-Mann.* Ed. by Ottavio Besomi and Hans Wysling. *Archivio Storico Ticinese*, No. 61 (March 1975), pp. 33–48. German text: Der Briefwechsel Croce-Mann. *Germanisch-Romanische Monatsschrift*, N. S., Vol. 25, No. 2 (1975), pp. 129–150

Debenedetti, Giacomo. "Il grande gioco." *Il Contemporaneo*, Vol. 2, No. 23 (June 4, 1955), p. 6

Della Volpe, Galvano. "Amor fati." *Il Contemporaneo*, Vol. 2, No. 23 (June 4, 1955), p. 7

De Toni, Gianantonio. "Al lettore di Zauberberg." *aut aut*, No. 29 (September 1955), pp. 405–422

Devescovi, Guido. *Il Doktor Faustus di Thomas Mann*. Trieste: Borsatti, 1955

Dyson, A. E. "The Stranger God: *Death in Venice*." *Critical Quarterly*, Vol. 13 (1973), pp. 5–20

Eilers, Egon. *Perspektiven und Montage: Studien zu Thomas Manns Schauspiel 'Fiorenza,'* Ph.D. Dissertation, University of Marburg, 1967.

Fertonani, Roberto. "Introduzione." In Thomas Mann: *La morte a Venezia, Tristano, Tonio Kröger*, pp. 7–52. Milano: Mondadori, 1970

Flora, Francesco. "Il Premio dell'Accademia dei Lincei a Thomas Mann nel 1952." *Letteratura Moderna*, Vol. 6, No. 3 (May-June 1956), pp. 343–345

Fortini, Franco. "La selva ironica." *Il Contemporaneo*, Vol. 2, No. 23 (June 4, 1955), p. 6

Fourrier, Georges. *Thomas Mann: Le message d'un artiste-bourgeois*. Paris: Les Belles Lettres, 1960

Frenzel, Herbert A. "Gerhart Hauptmann e Thomas Mann." *Convivium*, Vol. 23, No. 3 (May-June 1955), pp. 297–310

Furst, Lilian R. "Italo Svevo's *La coscienza di Zeno* and Thomas Mann's *Der Zauberberg*." *Comparative Literature*, Vol. 9, No. 4 (1968), pp. 492–506

Gozzi, Federico. "Il liberale Thomas Mann." *Il Mondo*, Vol. 7, No. 34 (August 23, 1955), pp. 1–2

Gronicka, André von. "Myth plus Psychology: A Stylistic Analysis of *Death in Venice*." In Henry Hatfield, ed., *Thomas Mann: A Collection of Critical Essays*, pp. 46–61

Günther, Joachim. "*Der Tod in Venedig:* Randbemerkungen zu Film und Buch." *Neue Deutsche Hefte*, Vol. 18, No. 132 (1971), pp. 89–99

Hatfield, Henry. *Thomas Mann*. Norfolk: New Directions, 1951

Heller, Erich. *The Ironic German: A Study of Thomas Mann*. Boston: Little, Brown, 1958

Hergershansen, Lore. "Au sujet de *Mario und der Zauberer* de Thomas Mann: Cesare Gabrielli—Prototype de Cipolla?" *Etudes Germaniques*, Vol. 23, No. 2 (April-June 1968), pp. 268–275

Hilscher, Eberhard. *Thomas Mann: Leben und Werk*. Berlin: Volk und Wissen, 1975

Hirschbach, Frank D. "The Education of Hans Castorp." *Monatshefte*, Vol. 46, No. 1 (January 1954), pp. 25–34

Hocke, Gustav René. "Thomas Mann bei Pius XII." In Klaus Schröter, ed., *Thomas Mann im Urteil seiner Zeit: Dokumente 1891 bis 1955*, pp. 418–420. Hamburg: Christian Wegner, 1969.

Hoffmann, Ernst Feodor. "Thomas Mann's *Gladius Dei*." *PMLA*, Vol. 83, No. 5 (October 1968), pp. 1353–1361.

Holthusen, Hans Egon. "The World Without Transcendence." In Henry Hatfield, ed., *Thomas Mann: A Collection of Critical Essays,* pp. 123–132. Englewood Cliffs, N.J.: Prentice-Hall, 1964.

Hösle, Johannes. "Thomas Mann critico ovvero 'Joseph em Hab'." *Critica e storia letteraria: Studi offerti a Mario Fubini,* pp. 744–754. Padua: Liviana Editrice, 1970

Jesi, Furio. *Letteratura e mito.* Torino: Einaudi, 1973

Jonas, Ilsedore B. *Thomas Mann und Italien.* Heidelberg: Carl Winter, 1969

Jonas, Klaus W. *Fifty Years of Thomas Mann Studies: A Bibliography of Criticism.* Minneapolis: University of Minnesota Press; New York: Kraus Reprint, 1969

———, and Ilsedore B. Jonas. *Thomas Mann Studies, Volume Two.* Philadelphia: University of Pennsylvania Press, 1967

———. *Die Thomas Mann-Literatur: Bibliographie der Kritik 1896–1955.* Berlin: Erich Schmidt Verlag, 1972

———. *Die Thomas Mann-Literatur: Bibliographie der Kritik 1956–1975.* Berlin: Erich Schmidt Verlag, 1979

Kasdorff, Hans. *Der Todesgedanke im Werke Thomas Manns.* Leipzig: Eichblatt, 1932

Kerényi, Karl. "Thomas Mann und der Teufel in Palestrina." *Neue Zürcher Zeitung,* No. 3 (January 1, 1961), p. 3

———. *Tessiner Schreibtisch.* Stuttgart: Steingrüben, 1963

———. "Thomas Mann zwischen Norden und Süden." *Neue Zürcher Zeitung,* No. 2, 850 (July 4, 1965), p. 3

Kirchberger, Lida. "*Death in Venice* and the Eighteenth Century." *Monatshefte,* Vol. 58, No. 4 (1966), pp. 321–324

Koopmann, Helmut. *Die Entwicklung des intellektualen Romans bei Thomas Mann.* Bonn: Bouvier Verlag H. Grundmann, 1971

Koppen, Erwin. "Quest'idioma celeste." *Arcadia,* Vol. 1, No. 2 (1966), pp. 192–209

Kristiansen, Børge. "Zur Bedeutung und Funktion der Settembrini-Gestalt in Thomas Manns Roman *Der Zauberberg.*" *Gedenkschrift für Thomas Mann,* ed. Rolf Wiecker, pp. 95–135. Kopenhagen: Text & Kontext, 1975.

Lehnert, Herbert. "Thomas Mann's Interpretations of *Der Tod in Venedig* and their Reliability." *Rice University Studies,* Vol. 50, No. 4 (1964), pp. 41–60

———. *Thomas Mann: Fiktion, Mythos, Religion.* Stuttgart: Kohlhammer, 1965

Leppmann, Wolfgang. "Time and Place in *Death in Venice.*" *German Quarterly,* Vol. 48, No. 1 (January 1975), pp. 66–75

Lion, Ferdinand. "Thomas Mann come filosofo." *aut aut,* No. 29 (September 1955), pp. 376–383

Loose, Gerhard. "Glocken über Rom." *Modern Language Notes,* Vol. 74, No. 7 (November 1959), pp. 633–636

———. "Ludovico Settembrini und *Soziologie der Leiden* [by Franz-Carl Müller-Lyer]: Notes on Thomas Mann's *Zauberberg.*" *Modern Language Notes,* Vol. 83, No. 3 (April 1968), pp. 420–429

Lukàcs, Georg. *Thomas Mann e la tragedia dell'arte moderna.* Milano: Feltrinelli, 1956

Maione, Italo. *Contemporanei di Germania.* Torino: Bocca, 1931

Malvezzi, Piero, and Giovanni Pirelli. *Lettere di condannati a morte della Resistenza europea.* Torino: Einaudi, 1956

Mann Borgese, Elisabeth. "Infanzia con mio padre." *Il Ponte*, Vol. 11, No. 6 (June 1955), pp. 899–902

——. Letter to Ignazio Silone. *Tempo Presente*, Vol. 3, No. 3 (1958), pp. 219–225

Mann, Michael. "Der verfilmte *Tod in Venedig:* Offener Brief an Luchino Visconti." *Süddeutsche Zeitung*, Vol. 27, No. 278 (November 20/21, 1971).

Marianelli, Marianello. "Presentazione." In Thomas Mann: *Considerazioni di un impolitico*, pp. vii–xxviii. Bari: De Donato, 1967

Matenko, Percy. "The Prototype of Cipolla in *Mario und der Zauberer.*" *Italia*, Vol. 31, No. 3 (September 1954), pp. 133–135

Matter, Harry. *Die Literatur über Thomas Mann: Eine Bibliographie 1898–1969*. Berlin: Aufbau Verlag, 1972

Mazzucchetti, Lavinia. "L'uomo Thomas Mann." *Il Ponte*, Vol. 11, No. 6 (June 1955), pp. 895–898

——. "Ricordo di Thomas Mann." *aut aut*, No. 29 (September 1955), pp. 400–401

——. *Novecento in Germania*. Milano: Mondadori, 1959

——. "Grenzgängerin zwischen Italien und Deutschland." *Die Zeit*, Vol. 17, No. 8 (February 23, 1962), p. 9

——. "La Mostra "Thomas Mann" in Italia." *Lo Smeraldo*, Vol. 17, No. 1 (January 1963), pp. 18–21

——. "Thomas Mann al Forte dei Marmi." *La Provincia di Lucca*, Vol. 4, No. 2 (1964), pp. 48–54

——. *Die andere Achse*. Hamburg: Claassen, 1964

——. "Thomas Mann und der Zauberer." *Die Zeit*, Vol. 20, No. 32 (August 6, 1965), p. 11

——. *Cronache e saggi*. Milano: Il Saggiatore, 1966

Mendelssohn, Peter. *Der Zauberer: Das Leben des deutschen Schriftstellers Thomas Mann*. Frankfurt: S. Fischer, 1975 [Part One]

Meyer, Herman. *The Poetics of Quotation in the European Novel*. Princeton, New Jersey: Princeton University Press, 1968

Mittner, Ladislao. *L'Opera di Thomas Mann*. Milano: Sperling & Kupfer, 1936

Mundt, Carl. "Thomas Mann als roter Sturmbock." *Stuttgarter Nachrichten*, No. 145 (June 28, 1961), p. 8 [Centro Thomas Mann in Rome]

Necco, Giovanni. "Thomas Mann in italiano." *Gazzetta del Mezzogiorno*, March 16, 1956

Nicklas, Hans W. *Thomas Manns Novelle "Der Tod in Venedig": Analyse der Motivzusammenhänge und der Erzählstruktur*. Marburg: Elwert, 1968

Paci, Enzo. "L'ironia di Thomas Mann." *aut aut*, No. 29 (September 1955), pp. 363–375

Pikulik, Lothar. "*Thomas Mann und die Renaissance.*" In Pütz, Peter, Ed. *Thomas Mann und die Tradition*, pp. 101–129. Frankfurt: Athenäum, 1971

Piper, Myfanwy. *Death in Venice: An Opera in Two Acts (Libretto)*. London: Faber Music, 1973

Pocar, Ervino. "Le mie traduzioni da Thomas Mann." *Babel*, Vol. 21 (1975), pp. 160–162

Porena, Boris. "Thomas Mann e la musica contemporanea." *Musica d'oggi*, Vol. 1, No. 2 (February 1958), pp. 91–95

Pütz, Peter. "Die teuflische Kunst des *Doktor Faustus* bei Thomas Mann." *Zeitschrift für Deutsche Philologie,* Vol. 82, No. 4 (1963), pp. 500–515

Reed, T. J. "Introduction." In Thomas Mann: *Der Tod in Venedig,* pp. 158–180. London: Oxford University Press, 1971

————. *Thomas Mann: The Uses of Tradition.* London: Oxford University Press, 1974

Rehm, Walther. "Der Renaissancekult um 1900 und seine 'Überwindung.' " *Zeitschrift für Deutsche Philologie,* Vol. 54 (1929), pp. 296–328

Ringger, Kurt. "Ein Echo aus Thomas Mann in Giuseppe Tomasi di Lampedusas *Gattopardo.*" *Germanisch-Romanische Monatsschrift,* N. S., Vol. 13, No. 4 (October 1963), pp. 423–432

Ritter-Santini, Lea. "Das Licht im Rücken: Notizen zu Thomas Manns Dante-Rezeption." In Helmut Koopmann [et al.], ed. *Thomas Mann 1875–1975: Vorträge in München, Zürich und Lübeck,* pp. 349–376. Frankfurt: S. Fischer, 1977

————. *L'italiano Heinrich Mann.* Bologna: Il Mulino, 1965

Rizzo, Franco. *Nazionalismo e democrazia.* Bari: Lacaita, 1960

Rosa, Alberto Asor. *Thomas Mann o dell'ambiguità borghese.* Bari: De Donato, 1971

Rüdiger, Horst. "Thomas Manns *Mario* als Melodrama." *Frankfurter Allgemeine Zeitung,* Vol. 8, No. 55 (March 5, 1956), p. 8

Rudman, Harry W. "A Possible Prototype of Mann's Settembrini." *Germanic Review,* Vol. 25, No. 4 (December 1950), p. 299

Sagave, Pierre-Paul. "Thomas Mann et le monde latin." In *Mélanges Etienne Gros.* Aix-en-Provence, 1959, pp. 261–269

Sanesi, Roberto. "Omaggio a Tonio Kröger." *aut aut,* No. 29 (September 1955), pp. 402–405

Santoli, Vittorio. *Philologie und Kritik: Forschungen und Aufsätze.* Bern: Francke, 1971

Schmidt, Ernst A. "Platonismus und Heidentum in Thomas Manns *Tod in Venedig.*" *Antike und Abendland,* Vol. 20, No. 2 (1974), pp. 151–178

————."Künstler und Knabenliebe: Eine vergleichende Skizze zu Thomas Manns *Tod in Venedig* und Vergils zweiter Ekloge." *Euphorion,* Vol. 68, No. 4 (1974), pp. 437–446

Schröter, Klaus. *Thomas Mann.* Reinbek: Rowohlt, 1964

Schultz, H. Stefan. "On the Interpretation of Thomas Mann's *Der Zauberberg.*" *Modern Philology,* Vol. 52, No. 1 (November 1954), pp. 110–122

Schwarz, Waltraut. *Deutsche Dichter in Bologna: Bologna in der deutschen Dichtung.* Bologna: Tecnofoto Bologna, 1972

Seckelmann, Klaus D. "Ein Tusculum für Dichter und Künstler: Aus der Geschichte des Sanatoriums Dr. med. Christoph von Hartungen." *Deutsches Ärzteblatt,* Vol. 66, No. 5 (February 1, 1969), pp. 306–309; No. 6 (February 8, 1969), pp. 382–385

Seidlin, Oskar. *Von Goethe zu Thomas Mann.* Göttingen: Vandenhoeck & Ruprecht, 1963

Silone, Ignazio. "Thomas Mann e il dovere civile." *Tempo Presente,* Vol. 3, No. 1. (January 1958), pp. 1–5

————. "Rettifiche e conferme su Thomas Mann." *Tempo Presente,* Vol. 3, No. 3 (March 1958), pp. 219–225

Sommavilla, Guido. *Parabole dell'ateismo: Friedrich Hölderlin, Friedrich Nietzsche, Italo Svevo, Thomas Mann*. Padua: La Garanzola, 1973

Stockum, Th. C. van. *Von Friedrich Nicolai bis Thomas Mann*. Groningen: J. B. Wolters, 1962

Stresau, Hermann. "Il motivo della "irruzione" nell'opera di Thomas Mann." *Il Ponte*, Vol. 11, No. 6 (June 1955), pp. 888–894

Tansini, Giorgio. "Appunti su Thomas Mann." *Humanitas*, Vol. 16, No. 12 (December 1961), pp. 993–1019

Tecchi, Bonaventura. *L'arte di Thomas Mann*. Torino: Eri, 1961

Teichmann, Alfred. *Savonarola in der deutschen Dichtung*. Berlin: De Gruyter, 1937

Tiburzio, Enrico. "Note su *Doktor Faustus*." *Belfagor*, Vol. 24 (1969), pp. 249–292

———. "Il Primo dopoguerra di Thomas Mann: Note su *La Montagna Incantata*." *Belfagor*, Vol. 26, No. 1 (January 31, 1971), pp. 6–38

Tollinchi, Esteban. "Thomas Mann y los ojos Romanos." *Sin Nombre*, Vol. 6, No. 2 (October-December 1975), pp. 33–47

Traverso, Leone. "In memoria di Thomas Mann." *Studi Urbinati*, Vol. 29, No. 2 (1955), pp. 139–154

———. "Thomas Mann, Schönberg e le teorie musicali di *Doktor Faustus*." *Studi Urbinati*, Vol. 45 (1971), pp. 348–351

Vaget, Hans Rudolf, and Ernst Feodor Hoffmann. "Thomas Mann's *Gladius Dei* Once Again: An Exchange." *PMLA*, Vol. 88, No. 4 (September 1973), pp. 482–484

Vetrano, Giuseppe. "La dinastia borghese dei Mann." *Communitá*, Vol. 15, No. 91 (July 1961), pp. 78–88

Vincenti, Leonello. "I settant'anni di Thomas Mann." *Nuovi saggi di letteratura tedesca*, pp. 281–290. Milano: U. Mursia, 1968

Völker, Ludwig. "Ein Missverständnis und seine Folgen: *placet experiri* als Wahlspruch Petrarcas in Thomas Manns Roman *Der Zauberberg*." *Euphorion*, Vol. 67, No. 3/4 (1973), pp. 383–385

Wagener, Hans. "Mann's Cipolla and Earlier Prototypes of the Magician." *Modern Language Notes*, Vol. 84, No. 4 (October 1969), pp. 800–802

Walzel, Oskar. *Florenz in deutscher Dichtung*. Stuttgart: Deutsche Verlags-Anstalt, 1937

Weigand, Hermann J. *The Magic Mountain: A Study of Thomas Mann's Novel Der Zauberberg*. Chapel Hill: University of North Carolina Press, 1964

———. "Thomas Mann's Gregorius." *Germanic Review*, Vol. 27, No. 1/2 (February-April 1952), pp. 10–30, 83–93

Witte, William. "Introduction." In Thomas Mann: *Two Stories*, pp. xi–xxiv. New York: Rinehart, 1959

Wittkowski, Victor. "Un borghese e la classicità." *La Fiera Letteraria*, Vol. 8, No. 43 (October 25, 1953), pp. 1, 6

Wolf, Ernest M. "Savonarola in München: Eine Analyse von Thomas Manns *Gladius Dei*." *Euphorion*, Vol. 64, No. 1 (1970), pp. 85–96

Wysling, Hans. *Quellenkritische Studien zum Werk Thomas Manns* [with Paul Scherrer]. Bern, München: Francke, 1967 (Thomas-Mann-Studien, Bd. I)

———. *Dokumente und Untersuchungen. Beiträge zur Thomas-Mann-Forschung*. Bern, München: Francke, 1974 (Thomas-Mann-Studien, Bd. III)

————, and Yvonne Schmidlin: *Bild und Text bei Thomas Mann. Eine Dokumentation*. Bern, München: Francke, 1975
————, and Marianne Fischer: *Dichter über ihre Dichtungen: Thomas Mann*. Teil I: 1889–1917. München, Frankfurt: Heimeran/S. Fischer, 1975
————. *Thomas Mann. Sieben Vorträge*. Bern, München: Francke, 1976
————"Die Technik der Montage: Zu Thomas Manns 'Erwähltem'." *Euphorion*, Vol. 57, No. 2 (1963), pp. 156–199
Zampa, Giorgio. "Parodia e verità." *Il Mondo*, Vol. 7, No. 34 (August 23, 1955), p. 3
Zerner, Marianne. "Thomas Mann's *Der Bajazzo*." *Monatshefte*, Vol. 56, No. 6 (November 1964), pp. 286–290.
Zoller, Elemire. "Thomas Mann." *Letterature Moderne*, Vol. 4, No. 2 (March-April, 1953), pp. 146–153

III. Works by Italian Writers

Alighieri, Dante. *La Divina Commedia*. Florence: Società Editrice Toscana, 1938
————. *Die Göttliche Komödie*. German translation by Karl Vossler. Zürich: Atlantis, 1948
Alvaro, Corrado. *Quasi una vita*. Milan: Bompiani, 1951
————. *Ultimo diario*. Milan: Bompiani, 1961
Bettiza, Enzo. *La campagna elettorale*. Milan: Bianchi-Giovini, 1953
————. *Il fantasma di Trieste*. Milan: Longanesi, 1958
Boccaccio, Giovanni. *Il Decamerone*. Milan: Hoepli, 1942
Borgese, Giuseppe Antonio. *Tempesta nel nulla*. Milan: Mondadori, 1950
Carducci, Giosuè. *Edizione nazionale delle opere*. Bologna: Zanichelli, 1939
Falqui, Enrico. *Tra racconti e romanzi del novecento*. Messina: G. D'Anna, 1950
Ginzburg, Natalia. *Lessico famigliare*. Turin: Einaudi, 1963
Lampedusa, Giuseppe di. "Lezioni su Stendhal," *Paragone*, No. 112 (1959), p. 49ff.
————. *Il Gattopardo*. Milan: Feltrinelli, 1963
Moravia, Alberto. *Racconti romani*. Milan: Bompiani, 1958
————. *Gefährliches Spiel*. Hamburg: Rowohlt, 1962
Pasolini, Pier Paolo. *Passione e ideologia*. Milan: Garzanti, 1960
Pavese, Cesare, *La letteratura americana e altri saggi*. Turin: Einaudi, 1953
————. *Racconti*. Turin: Einaudi, 1960
————. *Il mestiere di vivere*. Turin: Einaudi, 1962
————. *Das Handwerk des Lebens*. Munich: Deutscher Taschenbuch-Verlag, 1963
Pratolini, Vasco, *Diario sentimentale*. Milan: Mondadori, 1962
Prezzolini, Giuseppe. *Dal mio terrazzo*. Florence: Vallecchi, 1960
Schmitz, Ettore. See Svevo, Italo
Settembrini, Luigi. *Opere scelte*. Turin: Editr. Torinese, n.d.
————. *Lezioni di letteratura italiana*. Florence: Sansoni, 1964
Svevo, Italo, *La coscienza di Zeno*. Milan: dall'Oglio, 1969
Vittorini, Elio. *Diario in pubblico* Milan: Bompiani, 1957

IV. General Secondary Literature

Alker, Ernst. *Die deutsche Literatur im 19. Jahrhundert*. Stuttgart: Kröner, 1961

Apollonio, Mario. *Letteratura dei Contemporanei.* Brescia: Società Editrice 'La Scuola', 1957

Barzini, Luigi. *The Italians.* New York: Athenaeum, 1964

Bennett, E. K. *A History of the German Novelle.* Cambridge: University Press, 1961

Bertram, Ernst. *Nietzsche.* Berlin: Georg Bondi, 1922

Bickerstath, G. L. *Carducci.* New York: Longmans, Green, 1913

Butler, E. M. *The Tyranny of Greece over Germany.* New York: Macmillan, 1935

Carli, Plinio (and) Augusto Sainati. *Scrittori italiani.* Vol. III. Florence: F. Monnier, 1952

Croce, Benedetto. *La letteratura della Nuova Italia.* Vols. I and II. Bari: Laterza, 1943-1948

De Michelis, Euralio. *Introduzione a Moravia.* Florence: La Nuova Italia, 1954

De Robertis, Giuseppe. *Altro novecento.* Florence: F. Monnier, 1962

De Sanctis, Francesco. *La letteratura italiana del secolo XIX.* Naples: Morano, 1922

———. *Geschichte der italienischen Literatur.* Stuttgart: Kröner, 1941

———. *Storia della letteratura italiana.* Vol. II. Bari: Laterza, 1954

Emrich, Wilhelm. *Geist und Widergeist.* Frankfurt a. M.: Athenäum, 1965

Fiorentino, Luigi. *Narratori del novecento.* Milan: Mondadori, 1960

Flora, Francesco. *La poesia e la prosa di Giosuè Carducci.* Pisa: Nistri-Lischi, 1959

Frischauer, Paul. *Garibaldi.* New York: C. Kendall, 1935

Gioberti, Vincenzo. *Del rinnovamento civile d'Italia.* Bari: Laterza, 1911–1912. 3 vols.

Hatfield, Henry. *Aesthetic Paganism in German Literature.* Cambridge, Mass: Harvard University Press, 1964

Hauptmann, Gerhart. *Und Pippa tanzt.* In: Hans-Egon Hass, Ed.: *Gerhart Hauptmann: Sämtliche Werke. Centenar-Ausgabe.* Vol. II. Berlin: Propyläen Verlag, 1965

Hinderberger, H. *Michelangelo.* Zürich: Manesse, 1947

Hinterhäuser, Hans. *Italien zwischen Schwarz und Rot.* Stuttgart: Kohlhammer, 1956

Hösle, Johannes. *Cesare Pavese.* Berlin: De Gruyter, 1961

Mann, Heinrich. *Die kleine Stadt.* Berlin: Zsolnay, 1925

Marriott, J.A.R. *The Makers of Modern Italy.* London: Oxford University Press, 1931

Martini, Fritz. *Deutsche Literaturgeschichte.* Stuttgart: Kröner, 1958

Mazzucchetti, Lavinia. "Mignon von Goethe bis Hauptmann," *Schweizer Monatshefte,* VI, No. 4 (July 1965), pp. 359–372

Mittner, Ladislao. *La letteratura tedesca del Novecento.* Turin: Einaudi, 1960

Momigliano, Attilo. *Antologia della letteratura italiana.* Milan: Principato, 1952

Nicolini, Fausto. "Luigi Settembrini," *Enciclopedia Italiana,* Vol. XXXI, pp. 541–543. Rome, 1936

Nolte, Ernst. *Der Faschismus in seiner Epoche.* Munich: Piper, 1963

Olschki, Leonardo. *The Genius of Italy.* New York: Oxford University Press, 1949

Omodeo, Adolfo. *L'Età del Risorgimento italiano.* Naples, 1960

Pacifici, Sergio. *A Guide to Contemporary Italian Literature.* Cleveland: World, 1962

Petriconi, Helmut (and) Walter Pabst. "Die Einwirkung der italienischen auf die deutsche Literatur," in W. Stammler, *Deutsche Philologie im Aufriss*, Vol. III, pp. 223–260. Berlin: E. Schmidt, 1965

Platen, August von. *Sämtliche Werke in vier Bänden.* Stuttgart: J. G. Cotta, 1882
———. *Die Tagebücher.* Eds.: G. von Laubmann and L. von Scheffler. Leipzig: Insel, 1930

Prezzolini, Giuseppe. *The Legacy of Italy.* New York: S. F. Vanni, 1948

Rehm, Walther. *Späte Studien.* Bern: Francke, 1964

Requadt, Paul. *Die Bildersprache der deutschen Italiendichtung.* Bern: Francke, 1962

Russo, Luigi. *I classici italiani.* Florence: Sansoni, 1951, Vol. III, Part 2

Schiller National Museum, Marbach am Neckar. *Auch ich in Arcadien.* Stuttgart, 1966

Seuffert, Thea von. *Venedig im Erlebnis deutscher Dichter.* Cologne: Petrarca-Haus, 1937

Sforza, Count Carlo. *Contemporary Italy.* New York: E. P. Dutton, 1944
———. *Italy and Italians.* New York: E. P. Dutton, 1949

Solmi, Sergio. *Scrittori negli anni.* Milan: Il Saggiatore, 1963

Squarotti, Giorgio Barberi. *Poesia e narrativa del secondo novecento.* Milan: Mursia, 1961

Steinmann, Ernst. *Ghirlandaio.* Bielefeld: Velhagen & Klasing, 1897

Tecchi, Bonaventura. *Scrittori tedeschi moderni.* Rome: Edizioni di Storia e Letteratura, 1959

Villari, Pasquale. *Studies Historical and Critical.* London: F. Unwin, 1907

Vollenweiler, Alice. *Italienische Erzähler.* Stuttgart: Reclam, 1964

Volpe, Gioacchino. *Italia moderna.* Vol. I. Florence: Sansoni, 1958

Vossler, Karl. *Italienische Literaturgeschichte.* Berlin: De Gruyter, 1927

Waetzold, Wilhelm. *Deutsche Kunstwerke beschrieben von deutschen Dichtern.* Leipzig: Diederich, 1940

Weisstein, Ulrich. *Heinrich Mann.* Tübingen: Niemeyer, 1962

Wiese, Benno von. *Novelle.* Stuttgart: J. B. Metzler, 1963

Wilkins, Ernest Hatch. *A History of Italian Literature.* Cambridge, Mass., Harvard University Press, 1962

Wocke, Helmut. *Rilke und Italien.* Giessen: Münchow, 1940

Wonderly, A. Wayne. "Das Problem des Aussenseiters der Gesellschaft in Thomas Manns *Gladius Dei*." *Philobiblon*, Vol. 17, No. 4 (December 1973), pp. 275–278

INDEX OF PERSONS

ILLUSTRATIONS

Thomas Mann and his Family in their home in Pacific Palisades, Christmas 1944.
From left to right: Thomas Mann (standing), Giuseppe A. Borgese (seated), Frido
Mann, Katia Mann, Angelica Borgese, Elisabeth Mann-Borgese, with Domenica
Borgese in her lap, Gret Mann with Tonio Mann, Michael Mann (standing). *Courtesy Thomas-Mann-Archives Zurich.*

Thomas Mann and his wife Katia with Arnoldo Mondadori (left) and Alberto Mondadori (right) during Thomas Mann's visit with his Italian publishers in Meina, Italy, July 1947. *Courtesy Thomas-Mann-Archives Zurich.*

Thomas Mann and his Italian translator, editor, and critic, Lavinia Mazzucchetti, in Meina, 1947. *Courtesy Thomas-Mann-Archives Zurich.*

Thomas Mann surrounded by Italian writers and critics in Meina, 1947. *Courtesy Thomas-Mann-Archives Zurich.*

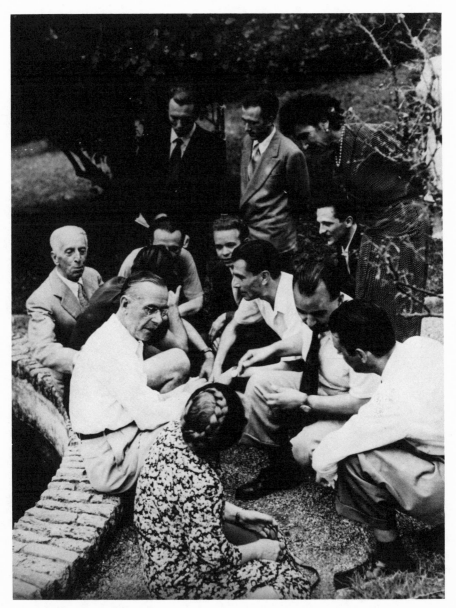

Thomas Mann speaking to Lavinia Mazzucchetti, with Italian critics, writers, and journalists looking on. On the right: Andrina Mondadori, the wife of Arnoldo Mondadori. *Courtesy Thomas-Mann-Archives Zurich.*

Thomas Mann and his wife Katia greeting the Italian novelist Alberto Moravia during their visit to Rome, April 1953. *Courtesy Thomas-Mann-Archives Zurich*.

Thomas and Katia Mann with Filippo Sacchi and Alberto Mondadori (in profile at the extreme right) at a party in Rome, April 1953. (Copyright Italy's News Photos, Rome)

Thomas Mann speaking to an Italian critic in Rome, April 1953.
(Copyright Italy's News Photos, Rome)